The Coming Fourth Reich

A layman's view of what's happening to the America I love.

By
Ray Grace

Copyright © 2012

Author: Ray Grace

All rights reserved.

ISBN-13:
978-1478266556

ISBN-10:
1478266554ISBN:

For my beloved family;
May they always live in a free America.

ACKNOWLEDGMENTS

To my dear wife, who suffered this, my first book with me, while recuperating from a broken hip. She has shown the very definition of love and patience. And to My parents, who taught me to love Truth, because it exposes evil just as sunlight drives away darkness.

Cover Art and poem by Ray Grace

When the Fourth Reich is come
Lady Liberty will be dead
Her lamp of Freedom extinguished
No longer inviting oppressed and weary
To Freedom, beside the Golden Door

The sign, *"Work Makes Free"*, is a translation of the German *"Arbeit Macht Frei"*; which was the sign above the entrance to Nazi Germany's infamous Auschwitz!

Table of Contents

Prologue   XI

PART ONE:
*If you don't know where you came from,
How can you know where you are?*

CHAPTER ONE
Why call it the Fourth Reich?   1

CHAPTER TWO
Right vs. Left. What is Right and what is Left?   11

CHAPTER THREE
America: Constitutional Republic or Democracy?   21

CHAPTER FOUR
Americans, what do we believe *now*?   29

CHAPTER FIVE
Just what is Fascism?   41

Table of Contents

PART TWO:

If you don't know where you are, how can you know where you're headed?

CHAPTER SIX
Revolution? It couldn't happen here, could it?   53

CHAPTER SEVEN
How did the seeds of Marxism come to the USA?   61

CHAPTER EIGHT
How do you Create a Socialist Revolution?
Part One: Basics   71

CHAPTER NINE
How do you Create a Socialist Revolution?
Part Two: Uncovering Termites, Moles, and Rats.   93

CHAPTER TEN
Who were the Kulaks? Why do we care about them?   119

Table of Contents

PART THREE:

If you know who blazed the trail you're following, you can tell where you're headed.

———————————

CHAPTER ELEVEN

Some people *do* know where they came from! 149

CHAPTER TWELVE

Fundamental Transformation was *never* Hope, only Change!   163

CHAPTER THIRTEEN

Who blazed the trail we're following Today?   189

Table of Contents

PART FOUR:

So, where are we *Now?*

CHAPTER FOURTEEN

The Map in the Mall says, "You are Here".   207

Research and Reference Notes.   219

Prologue

"That which has been is what will be, that which is done is what will be done, and there is nothing new under the sun."
King Solomon - Ecclesiastes 1:9

With all the historical and political books written this election year, why in the world does someone who is not a journalist, lawyer, or politician spend his time writing another?

Because too many of them have let you down and failed to give you history and current events undiluted with Political Correctness, or an agenda driven slant. Of course no one does this much work without a reason. Here is mine.

I am sick to death of listening to agenda driven "Professionals" giving 'non-answers' or answering a question with another question to obfuscate the answer to serious, life and death questions. I am a retired Professional Engineer; I make no claim to being a historian, only to loving history. I make no claim to being a legal scholar, an economist, or a professional politician, only to having become so disgusted with many in these professions, it caused me to do some research to find out why these people 'tick' me off. Besides, at seventy-four, I have no fear of the Political Correctness crowd. I have had a successful career, and do not need to prove anything. Having said that, my only agenda is to do my part to let in a little 'Sunlight', drive back some of the shadows, leaving a more "Correct" and less "Politically Correct" world for my children, grandchildren, and yes, great-grandchildren.

Prologue

For years I have watched in disbelief and utter disgust as entity after entity, both in the main-stream media and among elected officials, either dodged questions, or simple-mindedly parroted Marxist talking points and Socialist mantras instead of giving black and white "yes or no" answers concerning what's happening, why it's happening, and where it's taking the USA.

In my own plain-speaking, black and white world, I have never found an answer for such actions other than complicity, manipulation, or plain cowardice. Yet such devious methods have become familiar and even work in America because the public is anesthetized and lulled to sleep by a hundred years of compounded Marxist lies and subversion.

Because I do not believe the majority of American People are either European enough, or stupid enough to give up the free nation they inherited, I cannot understand why not anyone paying attention sees that tyranny has rapidly accelerated over the past decade.

The opinions in this book are 100% my own. They are long-studied and deeply considered before being committed to print. *If I am wrong, show me and prove my error. I will apologize and change my position.* However, let us at least have that debate instead of the weasel-worded Marxist mantras and sound bites currently in use!

Studied discourse and logical discussion are the only certain and civil methods for correcting misunderstandings or erroneous thinking. Sarcasm and "political correctness" instead of discourse is too often used today. However, sarcasm chokes discourse. It is resented by those intelligent enough to understand it and flies over the heads of those who do not.

Political Correctness, on the other hand, is an insidious weapon, whose aim is to destroy rational discourse and variant viewpoints. Its sole value is to stifle and obscure all viewpoints other than its own. Therefore, Political Correctness (PC) is a perfect tool for those in a position of power, who wish to keep their agenda hidden with subterfuge until it is an accomplished fact. The American People

Prologue

desperately need to refute PC along with every politician and media elite who uses this malignant weapon.

It is my considered personal opinion that Political Correctness is a virulent cancer metastasizing in our once-free society, invented and used by hard-core Marxist radicals to shut down discussion of all subjects where they wish to control the dialog. It is also obvious that if you try to debate a leftist idea or ideal based on their deceptive PC definition, the battle is lost before you speak. Accepting such outrageous parameters, accepts working from inside the box the parameters form, making valid information, counter-points, or even factual argument impossible and useless to raise, because PC's parameters are purposefully set to obscure, obfuscate, and control any true dialog.

Additionally, and more importantly, not only is PC a blatant frontal assault by Marxist Socialists on the American Constitution's First Amendment Freedom of Speech, but has also become the opening salvo in their battle to instigate and initiate "Thought-Crimes" as a criminal offense against the Marxist Revolution they slavishly serve, imitating Hitler's Gestapo and SS during the Third Reich.

Unfortunately, even this nefarious tool becomes unnecessary if repetitively utilized to the point of capitulation in people's consciousness. This happens when the majority allow themselves to be endlessly inundated by a State-Run Media without raising logical questions in fear of 'tripping over' Political Correctness. In such a situation, truth loses all meaning and value, while lies become an acceptable answer. Hitler said, *"By the skillful and sustained use of propaganda, one can make a people see even heaven as hell or an extremely wretched life as paradise".*

From my black and white point of view, the term "State-Run Media" in this book includes the majority of the American Media, who are willing prostitutes to Socialists and Marxists in positions of power in the US Government today, either as complicit Revolutionaries, or as what Lenin called "Useful Idiots".

Prologue

Nevertheless, what else can you expect of Media Elites? After all, they have historically hid, covered up, or simply non-reported the blood-soaked crimes against humanity committed by Lenin, Stalin, Hitler, Mao, Castro, Ho Chi Minh, and the whole Marxist Rogues Gallery, until the stench was overwhelming. Yet at the same time, they were 'uncovering' or inventing every possible fault or mistake allegedly made by the United States.

The propaganda campaigns we have witnessed for past decades were designed to *gradually* 'socially engineer' the American people into an emotional, Lemming like herd mentality, removing their ability to think rationally, and primarily ruled by emotions which may be skillfully ruled with Pavlovian certainty by those in charge.

Look around, from after-game riots and bloodshed, from crowds at merchandise sales turning into destructive, even deadly mobs, to today's school children, from pre-school to the University, chanting political mantras and staging demonstrations to support some socialist 'feel-good' cause, many Americans today completely ignore logical reasoning and facts. If truth is the first casualty of war, then the rational thinking process of the public is the first casualty of a successful Marxist Propaganda Campaign, blinding eyes to the truth and shutting down significant dialog, which might counter their lies.

Through development of emotional response replacing rationality, Americans have become trained to react emotionally to skillfully transmitted propaganda stimuli, until like Pavlov's dogs, they can instantly be triggered into *physical* reaction (like a lynch mob) by skillfully delivered stimulus. If you have not noticed that going on in today's political dialog, it is time to wake up and look around.

This book is not being written to prove my point, but to give my reader logical and thought provoking response to what I see happening. Not to blindly follow my opinion, but to care enough for our country and their posterity to research the facts and opinions given here, then to draw their own intellectually formed opinion.

Prologue

Unfortunately, I believe time is running out, both for reviewing the facts, and for rescuing our once free nation. Forces I see at work today are systematically erasing, airbrushing, and whitewashing what once was easily performed historical research on the internet. They did so because like sunlight, truth exposes the Marxist Socialist's efforts to destroy the USA from within. If their words and deeds are easily researched, analyzed, and distributed, their task of driving the 'Lemmings' into the sea becomes much more difficult, if not impossible. Truth's only agenda is to be exposed. From there it can stand tall without fearing the light of day. Like sunshine, Truth exposes details that remain hidden in half-light. What *you* do with the information when you have it is up to you.

For instance, when Hitler came to power in Austria, guns were quickly registered "for public safety". Not long after, he collected them because his government was becoming onerous. Collecting them was easy, as they were registered. If someone did not comply, the Gestapo or SS could take a wife or child hostage until the recalcitrant surrendered. Historically it is easy to disarm a populace with registered arms. Every potential tyrant knows that. Oh, by the way, did you know our Secretary of State is currently negotiating a "Small Arms Control Treaty" with the UN? In addition, such a Treaty if ratified by Congress will supersede the Second Amendment. Maybe you have been asleep!

I have been a reader all my life. I even subscribed to the communist "Daily Worker" in the '60's, where I learned to spot and interpret 'Marx-Speak', the supposedly intellectual language of the Hard Left. I also learned that the Seattle times and other US newspaper normally picked up headlines in the "Daily Worker" within a week or so. Today Reuters and the American press have so many Marxist Op-Ed Columnists you would think they were the Daily Worker!

George Santayana's famous quote then, *"Those who do not learn from history are doomed to repeat It.", is perfection, in* its simplicity and its clear and present truth.

Prologue

Studying both those I agreed with, and those with whom I seriously disagreed; along with economics and the surviving written histories of various world events has remained a lifelong habit.

Working overseas much of twenty years in my later working years greatly broadened my scope of understanding and bolstered my love of history and fascination with ethnic people groups and their history. Working in Venezuela in the early 80's, I watched the Venezuelan 'Guardia Rojo' (Red Guard) working hand-in-glove with the Syndicato (Union) as well as the government to bring disruption and violence to outlying areas, showing off their strength to the people. I watched in awe on one occasion, as one Syndicato Boss, a known Communist who spent time in Venezuelan jail, was hoisted to the top of a shipping container, and in less than 10 minutes had a snarling mob created out of some two or three thousand workers at shift change. The reason the Americans were supervising the job was because the Union and the South American Consortium had gotten the $1.5 Billion project more than two years behind schedule, threatening the whole Venezuelan economy. Because his venom and hatred was directed at the "Gringos" currently supervising the project, it was a very personal moment

So, for a twenty year period of my working life, I worked and communicated abroad with numerous nationalities and ethnicities, learned how to work with them and how they worked with others and each other. During years working overseas, we traveled whenever possible. We have set foot in some 50 nations in Europe, Middle East, North and East Africa, Central and South America, SE Asia, Australia, Russia, China, and the Pacific Rim. Our travels greatly enhanced my fascination with ethnic peoples and their histories, and enlarged my understanding of the human race. After all these years and miles, I truly believe there is *"nothing new under the sun."*

I would be sadly remiss to leave out my faith in this forward, as it has not only helped shape my argument, but also helped me personally, by steadying my hands at a time the world situation

Prologue

seems increasingly out of control. It was only after I came to belief there *is* a God, ultimately in control, not only of our lives but also of world history, that I was able to rest in rational thoughts rather than a pervading sense of hopelessness. Belief became a key for applying sanity to the tragedy I see progressing in the Nation I love.

I wrote this book because I have watched world events with a growing sense of concern for my whole adult life, as forces foreign to the Great American Experiment have infiltrated and inserted themselves into our lives. Self-appointed elites, considering themselves to be more intelligent than the "ignorant" masses have decided they are "obligated" to provide "Social Justice" to save us from our own stupidity. These self-appointed elites have laid full siege to the American Dream that citizens are intelligent enough to rule themselves if provided with only a Rule of Law and a Constitutionally Elected Representative Government. The Socialist Elite's ill-gotten plan is based in the ideology of Marxism, which has *never* created anything but tyranny, brutality, enforced mediocrity, mass suffering, and death.

I have seen few raise an alarm to this threat, and those being attacked mercilessly, by both the self-appointed elites and their sycophants. Nevertheless, as a watchman on the wall, I must raise a warning, or share guilt for the slavery and tyranny I believe to be coming. If I am wrong, in a few years, you can have a good laugh at this silly old man with his crazy warnings. However, if I am right, you or someone you know may be joining me in a "re-education" camp or pushing up dirt.

History is on my side in this argument, but that is only obvious if you have studied it. Therefore, I hope you read my book. You cannot refute the historical facts, however you do not have to agree with the conclusions I draw from them. These conclusions are my own. Nevertheless, maybe you will discover why I think as I do. Maybe you will even discover something you didn't know.

Ray Grace.

Part One:

If you don't know where you came from, how can you know where you are?

CHAPTER ONE

Why Call it the *Fourth* Reich?

> *"Those who do not learn from history are doomed to repeat it"*
> George Santayana

Certainly almost every literate American Citizen knows of the Third Reich. That paragon of evil, circa 1940 Germany under the rule of the Mad-Man Adolph Hitler, whose deluded, power hungry narcissism, and hatred of 'lesser, sub-human men', (Unter-Menschen) turned his name into anathema for a thousand years, even though his "Thousand-Year Reich" lasted only twelve. Some of us still believe his "Final Solution" murdered over six million Jews, although that fact seems to be in question to some people today. But why talk of a Fourth Reich?

Unfortunately, not every literate American understands the chronological context of the term Third and 'Fourth' Reich. That is to say, this much despised and feared 'place' was, in Hitler's (and others) eyes, an attempt to create a 'third whatever Reich means'. So, what is the definition of this mysterious word, still in selective use in Germany?

The Coming Fourth Reich

Even minimum research indicates 'Reich' is in a family of words, which may be defined as empire, realm, or rule. Definition of the Latin equivalent is 'regnum', as in the German Lord's Prayer, 'Deine Reich Komme' or in English, 'Thy Kingdom Come'. Also, from the German, the 'Heiliges Romisches Reich' in English is 'The Holy Roman Empire'. These two-thousand year old translations should conclusively indicate the English meaning of the word Reich to be Kingdom, Empire, or Realm. Although "reich" is not necessarily empire, we must consider that "Reich" (capitalized) definitely has that meaning.

Research also indicates true-believers in Hitler's "Thousand-Year Reich" believed the Roman Empire was the First Reich, the Kaiser's failed German Reich (defeated during WW I) was the Second Reich, and the Nazi (Nationalsozialistisches in German, National Socialist in English) was the Third Reich. However, these definitions were not widely used except in Nazi propaganda and writings.

So, although the word Reich is a German Word still in use, and Third (Drittes) Reich was known to have been Nazi Germany, without the continuity of the first and second Reichs, the meaning is seldom considered, let alone understood today.

So, with minimal study and research, it becomes obvious the power-mad 'Fuhrer' fully intended to re-create a "Thousand-Year Reich", or the Millennial Reign of a Revived Roman Empire, which historically ruled much of Europe, Africa, the Mid-East, and parts of Asia. This was close as the world ever came to a "One World" Government. As an interesting aside, Biblical Prophecy concerning the 'End-Time Days', pictures the Biblical Anti-Christ as the supreme ruler of just such a one world-wide revived Roman Empire.

But not in America, you say! Well, let us do a little historical research here as well. It is well documented, even though it has been "airbrushed" from most scholarly history taught over the past 50 to 60 years in order to keep the younger generation from asking too many embarrassing questions. More on that subject later.

The Coming Fourth Reich

I grew up listening to and reading about WW II on the radio, newspapers, and newsreels. After returning from the war my Dad always had new books on political history and national intrigue he was reading, and I began to read them as well. It was during those formative years my life-long love of history was born. Because they are so closely entwined, I also began to study economic systems as well. But, because the combination of the two necessarily includes politics, you cannot study one of these three without some understanding of the other two. So the die was cast.

America is no longer what she was founded to be. I make that statement comfortably because while it is obvious to all who have studied her founding history, it also becomes obvious that Progressives and other Marxists have taken a lot of care over most of the past century to denigrate and 'airbrush' American History, and to disassociate the Founders and Founding Documents from the current American generation's knowledge-base.

What reason could anyone have for deleting and denigrating all the successful history of the world's first nation founded on personal freedom with a true representative government?

In my long studied and considered opinion, the reason is the Santayana quotation above, i.e., if you refuse to learn from history (or were never told, or were lied to about it) you are liable to repeat it. There are a lot of people in the world who believe mankind is too stupid to rule himself, although they themselves are not only capable of ruling mankind, but are in fact obligated to do so.

Case in point, I remember meeting Tom Foley in 1969 when he was campaigning for his second term (he eventually served 30 years and became Speaker of the House). We debated the 'rights' of the Federal Government to impose onerous rules and restrictions on Americans in response to any whim popular at the time. I asked him why people should be forced to do whatever people like him arrogantly considered 'best' for us. His voice dripping with condescension, he responded with a statement, which I will never forget, "Well, *we* in government have the responsibility of 'taking-care-of' the people, because they aren't smart enough to take care of themselves". As I accused him of elitist arrogance, his campaign manager, seeing a crowd gather, worked to hustle him away. My argument was not what he wanted the crowd to hear.

That was the first time I came face to face with one of these hypocritical, self-appointed progressive elitists, but I have seen and recognized many over the years since. It rather reminds me of being a 'kid' on the farm, many times seeing a snake made me jump because it 'might' be a rattlesnake. But when you do see a rattlesnake, you *know*, you don't just 'think-so'.

Thomas Jefferson said, *"When the people fear their government, there is tyranny; when the government fears the people, there is liberty."*

Tom Foley, in his 30 year 'Reich' in the US House of Representatives, proved the truth and wisdom of Jefferson's statement, as he worked diligently to create and legislate a Statist, Socialist environment. One he intended to one day replace our government 'Of the People, By the People, and For the People', with the tyranny of self appointed elites, who, being superior, were therefore "obligated" to rule "the stupid masses".

To understand where you're going, you need to know where you came from and where you are now. Why is it, then, that we have generations who know nothing about US History except that the US is an evil, empire-building, colonialist nation who is likely guilty of everything wrong in the world all the way back to the fall of the Roman Empire.

Seriously too many High School and even (or especially?), university students don't know the US doesn't go back that far, but of course they've never been taught American History, only the Marxist history of the "Colonial Expansionism" and brutality of the United States.

When I was in high school, US history was still a required class for graduation. Yet today we have several generations who have never learned true US history. "Social Studies" became the required curriculum somewhere in the Sixties. Today, instead of studying US history our children study "how societies live and evolve", or "It takes a village", and other Marxist fantasies.

They currently study propaganda, like "how white Judeo-Christians have held down and enslaved all the poor masses of the world". I understand this sentence carries some personal sarcasm, but while social studies almost never say such things in clear, black and white terms, most people would be hard-pressed to read a significant amount of current "social studies" (propaganda) without drawing the same conclusion.

As an 'aside', did you know who developed the "Social Studies", which replaced US History as a required class? Karl Marx is credited, along with Émile Durkheim and Max Weber, as the three principal architects of modern social science. (1) Obviously, the average American has a lot more to learn about this man, most of which the self-appointed progressive elites really don't want you to learn.

That is because Socialism, in its various forms, whether Communism and Fascism, have provably slaughtered some 150 million people during the Twentieth Century. Also, while not completely recorded due to the news being cloaked in secrecy under the oppressive regimes under which it occurred, along with the complicity of the US and World Media, it likely starved or otherwise caused the deaths of at least an equal number.

Thomas Jefferson said, *"I predict future happiness for Americans if they can prevent the government from wasting the labors of the people under the pretense of taking care of them"*. Karl Marx said, "From each according to his ability, to each according to his need".

In other words, the Founders said, "Americans, even if you work hard and do well, you'll still only be safe if you keep a rein on runaway government, who will rip you off in the name of taking care of you". Meanwhile Marxists say, "If you work hard and do well, we will take everything you have, even your life, and give your goods to the non producers and non-performers who kiss up to us."

Lenin put this into practice in Russia in 1917, almost immediately causing the deaths of more than ten million people, which resulted in a famine that wiped out another five or so million people, and forced him to 'moderate' a little in order to keep the nation from collapse. Of course, when Stalin took over, because he was not only an ideologue, but a cold-blooded murderer as well, he dispensed with moderation, dramatically increasing the death count.

Following, I can only use 'averaged' numbers, as does the website relating those numbers quoted in various researches. But to give you a taste of the difficulty in finding the true sum of Socialist murders, at one point the website states, "(we) ignored any death toll under a quarter million as small change".

In God's Name, how often can we as civilized human beings, consider a quarter million deaths a rounding error, 'small-change'? Obviously, the answer is only when counting the deaths caused by Marxism's Statist Socialism during the Twentieth Century.

Following is a partial list of 20th Century deaths caused by socialist dictators of one stripe or another. Historical estimates vary greatly, as some leave out one or two 'Purges', 'Famines', or can't really find out how many people really died due to political cover-up or 'black-out of one 'Pogrom' or another. (2)

- The Russian Civil War (1917-1922) seven to ten million people (war, terror, famine and disease).
- Lenin's Regime (1917-24) five to ten million people (war, terror, famine, and disease. Add to or include in above? – Only God knows the total.)
- Soviet Union, Stalin's regime (1924-53): Estimates run from twenty to fifty million. Only God knows.
- Second World War (1939-45): fifty to sixty million people. These are better recorded and studied than the wanton murders by Russian Marxists, spread across their huge nation, because these mostly include war dead. But it's still unknown just how many civilians died from ancillary war actions and "Collateral Damage". Possibly this many more.

- Adolf Hitler: The Holocaust (1939-1945). Nuremberg Indictment accepts five point seven million Jews (includes only outright murders – not counting Gypsies, Poles, Hungarians, Russian prisoners, and all others who died as a result of direct or indirect actions of Hitler's SS, Gestapo, or the German Military, etc.,).

- Mao Zedong's regime (1949-1975): Originally reported as forty million, however this number is recently being revised upwards of seventy five million. Due to the closed situation inside China during those years, famines, purges, mobs, famines, and executions were left out of studies or simply never reported due to lack of available information (or will on the part of the complicit media).

These are merely the most 'shining' examples of life under a Socialist Dictator. I'll not attempt to give numbers for more recent 'heroes' of American Progressives, such as Fidel Castro, Ho Chi Minh, Pol Pot, Daniel Ortega, and others. Cold-blooded murderers, every one!

In addition, while Marxists do not openly claim Hitler as one of their heroes because he embarrassed them during WW II and the Holocaust, the current western form of Marxism more closely resembles National Socialism than Communist Socialism. That is because National Socialism allows some capitalist industry to create the wealth necessary to finance socialist programs and buy 'democratic' votes to keep them in power, as they may install their statist, socialist dictatorship, with less chance of economically imploding their nation.

Besides, Fascism, enriched by crony capitalism is far more rewarding to modern Statist Socialists than Communism ever was. Especially in today's politically correct regulatory environment, even though it was originally designed to destroy our free-market system. That is because a semi-free market is still able to create a certain amount of wealth, thus bringing greater economic rewards to the fascist leader who controls it. Whereas communism simply pools, and stagnates "equal" misery for the population, then drowns them in it, although the ruling oligarchy or dictator lives very well.

However, only the most dedicatedly corrupt and evil make it to the top in either form of socialism. I guess you might rephrase that by saying the scum raises to the top. Well, just a thought. However, both forms of government are equally destructive. First by utilizing purposefully created class and ethnic hatred to separate the populace into factions in order to gain control, and secondly, by keeping people's attention focused on a "straw-man", or "common enemy".

Adolph Hitler himself said,

> "The art of leadership...consists in consolidating the attention of the people against a single adversary and taking care that nothing will split up that attention." Or:

> "The great masses of the people will more easily fall victims to a big lie than a small one".

Benito Mussolini said,

> "It is the state which educates its citizens in civic virtue, gives them a consciousness of their mission and welds them into unity".

For those who do not understand crony capitalism, Wikipedia defines it as follows:

> "Crony capitalism is a term describing a capitalist economy in which success in business depends on close relationships between business people and government officials. It may be exhibited by favoritism in the distribution of legal permits, government grants, special tax breaks, and so forth."

If you cannot relate this to what has been happening increasingly in the USA over the past few decades, you had better read that again a few times. And under the current Administration, it has reached epidemic proportions.

The Coming Fourth Reich

Over the past three and one half years our government has stolen several trillion dollars from US taxpayers and *given* it to corrupt financial and quasi-public institutions (Fannie and Freddie, etc.) public employee unions, Government Motors, the UAW, GE, and many in the 'Green' industry. Not surprisingly, a sizeable percentage has inexplicably been recycled into huge multi-billion dollar campaign 'contributions', for Obama. And no one knows how many outright "Gifts" to our 'Crony' President. During this same period, our once-capitalist nation nationalized major financial institutions, auto companies, energy companies, and more. If this does not equate to crony capitalism, just how much proof do you need? Do you need to see another Holocaust? Well, you just might!

Additionally, this is not happening in a vacuum. There is a worldwide Socialist Statist movement simmering. Anti-Semitism is obviously on the rise to all who are paying attention. In nation after nation, socialism and crony capitalism have robbed the capital from productive working people until these nations can no longer tax enough from the 'rich' to pay for the promised welfare, pensions, and social programs for all who claim them.

Portugal, Italy, Ireland, and Spain (the infamous PIIGS), along with Britain are currently having violent riots in the streets. Angry and hate-filled crowds, encouraged by the socialists, are demonstrating destructively, adding to the bankruptcy of these nations. The out-of-control, rampaging crowds do not think they are doing anything wrong, they are angry for not getting what they have been told they 'deserved'. On being interviewed, looters admitted as much.

In May of 2012, the Socialists won back the government of France, and the Neo Nazi Party became a twenty percent player in a Greek coalition government. History repeats. I will leave you here with this prophetic and not too uplifting thought from a Founding Father:

> *"When we get piled upon one another in large cities, as in Europe, we shall become as corrupt as Europe."*
>
> Thomas Jefferson

CHAPTER TWO

Right vs. Left. What is Right and what is Left?

"Government is not reason; it is not eloquence; it is force. Like fire, it is a dangerous servant and a fearful master."

George Washington

If there is one Thing the Founding Fathers of the United States believed, it is encapsulated in the above statement by George Washington. The political spectrum considered by the Founders is completely different from the European model normally used by the political elites that have educated the last three or four generations of Americans.

The history of America from Plymouth Rock to the Revolutionary war was one of oppression to the point of slavery by the British government. Although the early colonists wished to retain close ties or even union with Britain, they were harassed and oppressed to the point of rebellion by the heavy-handedness of the Crown. *"Taxation without representation"* eventually became a rallying cry borne of desperation with tyrannical oppression. Some Americans appear to be comfortable with just that, while others are today feeling oppressed almost to that extent of desperation once again.

I find heartfelt agreement with Founder Ben Franklin, who said,

> "Those who would give up essential liberty to purchase a little temporary safety deserve neither liberty nor safety."

Because such treatment by the British Crown formed the basis of the Founding Fathers theory of what government should be, they considered a political spectrum based from anarchy (no government) on one extreme to any completely oppressive government (totalitarianism) on the opposite extreme.

That is to say, using a yardstick, Anarchy would be placed at the zero inches, and Totalitarianism at thirty-six inches, whether Communism, Fascism, or any other form of Totalitarianism. Democracy would then range from some twenty inches into the low thirties, ending in the early revolutionary stages leading to totalitarianism. Historically Democracy collapses into Anarchy, whereby people cry out for government to bring order, and that order ends in either Fascist or Communist Marxism and Tyranny.

The Republican form of government instituted by the founders between May 14 and September 17, 1787 was the American Founders' second attempt. That happened because the loose Articles of Confederation, which followed the end of the Revolutionary War, proved to be too close to the anarchy end of the spectrum, allowing too much lawlessness and rule by the strongest, best armed, or most evil amongst the people.

It is actually not surprising the colonies erred too far toward anarchy by seeking too much freedom from government after the heavy-handed treatment of the British Crown; it was merely the pendulum 'over-swinging', a completely natural reaction. But it quickly became obvious that some structure of government-instituted law was necessary for the common good.

So, while the American people understood too much government could signal a return to the oppression they had earlier suffered, they had also become aware that too little was the wrong answer as well. Therefore, they did everything possible to place the USA at eighteen inches, dead center on the scale. Neither too little, nor too much government power. Remember, the very *definition* of government is:

'A means to control a nation or a society'

And all governments must be hobbled by constitutional law, lest they wander too far afield. Left alone and uncensored by the people, government tends to grow oppressive. Allowed to grow unfettered, it will quickly end up resembling Washington's quotation at the beginning of this chapter, *"A fearful master"*.

The following European, progressive description of Left and Right Politics comes from Wikipedia:

> *"The left–right political spectrum is a common way of classifying political positions, political ideologies, or political parties along a one-dimensional line. ... Left-wing politics and right-wing politics are often presented as polar opposites ... the terms left and right are commonly used as if they described two globally opposed political families. In France, where the terms originated, the Left is called "the party of movement" and the Right "the party of order". ... Left and right in Western Europe is class. Those on the Left seek social justice through redistributive social and economic intervention by the state. Those on the Right defend private property and capitalism. ... Left-wing values include the belief in the power of human reason to achieve progress for the benefit of the human race, ... The Right is skeptical about the capacity of radical reforms to achieve human well-being while maintaining workplace competition."* (1)

Unfortunately, in today's world, the majority of US educators, media, and politicians, being progressives (socialists in disguise), still use the European, or French definition of the political spectrum, placing communism left, fascism right, and all others (even anarchists) in some 'middle'. That is because the Europeans have never really known true freedom as Americans have, and are unable to understand anything but one form of totalitarianism or the other.

Even when social reforms were brought about in Europe between 1800 and 1850, the Monarchy and the Aristocracy made certain that only people from their select groups or choice could run for parliament. When you consider that the Roman Empire was the first nation to define them as Fascist, that they governed most of Europe, the Middle East, North Africa, and Eurasia some 2000 years ago, you can understand why Europeans might consider Monarchy as Right wing (Conservative), and Fascism as Left wing.

Even though true freedom and free-markets proved itself quickly when adopted for a decade or more by the German people after their defeat in WW II, creating a remarkable period of growth, and allowing Germany to rapidly re-emerge as the European powerhouse, old habits die hard. Therefore, the socialists eventually revived their old ways, luring the people back into a socialist form of government, and then further, into a Socialist European Union.

Now Germany is desperately trying to reverse some of the damage done, but as a member of the new Socialist European Union they will quite possibly collapse into socialist/anarchy, revolution and bankruptcy, while trying to bail out the PIIGS (Portugal, Italy, Ireland, Greece, and Spain)

Foolishly, Europeans even believe democracy is a form of freedom. But as Thomas Jefferson famously said of Democracy:

> "A democracy is nothing more than mob rule, where fifty-one percent of the people may take away the rights of the other forty-nine."
>
> Thomas Jefferson

Personally, I have always remembered a classic example of democracy in action heard many years ago:

> *"The best example of democracy in action is a lynch-mob. Everyone but one agrees that he should be hung, and soon he'll be shut up."*
>
> Unknown (My personal favorite)

Here, we will move geographically from Europe to North Africa and the Middle East, where the farce of democracy as a viable form of freedom was advertised as well. That happened in large part, no thanks to our very own misguided foreign policy of spreading Democracy and nation building, something the Founders explicitly warned against if we intended to remain a free people. How can we "Spread Democracy" with a straight face when we were not even founded as a Democracy? Recently, a Middle-Eastern Leader, speaking of the 'Arab-Spring', said,

> *"Democracy is only a Trolley you ride until you get off at your destination".*

Unfortunately, during the Twentieth Century, that end destination has all too often been either a Military or Marxist Dictatorship, that is, either Fascist or Communist Totalitarianism.

Although I do not know who coined this saying first, the new *"Arab Spring"*, so heartily cheered on by our President, has sadly become:

> *"Democracy; One Man, One Vote, One Time"*

Totalitarian Sharia Law, as overseen by the Muslim Brotherhood, whose taproot reaches back into the Third Reich, is now obviously headed for power in most of North Africa. By the way, for those who know nothing of Sharia Law, it is totally and completely in opposition to, and destructive of all personal, economic, and religious freedoms, which form the very basis of our American Constitution.

As such, these last two examples indicate that democracy is merely an intermediate stage, in transition toward revolution and some type of socialist, totalitarian takeover. Since Islam under Sharia law is essentially a form of religious fascism, it could never become a democracy, as the two are incompatible. If Islam could never even become a democracy, how could it ever become a constitutional republic? But if a Constitutional Republic (like America) became a Democracy (as it nearly has), how could it then remain a free nation and not fall into chaos, revolution and thence into socialist totalitarianism like nearly every other democracy has done?

To my knowledge, our American Constitutional Republic is a result of the only time in recorded history that a group of men knowingly sat down to develop a government in which the common people would have the ultimate control. All known governments preceding it were instituted from the top down.

In direct contrast to all other known forms of government, ours was designed uniquely to *limit* the power that the government exerted over the people, not the other way around, because our Founders were neither anarchists nor revolutionaries, but Statesmen.

This was not strictly a surprise to the American People. The American experience had hit both extremes of government, both anarchy and tyranny. From the near tragedy of the first Plymouth Colony, governed by William Bradford, in which the settlers nearly starved under a socialist contract, to being driven into revolution writhing under the pain of the boot of the English Crown upon their necks. In addition, they nearly descended into anarchy under the "Articles of Confederation" in the wake of the Revolutionary War. How was it then a surprise that such a group of benevolent elder statesmen, who had lived through these trials with their people, would opt for freedom of the individual?

From May to September 17 of 1787, these men toiled together bring (and keep) harmony, balance needs and wants, and generally performing something never before done in the history of the human race, they developed a government of the People, by the People, and for the People.

They developed a government under which men were free to come and go, to own and utilize, or sell their own property, to vote for those who would represent (not rule) them from the local level to the national level. Given freedom of thought and speech, freedom from harassment by those elected to represent (not rule) them, freedom to worship freely and openly any god they chose, and so much more!

Americans became free men that September day in 1878! Without a doubt, the most free in the history of the world, although there was still a slavery problem to settle, which was eventually accomplished, although it cost of a bloody Civil War.

When queried whether America had a Republic or a Monarchy?" Benjamin Franklin responded, *"A Republic, if you can keep it."*

We mostly kept it for the first 120 years, during which time slavery was abolished by a bloody civil war. Then under the spell of European Marxists, Progressives began to slither their way into public office, and commenced the decay of our Republic into a Democracy.

From the beginning of recorded history, humankind has continually been subject to the brutality of those stronger, better armed, and more evil, or a combination of these traits. History is replete with examples of the brutality of kings, generals, and hereditary rulers. Many of the great monuments in the world were raised to the memory of someone of this category.

While the pyramids in Egypt are magnificent examples of architecture and construction, they were constructed at the cost of the slavery, pain, blood, and death for hundreds of thousands or more people. Yet their only value and their reason for being at the time of construction was as a monument to some hereditary ruler, a man who considered himself a type of god, somehow appointed to be absolute ruler, totally separated from the people of his nation or those his armies captured, yet a man just like the beggar in the street.

Throughout the Middle Ages most men who lived on the face of the planet were subjects of a king, generals, or some evil genius in command of an army (oft-times an army of villains and thugs). Very few men on this earth have lived in the freedom of what we in America considered normal. Yet we today in America have lost or given away huge amounts of our once-held freedoms. Worse yet, most do not even know the extent of, or which freedoms were taken from us during the past hundred years by insidious socialist progressives.

Today, generations of American youth have been taught neither US History, nor the US Constitution. They have instead been taught, at first 'closet' Socialism, and now even blatant Marxism. I understand that this year, Portland State University (Oregon) now has a class on Revolutionary Marxism. Of course, Portland Oregon also has Reed College. Wikipedia says of John Reed, the man Reed College was named to honor,

> "For the Communist movement to which he belonged, Reed became a symbol of the international nature of the Bolshevik revolution, a martyr buried at the Kremlin wall amidst solemn fanfare, his name to be uttered reverently as a member of the radical pantheon. (2)

John Reed was a "Workers of the World, Unite" radical activist, arrested in New York, then later, a Journalist cum propaganda writer, cum rifle toting helper in the Bolshevic Revolution in Russia, friend and helper of Trotsky and Lenin. I have seen his tomb near Red Square, along with other blood-soaked 'heroes' of the Russian Communist Revolution, not far from Lenin's crypt. Some 'hero'!

Today, Progressive teachers and professors pimp such totalitarian socialist murderers as Che Gueverra, Mao Tse Tung, and Ho Chi Minh as heroes of the modern world. In my own opinion, it is too bad the people teaching how wonderful those murderers were did not live under their regimes. Those who survived would likely be telling a different story from the glowing Marxist Socialist propaganda they now spout.

So, here we stand today. During the past century, many regions the world that have been the recipient of brutality, slavery, and death at the hand of the self-appointed Socialist Elites, yet today self-appointed Socialist Elites in our own nation pervert and lie about that history. They are hoping to propagandize and brainwash another new generation, to raise them up in revolution against the only nation on earth that has created a government of the People, by the People, and for the People.

Today, we have two disparate definitions of Right and Left, depending upon where your heart is. European Right and Left are both equally Tyranny, i.e., Fascism vs. Communism, or Monarchy vs. Socialism, with all other beliefs dumped indiscriminately into some 'center'. Both ends are merely different forms of totalitarian government, both exert total control over the lives of their subjects.

Fascism (National Socialism) and Communism ('Peoples' Socialism) are differing forms of totalitarian socialism, with the only difference being the dictator's 'excuse of a reason' for imposing totalitarian control, while monarchy is the elevation of some man to the point of god-hood, claiming that he therefore has the 'right-of-kings' to totally dictate the lives and property rights of his subjects. The Europeans have historically known no other forms of government.

However, the American founders saw the Left as *any* totalitarian form of government, whether socialism, monarchy or any other form of dictatorship. Our Founders saw the Right as a total lack of any government, as in anarchy, chaos, or mob-rule (rule of the 'jungle').

The American Constitution was purposefully placed as far as possible from either, in order to govern by a *Rule of Law, not a Rule of Men*. This placed the US Constitution in the center of the American political spectrum, with intentional error leaning slightly to the Right (less government control) instead of to the Left (more government control).

> *So, we have placed before us today, Life and Freedom or Slavery and Death, a Blessing, or a Curse.*
>
> Deuteronomy 11:26

Which will YOU Choose? Would you purposefully choose slavery?

CHAPTER THREE

America: Constitutional Republic or Democracy?

"A Republic, if you can keep it."
Benjamin Franklin's response to the question whether the United States had a Republic or a Monarchy.

"Democracy is two wolves and a lamb, voting on what's for dinner. Liberty is a well armed lamb contesting the vote."

Benjamin Franklin

A very small amount of research will give you volumes of information on this subject. Actually, the bigger question immediately becomes which form of government the Founding Fathers loathed and feared more, Monarchy or Democracy. They considered both to be forms of tyranny. Were you ever taught that in school? Probably not. (1) (2) (3)

This whole chapter could be made with Founders Quotes on this subject. There likely were more words written on the subject of democracy as a form of government for the simple reason that the American Colonists had everyday living, breathing, (not to speak of arms-bearing and threatening) examples of the oppression a Monarchy was capable of.

But the Founders were at least equally skeptical of democracy, as shown below. Nothing I could say would be better education than the founder's own words. Here are several more quotations, because they do not emphasize this in the US Education System, if they teach it at all:

> "A democracy is nothing more than mob rule, where fifty-one percent of the people may take away the rights of the other forty-nine."
>
> Thomas Jefferson

> *Democracy...while it lasts is more bloody than either [aristocracy or monarchy]. Remember, Democracy never lasts long. It soon wastes, exhausts, and murders itself. There is never a democracy that did not commit suicide"*
>
> John Adams

> "The democracy will cease to exist when you take away from those who are willing to work and give to those who are not."
>
> Thomas Jefferson

Additionally, two of the eighty-five Federalist Papers deplored the manner by which several States' Elected Legislatures were imposing what the writer Madison called, the Tyranny of "Majority Faction" on American Citizens. That is to say, whoever gained the majority by any means, did as they pleased without regard to its affect on the minority of the people. This Madison named as a form of democratic tyranny, and therefore an aberration of the Founder's Constitutional Principles, the potential roadway back to tyranny.

Here, we will insert a capsule history of the Federalist Papers as a starting point, because too many readers not only have *never read the Federalist Papers*, but also because some may not even know *what they are!*

Such a dearth of knowledge about our Founding Documents is due to decades of American schoolchildren purposefully having been taught Marx inspired, "Social" Studies, "Ethnic" Studies, and "Diversity", instead of American and World History. It is a travesty of epic proportions and the paramount reason I consider the current American Education System a State-run Propaganda tool, *not* an Education System.

The fact that we need to define and describe the quintessential descriptions of, and arguments for, our Constitutional Republic, written by several Founding Fathers during a critical time in our nation's formation is proof of a gigantic hoax upon the American Nation by those charged with educating our children.

Because the Federalist Papers are so important to understanding the foundations and structure of our government, and are such a deep well at which to drink, this short 'refresher course' will only serve to revive information the reader previously knew. We cannot here re-construct a lifetime of historical apathy and illiteracy, from which all too many Americans suffer. Referring again to the "Majority Faction", this is the term James Madison utilized in Federalist #10, in which he strongly deplored and argued against the "mortal disease' of popular governments" and argued for a republic instead of majority tyranny (democracy).

Simply, his argument was that no matter how large or small any group of people, each individual had their own biases, based on their own mortality, morality, station, and situation in life. Not evil, simply personal. He stated however that,

> *"public assemblies have been infected with the vice of majority tyranny: ... measures are too often decided, not according to the rules of justice, and the rights of the minor party; but by the superior force of an interested and overbearing majority*."

This, he called, the *"Majority Faction"* in an argument against democracy and in favor of our republican form of government, which moves with the majority, but must also be certain to protect the rights of minorities.

The Republican form of government instituted by the founders during the Constitutional Convention between May 14 and September 17, 1787 was, as noted earlier, a second attempt, necessary because the loose Articles of Confederation that followed the end of the Revolutionary War proved to be too close to the anarchy end of the spectrum.

That situation threatened either too much lawlessness and rule by the strongest, best armed, or most evil amongst the people on one hand, or heavy-handed, even though possibly well meaning "Majority Faction" rule of the whole people by the faction or coalition able to win elections (much the same as we suffer today).

This latter situation is essential democracy, meaning those who are able to grasp power by any means, may then force their will on everyone else. Remember the lynch mob example (majority of people in agreement, one dissenter – but he will soon be shut up?), that is simple, basic democracy in action. A herd of Lemmings stampeding over a cliff is a similar example.

The Federalist Papers, written by three men (Madison, Hamilton, and Jay) during the year following the 1787 Constitutional Convention, were to educate and inform voters in all the states of the reasoning followed by the Convention in the drafting a new Constitution. It was critically important at the time, as the ratification process for the several states was on going during that time, and as they should be, the American People were highly interested and involved in the process. American Citizens had raised questions, and this series of articles was written to answer, to influence the vote in favor of ratification, and to help shape future interpretations of the Constitution.

Most of these essays were published serially in The Independent Journal and The New York Packet between October 1787 and August 1788, then compiled into a book, originally called "The Federalist", and later the Federalist Papers. So, if you want to understand how and why the United States was founded as a Constitutional Republic, the Federalist Papers is a glimpse into the minds and rationale of several of the men who were prime movers in our Constitution.

Returning to the "Majority Faction", this was obviously problematic to Madison, as well as Jefferson, two men who were very involved in forming our government. Two of the 85 articles in the federalist papers, discussed the "Majority Faction", as a *negative* result in the representational republic the Founders hoped to complete in America. In Federalist Number Ten, James Madison actually quoted Thomas Jefferson's "Notes on The State of Virginia" (1781-2), in which Jefferson wrote to admonish a creeping form of democracy there by saying,

> *"An elective despotism was not the government we fought for . . ."* and, *"All the powers of government, legislative, executive, judiciary, result to the legislative body. The concentrating these in the same hands are precisely the definition of despotic government. It will be no alleviation that these powers will be exercised by a plurality of hands, and not by a single one. 173 despots would surely be as oppressive as one. Let those who doubt it turn their eyes on the republic of Venice."*

Even though he made no mention of the term democracy here, tyranny by the majority is *precisely* the definition of true democracy as Jefferson's earlier 'fifty one percent democracy rule' quote says, in so many words.

In Federalist 14, Madison rebuts arguments *against* the confederation of states into a new constitutional republic. Mentioning monarchists who try to compare the, *"... the turbulent democracies of ancient Greece and modern Italy"* to the new America. So the nature of democracies was understood well enough by average American Colonists that adversaries of the United States tried to use it to their own advantage.

In Federalist Number Fourteen however, Madison's primary point was the discussion of, *"rash"* attempts by *"subjects of either an absolute or limited monarchy"* to intimate that the new continent was too large, and the states too scattered to form one national government. That we should instead, form a series of smaller nations (like Europe?), or as he stated, *"render(ing) us in pieces in order to preserve our liberties and promote our happiness"*. This idea he completely refused to consider.

Democracy or Constitutional Republic? America was founded as a Constitutional Republic, with the States ratifying and accepting the 1787 Constitution. That happened after a serious national debate, in which such a Republic was argued in print for a year. It was not done blindly, nor in a dark corner. How could it even be a question today? We have been lied to, that is how!

Dedicated Marxists and Statists never quit. Like cockroaches, termites, and maggots, they are continually at work, under the surface and in the shadows, stealing, undermining, and taking their sustenance from any form of death or decay they can bring about in the body politic of a free society.

Marxists and Statists must ever use subterfuge to survive until they have caused and consolidated sufficient economic destruction and the disenchantment of those they have thrown out of work in order to bring class hatred and warfare to play, with which to cause marches in the street and eventually revolution. This is the Statists historically proven method to bring down a free nation and place its once-free people under their boot heels.

The definition of Statism is:
> *"centralized political control: the theory, or its practice, that economic and political power should be controlled by a central government leaving regional government and the individual with relatively little say in political matters"*.

And of course, the Self-Important, Self-Appointed Elites believe they must be in charge of such a centralized government because they are mentally superior to the 'stupid' common-man.

Today in the once-free United States, we have been manipulated into just such a central government run by an oligarchy of Statists, Professional Politicians and Lawyers in Washington DC.

Americans, in their complacency have continually elected and re-elected scoundrels, allowing them to remain in office until they develop a 'god-complex' and assume they have attained deity. As is obvious by even cursory study of America's Founders and their recorded documents, this is an error of tragic proportions.

While there is an instinctive sense of right and wrong to caution them against the tyranny of Statism, a free people may become complacent by living the 'good-life' over several generations. During my lifetime, Harry Truman is the last President I can remember using the term, "Republic" when speaking of our nation. Since that time the term democracy has gained supremacy, even though the very word was anathema to the Founders.

And today, too many Americans under fifty actually believe the US was *founded* as a democracy! Yet the truth is that our Constitutional Republic has been stealthily, and insidiously *perverted* into a democracy over the past hundred years by Socialists and Statists. But you do not know them as Socialists, because they changed their names to Progressives a century ago in order to disguise their devious ways of placing the American People into Statist bondage.

However, early in the Wilson Administration Progressives frightened the American People with their overt, gushing praise of Lenin and Mussolini, and stopped using the 'Progressive' word for a time and began to refer to themselves as 'Liberals'. Essentially, they took off their black hats, put on white hats, and then announced they were really the good people. Another Socialist lie!

The 'new' form of Socialism (called Communism), born during the Revolution against the French Monarchy (French First Republic), was so horrific and bloody that the French eventually ended up executing the demonic firebrand Robespierre and re-installing a member of the French Nobility (Napoleon Bonaparte) as Emperor. But not before tens of thousands of French Citizens, innocent and guilty alike, were executed by various methods, from the guillotine to simply being shot, stabbed, or beat to death by out of control lynch-mobs administering democracy-in-action.

At first these revolutionaries tried to court the US Founding Fathers, however more than a simple glance at what they were doing, showed their revolution to steeped in terror and murder, and bringing as much or more tyranny on the common people as the Monarchy had ever done.

I remember a saying from the Fifties, "The Communist Kitten that was born in France, grew to become a Tiger in Russia". First, France, then Karl Marx and Friedrich Engels authored the "Communist Manifesto" to distill the theoretical essence of this 'new' form of Statism called Communism. Lenin in turn experimented with Communism with varying success, instigating horrific life and death situations with which to collectivize Russia. Success meant collectivation, slave labor, and grinding of his heel into the faces of the Russian People, failure meant massive death tolls by murder, starvation, and colossal destruction of whole regions.

After Lenin's death, Josef Stalin, likely the most conscienceless human to ever live, had no compunction about enforcing Marxist/Communist Statism with brutal civilian slaughter reaching into many tens of millions. To this day, no one knows how many people the Soviet 'Experiment' in Russia slaughtered, but slaughtered is the correct term. Progressives do not want you to really study that history and see the parallels to what they have done over and over again in many nations of the world and are working to instill in the United States.

When you hear American politicians today glowingly extol how Marxism will bring back the equality and freedoms that capitalism has diminished, you should recall the hundred and fifty million souls slaughtered by various brands of Socialism and Marxism during the twentieth century.

The only Equality and Freedom that has historically been true under Marxism is the Equality and Freedom do die for the "Cause", which can happen to you equally whether you're bourgeoisie or proletarian.

Somehow that is not my idea of equal and free, and somehow I do not believe it was the Founders definition either.

CHAPTER FOUR

Americans, what do we believe *now*?

We hold these truths to be self-evident, that all men are created equal, that they are endowed by their Creator with certain unalienable Rights, that among these are Life, Liberty and the pursuit of Happiness. That to secure these rights, Governments are instituted among Men, deriving their just powers from the consent of the governed... —

Opening: Declaration of Independence

It is no secret what Americans *used* to think. The thought processes that freed the American People, along with their Spirits to build the greatest, richest nation in the history of the planet are enshrined in our Declaration of Independence, our Constitution, The Federalist Papers, and in a myriad of letters and documents now preserved into a personae of our beliefs. These precious documents, written by wise, yet humble men who labored (and died in many cases), to set future generations free, have then become a legacy to those who birthed a nation so free and rich that emigration to America has been a worldwide dream for both rich and downtrodden from all over the world for more than two centuries.

The majority of Americans are still a freedom-loving, center-right people measured by the American political spectrum (not the European). According to two polls reviewed, Americans are roughly 40% Conservative, 40% Moderate, and 20% Liberal. (1)

Yet there are three places in the nation where those polls are 'stood on their heads'. They are the Washington DC Beltway, the so-called 'Main-Stream Media', and College and University Campuses across the Nation. In these places, Conservatives and even Moderates are an unwelcome species. That is because 'big-government' is job security in the Beltway; the Media have cleansed their ranks of non-Marxists and Pro-Americans continually over the past 50 or more years, as have most Colleges and Universities across our Nation.

It is no secret to people as old as I am, who were politically aware in the Forties, Fifties, and Sixties that Lenin and his Bolshevik Revolution was greatly lauded in America in the 1920's. The majority of the self-appointed Elites from both the Education Establishments and the American Media who felt 'intellectually superior' to us 'ignorant masses' of common people, believed they had the obligation to *'socially engineer'* our lives and our future.

Of course, it is more difficult to find those articles and editorials today. It is even hard to find research articles I found on the internet as little as 3 years ago when I began to study Obama's background. Where have they gone? Only the Progressives know. Records today are only found in old journals and currently out-of-print books mainly found in old bookstores and garage sales. There's 'no-need' for *real* history when progressives can teach Marxist 'Social Studies'. That way you do not confuse young, malleable minds with some old, outdated version of the "facts" (even if those writers were eyewitnesses to the history). That way Progressives do not have to 'un-explain' their lies and perversions to new generations.

Personal Case-in-Point: Do you remember Washington State Representative Tom Foley? Well, he was the first of these to reveal his *self-important superiority* to me, certainly not the last. Fans of Lenin Think-Tanks and Universities became Lenin Fan Clubs, Fan

Clubs became Marxist-Leninist Cliques, and Marxist-Leninist Cliques became Underground Communist Movements, and so on throughout the Twentieth Century. Did you know the Communist Party USA (CPUSA) was formed with Soviet cash grants almost immediately after Lenin formed the Communist International (Comintern).

As these groups in-bred and grew, they obviously brought in like-thinking friends. And then, even in the 1920's, because the American People have always been suspicious of Communism and Marxism, even if they didn't care enough to understand it, they tried to 'disappear' by changing their names to "Progressives".

Sounds really 'hip', and of course, NOBODY could be against something called progress, or "Progressive" could they? That would like being against motherhood, or for child labor. Just like asking 'Joe Citizen', "When did you stop beating your wife"?

The Lefties in the Sixties loved that type of question, endlessly using it to change the subject when asked why Marxism had always failed and had killed so many millions since the French Revolution. There is no correct answer to that question which will completely settle the suspicion planted with the question that 'Joe Citizen' *is*, somehow a wife-beater (or whatever the planted allegation).

That type of question, instead of giving a simple yes, no, or any rational form of answer, is a major give-away you are talking to a Marxist, trained to propagandize, but *never* to answer a question. When asked simple, direct, questions, you hear that response endlessly from Leftist political candidates, consultants, or authors. Did you never notice that they usually answer a direct question with another question? It makes it easier than gagging on the truth if they would actually respond. How many times a day do you hear that on the evening news? If you have not been hearing it, you are not paying attention to what is happening around you.

It was, and still is a very smooth operation, because the American People have allowed that dodge as an acceptable form of dialogue. Thus, Marxists have been enabled to work like termites and cockroaches, (more correctly, deadly viruses) corrupting and polluting the very structure and fabric of American Life for almost a century now. This is their strategy as they await the 'perfect-storm' they have patiently been creating to collapse the American System of Constitutional Republican Government and place America under the tyranny of socialism. Do you *not* remember that when the Soviet Union collapsed upon itself in 1989 and the only people who mourned besides the ruling Soviet Oligarchy were the US 'Halls of Ivy'?

The 'Lame-Stream' American Media was in such deep shock that it could have happened, that they were virtually unable to react or respond intelligently for some months, yet most Americans simply shrugged off the Idiocy of being under Communism in the first place and continued what they do the best, Wealth Building! The very term "Making Money" came from the ability of Americans, using their own sweat, ingenuity, and freedom to Create Wealth instead of simply stealing the resources of the land or the labor of its people. That was something that had never occurred in the history of the world.

Unlike Europeans, who seem to worship at the ant-colony of socialism, Americans are competitive, filled with problem solving, and initiative, as well as a natural suspicion of too much government authority and too much power in government. America and Americans, under a free enterprise economy have created many times more wealth for this nation of free, private, individuals to spend as they wish than all the socialist or monarchist governments in recorded history.

I state that without fear of contradiction because socialist or monarchist societies themselves always put ordinary people into bondage, absorbing, and enriching themselves with all wealth gathered, leaving only a survival stipend for the citizen subjects who do the necessary labor.

America is, as Ronald Reagan said, a "Shining City, set upon a hill", where any man, by hard work and determination can become anything he is capable of becoming, including President. America is not a socialist anthill, with all the workers living and expending their lives in the service of the "Queen" and her "Consort". Europeans and Americans are galaxies apart in their concept of freedom. Nevertheless, there are always those who lust for power over others, and who will lie, cheat, kill, and steal to attain it. Their evil ways must be guarded against, always!

Therefore, the operative word in the title of this chapter is *"now"*, for the simple reason that too many Americans obviously no longer believe in or subscribe to the Declaration Statement above, which trumpeted the beliefs of Americans to the world back in 1776.

Unfortunately, greed and envy have replaced those American's belief that all men were endowed by their Creator with life, liberty, and the pursuit of happiness. They have instead, come to believe that only a government who takes from those who are productive will 'redistribute' to them the wealth after which they lust.

Although there were obviously some things left to correct, the American Revolution that began on Concord Bridge that day has given more personal freedom than previously existed, to more human beings on the face of the earth than in all of recorded history.

Unfortunately, our once-free nation it is now under siege by a group of people to whom the masses of people are nothing but cheap pottery chessmen in their history-long quest to rule the earth. Their support comes from those who have no wish to earn their 'daily bread' but to have it ripped from the hands of those who make it and given to them for that support.

That is a sad but true statement. However today, if you listen to the snarling, hate-filled, anti-Semitic rhetoric spouting from the "Occupy Wall Street" protesters, it reveals much to those who are paying any attention. It is an undiluted warning spoken directly by Anarchists, Marxists, and their (in many cases paid) lackeys. Their message is not at all vague, but very clearly spoken. Simply stated, the message I hear from Occupy Wall Street (OWS) follows:

- *We are here, working to subvert and collapse the hated system of Capitalism, which made America the richest, the strongest and most free nation on earth.*
- *We are here to replace Capitalism with a Socialist government that will quickly redistribute all the wealth created by others to ourselves in exchange for our support in this effort.*
- *We are not afraid to use the names Communist and Marxist, because we believe we now have a like-minded champion in the Oval Office, the numbers, and the perfect economic storm with which to destroy evil Capitalism, which we say is controlled by the hated "Jew Bankers" of Wall Street.*
- *We intend to fully use and abuse our system of laws and freedoms to protect us while we riot, rob, destroy, and pillage.*
- *We are here to promote and promulgate a Marxist Revolution to sweep the American "Rule of Law" away and replace it with Marxist "Social-Justice".*
- *The brand of "Social Justice" we seek will allow those filled with envy hatred, and greed, (it was never Hope and change) to destroy and steal any and everything from those who earned or created it the American Way (i.e., by hard work, not utilizing federal theft and welfare programs).*
- *We will utilize all means to antagonize and provoke a reaction from the police who protect the rest of America from our depredations.*
- *If able to provoke a police incident, we will infect, inflame, and lie about it, turning it into a cause célèbre in order to create more violence so we can invite governmental intervention.*
- *If the government intervenes, we will as well use that as a cause célèbre by which we can bring our professional leftist agitators, legislators, and charlatans to exacerbate and enflame further Revolution.*
- *Ad infinitum, ad nauseum!*

As I listen to OWS, the message I clearly hear, is Do you perhaps hear something different? Just what would that be?

In New York City, Police overtime topped $17 Million by Mid-March 2012, and still counting. Murders, rapes, and robberies continue, the hate-filled rhetoric escalates, and private and municipal property damage increases. Where does this end? The Socialists hope to create a Civil War. These 'regular' scenes on the nightly news remind me of so many things I have studied over the years. Read your history; watch the news of the riots in Greece. Look around you!

You can even watch movies of the Communist Revolution in Russia, such as *Dr. Zhivago*, or *"The Way Home"*, or the history of the Third Reich, in Hermann Wouk's two-part mini-series, *Winds of War, and War and Remembrance*, or *The Diary of Ann Frank*, or the finding of Auschwitz death-camp by American GI's at the end of WW II, from the mini-series, *Band of Brothers, or "The Great Escape"*. There are more, but these stand out as history lessons, even with a fictional story base. They are 'fiction-based-on-fact', so to speak.

If you have not read the history, or do not want to, at least spend a few dollars and see these movies (as kind of a 'painless history lesson'). However, realize they do depict documented historical events, easily separated by thinking people from the fictional story lines. Nevertheless, do not watch them just before dinner when they are showing the Gulags or the Gas Chambers!

Also, there are many history books out there, languishing on shelves unread because the 'Average American' is too earning a living all day so he can pay his socialist taxes, and then too busy watching sports and junk TV at night rather than study to see what he is being robbed of by America's corrupt "Free-Universal Education System".

Still think they are just unhappy students and out of work people looking for the government to help them out by correcting the economy?

Following is a list of Occupy Wall Street's Supporters, Sponsors and Sympathizers for your reading pleasure: (2)

- **Communist Party USA** Sources: Communist Party USA, OWS speech, The Daily Caller
- **American Nazi Party** Sources: Media Matters, American Nazi Party, White Honor, Sunshine State News
- **Ayatollah Khamenei,** Supreme Leader of Iran Sources: The Guardian, Tehran Times, CBS News
- **Barack Obama** Sources: ABC News, CBS News, ForexTV, NBC New York
- **The government of North Korea** Sources: Korean Central News Agency (North Korean state-controlled news outlet), The Marxist-Leninist, Wall Street Journal, Times of India
- **Louis Farrakhan, Nation of Islam** Sources: Black in America, Weasel Zippers, Philadelphia Weekly
- **Revolutionary Communist Party** Sources: Revolutionary Communist Party, Revolution newspaper, in-person appearance
- **David Duke** Sources: Talking Points Memo, video statement, davidduke.com
- **Joe Biden** Sources: Talking Points Memo, video statement, Mother Jones
- **Hugo Chavez** Sources: Mother Jones, Reuters, Examiner.com
- **Revolutionary Guards of Iran** Sources: Associated Press, FARS News Agency, UPI
- **Black Panthers (original)** Sources: in-person appearance, Occupy Oakland, Oakland Tribune
- **Socialist Party USA** Sources: Socialist Party USA, IndyMedia, The Daily Caller
- **US Border Guard** Sources: White Reference, www.usborderguard.com, Gateway Pundit, Just Another Day blog *(NOT to be confused with the US Border Patrol!)*

Industrial Workers of the World Sources: IWW web site, iww.org, in-person appearances

CAIR Sources: in-person appearance, Washington Post, CAIR, CAIR New York

Nancy Pelosi Sources: Talking Points Memo, video statement, ABC News, The Weekly Standard

Communist Party of China Sources: People's Daily (Communist Party organ), Reuters, chinataiwan.org, The Telegraph

Hezbollah Sources: almoqawama.org, almoqawama.org, almoqawama.org , wikipedia

9/11Truth.org Sources: 911truth.org , 911truth.org , 911truth.org

International Bolshevik Tendency Sources: bolshevik.org, Wire Magazine

Anonymous Sources: Adbusters, The Guardian, video statement

White Revolution Source: whiterevolution.com

International Socialist Organization Sources: Socialist Worker, socialistworker.org, in-person appearance

PressTV (Iranian government outlet) Sources: PressTV, wikipedia

Marxist Student Union Sources: Marxist Student Union, Big Government, marxiststudentunion.blogspot.com

Freedom Road Socialist Organization Sources: FightBack News, fightbacknews.org,

ANSWER, Sources: ANSWER press release, ANSWER web site, Xinhua

Party for Socialism and Liberation Sources: pslweb.org, The Daily Free Press, Liberation News

This is a privately compiled list by a few anti-Marxist groups of people with several days of research, and within *less than sixty* days of the OWS movement beginning.

It was published for informational purposes and has *does not* claim to be anything like a complete list (after all, there are *hundreds* of these Pro-Marx-Anti-American groups out there. Not only do they not hide who they are, many of them are actually receiving multi-million dollar funding from the US Government, (your Tax-Dollars at work!) Check it out!

As an up-standing, hard-working, taxpaying American, doesn't it make you proud to have your sitting President, Vice President, and Former Speaker of the House cheering for and assisting this openly Anti-American, Marxist, Communist, Hate-America group? It assuredly makes me want to vomit! But, neither is it unexpected. I have been studying these people for over 50 years, and they always seem to move forward with the assistance of Washington DC. Sometimes two steps forward then one-step back, whatever is necessary. But notice they always gain a step in such a move.

Unfortunately, too-few good Americans are aware enough to do anything. Actually, altogether, too-many Americans are so illiterate of history and politics they are unable to see the gigantic 'Freight-Train' barreling down the track to destroy them.

That is no surprise either. This Plan was published years ago. Following Marx, who is credited with the "invention of Social-Studies", and beginning from the top down (now down to kindergarten), school children began years ago being taught social studies (and later 'Ethnic-Studies', and 'Diversity') instead of US History. Now they do not study World History either.

Since recorded History has repeated itself in recognizable patterns since long before King Solomon said, "There is nothing new under the Sun", there is also a predictable result to such a situation, and Karl Marx was very well aware of it. *"Those who refuse to learn from history are doomed to repeat it"*. Yes, there is a reason I chose those quotations for this book.

Predictably, if people do not know, or are not taught about these cycles, they may easily be herded off a cliff into some form of despotic, totalitarian bondage. There are always evil men willing to do so, and there are always strong and powerful men willing to be used, gaining from aiding and abetting them. There are also others, uneducated in this knowledge, and easily led by smooth words from properly prepared Marxist teachers and especially those spouting clichés filled with grand-sounding themes. The term, "Useful Idiots" (coined by Lenin) comes to mind as I listen to these people (young and old), who have been used to the benefit of Socialism.

At first stealthily, then openly, Marxism was taught in the Universities of the American Education System, generation after generation for the past hundred years. Many believe today that Communism and Fascism are a viable form of government and will give them 'Social Justice' and set them free to rob, riot, and essentially take everything they want from anyone who has more than they do.

Of course, as it historically works out, Socialism usually ends up taking *everything* away from *anyone* who has *anything*, and "Useful Idiots" end up shot or imprisoned as "Enemies of the Government". Because while once helpful, these idiots are now impeding those who are in charge. Besides, they also have anti-government attitudes. Too bad, they didn't study their history!

The American people are not generally in favor of such things, but most have simply been too busy, either earning a living and having only so much extra energy to expend, or have been lulled into complacency by having had it so good for so many generations, they still trust the Lame-Stream Media. Many of these are ideologically or financially complicit with Marxist Communism, Fascism, Anarchism, or any other form of darkness that helps destroy the USA. Yet the Average American simply cannot (or will not) believe this could happen to the USA.

Last, but certainly not least, I have inserted a copy of Ten Planks from Karl Marx's Communist Manifesto into the Appendix. Please look there and review it. You may be surprised at how many you recognize in our own nation.

If these are in forceful effect, the societies are practicing Communism, whether they realize it yet or not.

The Ten Planks of the Communist Manifesto, (3) written in 1848 by Karl Heinrich Marx and Friedrich Engels, (also known as the 10 Pillars of Communism) are stated below:

The Coming Fourth Reich

1. Abolition of property in land and application of all rents of land to public purposes.

2. A heavy progressive or graduated income tax.

3. Abolition of all right of inheritance.

4. Confiscation of the property of all emigrants and rebels.

5. Centralization of credit in the hands of the State, by means of a national bank with State capital and an exclusive monopoly.

6. Centralization of the means of communication and transport in the hands of the State.

7. Extension of factories and instruments of production owned by the State; the bringing into cultivation of waste- lands, and the improvement of the soil generally in accordance with a common plan.

8. Equal liability of all to labor. Establishment of industrial armies, especially for agriculture.

9. Combination of agriculture with manufacturing industries; gradual abolition of the distinction between town and country, by a more equitable distribution of the population over the country.

10. Free education for all children in public schools. Abolition of children's factory labor in its present form and combination of education with industrial production.

~~~~~~~~~~~~~~~

Do any of these sound familiar? Can you identify which ones are already place, to what extent they are in force in US law, and for just how long the American People have been gradually and increasingly accepted them? Are you stunned into disbelief and hopefully to action, or will you merely retreat into a grand canyon of denial.

You know that song by now, *"It can't happen here!"* Oh, Really?

CHAPTER FIVE

Just what is Fascism?

> Fascism: *any movement, ideology, or attitude that favors dictatorial government, centralized control of private enterprise, repression of all opposition, and extreme nationalism.*
>
> The Encarta World English Dictionary

Such a clinical definition is like defining the elephant as a large grey beast. It gives you a vague picture, but totally fails to describe a highly intelligent, social animal, sometimes docile, and sometimes rampaging, with few things able to stop it.

However, the following two statements written by Benito Mussolini, one of the two best-known Fascists in world history, while much less clinical and precise, chillingly demonstrate the exact totalitarian, anti individual liberty state of fascism. Writing in *the Fascist State versus individual liberty*:

> "The Fascist conception of the State is all-embracing; outside of it no human or spiritual values can exist, much less have value. Thus understood, Fascism is totalitarian, and the Fascist State—a synthesis and a

unit inclusive of all values—interprets, develops, and potentiates the whole life of a people."
                         Benito Mussolini; Doctrine of Fascism

Additionally, in "The Fascist State versus social, educational, political, and economic facets of life", Mussolini states:

"The Fascist State lays claim to rule in the economic field no less than in others; it makes its action felt throughout the length and breadth of the country by means of its corporate, social, and educational institutions, and all the political, economic, and spiritual forces of the nation, organized in their respective associations, circulate within the State."

Fascist Socialism is, first, and foremost a religious belief. Never forget that! Even though Socialism considers itself Atheistic, Socialism's adherents consider the Socialization of World Society to be the culmination of the World Society's Collective Salvation. That is why you cannot use logic to argue with a Socialist. They can only respond to what is a religious argument emotionally. It is also why Socialists can ignore, overlook, or blindly minimize the cost in human lives and suffering 'necessary' to bring about the Socialist End Game, because they believe they are bringing about a millennium in which salvation for the total nation (or total world) will be accomplished.

Described in another way, Socialists believe they are bringing about a millennial reign (Thousand Year Reich, anyone?), of a Utopian world, with freedom, equality, and collective salvation for all. In essence, Fascism resembles the Kingdom prophesied in the Bible, except this one is ruled with tyranny to complete its collective salvation. Digest that, and then tell me it is not a religious belief.

Therefore, just as Christianity is endowed with the character of Christ, Buddhism with the character of Buddha, and Communism with the character of Marx, Lenin, Stalin, et al, failure to recognize modern National Socialism (Fascism) as a religious cult, is to see a few trees, but never the 'forest'. Fascists follow a charismatic leader determined to cleanse and purify his Nation/State with his own form of "Collective Salvation". Historically, millions have died because they failed to recognize this. This knowledge is critical to survival.

Islam as well, from my personal experience living and working in a Muslim Country, is certainly endowed with the character of Mohammed. It is a form of religious government, fascist in nature, in which the life and meaning of all people living inside its boundaries is forcibly projected into formation of the Islamic state, where the 'salvation' of its members is accomplished through minute control of every facet of life by the mullahs and the religious police. Life under these conditions consists of strict living rules for Muslims, under threat of death for straying, whether by the religious authorities, or even by their own family, devoutly killing their own members in 'honor' killings to absolve Islam of their 'sins'.

For Non-Muslims, conquered by and living under Islamic Rule, life is ruled in Dhimmitude, a form of third-class citizenry in lieu of death for Non-Muslim minorities unwilling to convert to Islam. Again, never forget that radical Islam happily allied itself with Adolph Hitler during WW II because he was anti-Christian and Anti-Jew.

In today's essentially anti-Christian USA, where a majority scoff at Christianity and Judeo/Christian values as 'exclusive', yet consider themselves to be 'tolerant' of all religions, it might be difficult to realize Americans could be lured or pushed into a quasi-religious political movement.

However, historically speaking, nations founded on any other set of moral values than our Founding Documents are highly susceptible to devolving into a democracy, thence into a statist tyranny, by following a charismatic leader into a dictatorship, where they are ruled by a coalition of the strong and the wicked in the name of national unity, or whatever.

Founder John Adams stated,

> "Our Constitution was made only for a moral and religious people. It is wholly inadequate to the government of any other."

Notice that his statement did *not* invoke Christianity or Judaism, from which the basic tenets for morality have stemmed for millenniums, but merely indicated that morality was a critical foundation for the survival of our Constitutional Republic. An old saying, illustrated repeatedly in many nations is, *"He who believes nothing will fall for anything"*.

After all, people are drawn to the idea of bettering themselves as well as their society through some form of hard work, self-denial, and or sacrifice, whether consider themselves religious or not. It is therefore no large leap for people who serve no omnipotent god, to substitute national, world, or ecological allegiance as a deity deserving of homage and sacrifice, especially given a charismatic, smooth talking, leader like the Pied Piper of Hamlin leading them. Review the Mussolini and Hitler's beliefs here (1)

Concerning Fascism, while Hitler and the word Nazi (which is a simple contraction of the two German words, National Socialism) is best known, it is more likely proper, and many scholars do, to consider Benito Mussolini as the 'father' of twentieth century fascism. It is true that both men were atheistic, brutal, arrogant, narcissistic, and shared numerous other traits with power-mad tyrants, but Mussolini's rather large collection of writings on fascism are more easily readable and understandable, even if you don't agree with his premise, whereas Hitler's are recognized (by most) as the lunatic ranting of a madman in most cases. However, Hitler is the one best remembered, due to the magnitude of his evil, although increasingly today, not always in a negative way.

Most Americans think first of Adolph Hitler when the word fascism is mentioned, and that is proper, because he was the most notorious, bloodstained, evil face of fascism in the twentieth century. But did you know that today, deniers of the Holocaust are re-building Hitler into a cult-hero, and that Mein Kampf is a recent a best seller in Turkey, the Palestine Territories, and some eastern European nations, and that in 2009, Mein Kampf topped Amazon's Best-Seller list in Kindle, and is a huge seller internationally in the Arabic Version?

This adds up to a corresponding upsurge in anti-Semitism worldwide. Have you actually listened to the anti-Semitic, hate filled "Jew Banker" type comments recently coming from the Occupy Wall Street Movement? Are Americans paying attention to anything but their own lifestyles and major sports events? Alternatively, do they even care? Most of the time, it is hard to tell.

Please remember we said at the beginning of this chapter, historically, the failure to recognize fascism for what it is has proven itself to be is a deadly error. Millions have died because they failed to recognize these signs. That haunts this writer as days pass, because I cannot help but see this and other things as major warning signs, readable because I have studied their results in history.

Therefore, while Mussolini better defined fascism, his rhetoric is still more than a little difficult to digest. Not in part because of his repetitive concept of the All-Powerful State (or Nation) as a type of god-figure, embodying the 'spirit' of its collective individuals, who are either *'progressive'*, moving into their Fascist future, or *'static'*, i.e., not moving forward (where to him such inactivity equates to death), and of himself as being that Fascist State's supreme protector, i.e.;

> *"Primarily, Fascism, the more it considers and observes the future and the development of humanity quite apart from political considerations of the moment, believes neither in the possibility nor the utility of perpetual peace. It thus repudiates the doctrine of pacifism—born of a renunciation of the struggle and an act of cowardice in the face of sacrifice. War alone brings up to the highest tension all human energy and puts the stamp of nobility upon the peoples who have the courage to meet it. All other trials are substitutes, which never really put men into the position where they have to make the great decision—the alternative of life or death.*
>
> Benito Mussolini

The Coming Fourth Reich

One of the hardest thing for an American to conceive in Mussolini's writings is not something Mussolini did himself, but what the American Progressives (Socialists) did to America almost a century ago in order to camouflage their rhetoric and methods. The meaning of the words Liberal and Conservative are totally reversed since Mussolini wrote his doctrine. The word Liberal was then roughly equivalent to today's term 'Libertarian', as in those seeking the greatest individual liberty and personal freedom for all citizens, whereas the term Conservative defined at that time someone who sought to retain the old ways, for instance, those in Colonial America who wished to keep a Monarchy instead of setting up a Constitutional Republic. By today, those definitions are, in American common usage, totally reversed.

Consider his following statement:

> "The **"Liberal State"** is not a directing force, guiding the play and development (both material and spiritual) of a collective body, but merely a force limited to the function of recording results. On the other hand, the Fascist State is itself conscious, and has itself a will and a personality—thus it may be called the "ethical" State"
>
> Doctrine of Fascism, Benito Mussolini

The bold emphasis was added to point out that what he is saying is impugning **freedom**, not what we today call liberalism.

In another place in this document, to prove that he was speaking negatively of the freedom given the citizens of the USA, Mussolini also refers to the 'Liberal State', while including the year *"1789, the date which seems to be the opening years of the semi-Liberal century."* To me, this indicates Mussolini is speaking of the founding of the American government, as our current federal constitution was written in 1787 and ratified in 1789, creating a (then) 'Liberal' i.e., Freedom Loving, class of people in the United States of America. Today it is the "Liberal" Americans, of both parties who are working stealthily to destroy individual liberty and freedom in America, returning us to statist tyranny under Marxist control.

> *Personal Warning!* Excessive study of either Mussolini or Hitler's writings can lead to severe mental confusion and potential gastric distress!   rg

While the Roman Empire was technically the first fascist nation/state, that statement is not today a straightforward truth. My study indicates to me that the Roman Empire never equaled the fascist form of government Benito Mussolini set up in Italy in the 1920's, but was a simpler form of fascism. I admit this is a very rudimentary political glance at the Roman Empire, but let us do it to put today into context.

Rome was first a monarchy, which commoners and aristocracy overthrew in order to install a form of representative republic, still mostly controlled by the aristocracy. However, the republic deteriorated by political intrigue into a form of democracy, then into fascism with its first emperor, only to disintegrate further as power factions continued to battle or assassinate one another. However, Rome survived over two millenniums as a nation in one form or another, from 750 BC to 1450 AD although latter centuries observed the slow, incremental collapse of a dying colossus.

Only a part of Rome's history was fascist, and while it was a form of fascism, it does not appear to be the fascism re-invented in the twentieth century by Mussolini. It appears more likely to be an attempt by rulers bent on controlling an ever fragmenting populace, partly by recalling and appealing to the loyalty for earlier Rome, and by the brutality of power when necessary. Consider that in the later condition the Caesars mollified angry crowds who were ready to riot in the streets by going atop a tower and throwing gold coins to the crowds until the rioters had enough money in hand to go away and spend it. Yet we know that government brute-force ripped that gold was from another citizen's hands, just as today we see "tax rebates" going to those who pay no taxes. As King Solomon said, "there is nothing new under the sun".

There can be no greater historical comparison lesson here than to relate a number of quotations from the two 'great' fascist leaders of the twentieth century, Adolph Hitler and Benito Mussolini (by the way, did you know that their titles, Der Fuehrer, and Il Duce) are the same word in their respective languages? The "Leader"!

Adolph Hitler Quotes:

- "By the skillful and sustained use of propaganda, one can make a people see even heaven as hell or an extremely wretched life as paradise".
- "He alone, who owns the youth, gains the future."
- "How fortunate for leaders that men do not think."
- "The art of leadership...consists of consolidating the attention of the people against a single adversary and taking care that nothing will split up that attention."
- "If you tell a big enough lie and tell it frequently enough, it will be believed."
- "The great masses of the people will more easily fall victims to a big lie than to a small one."
- "The leader of genius must have the ability to make different opponents appear as if they belonged to one category."
- "I use emotion for the many and reserve reason for the few."
- "The great strength of the totalitarian state is that it forces those who fear it to imitate it."
- "There must be no majority decisions, but only responsible persons, and the word 'council' must be restored to its original meaning. Surely every man will have advisers by his side, but the decision will be made by one man." "Success is the sole earthly judge of right and wrong."
- "The [Nazi party] should not become a constable of public opinion, but must dominate it. It must not become a servant of the masses, but their master!"
- "Demoralize the enemy from within by surprise, terror, sabotage, assassination. This is the war of the future."
- "Humanitarianism is the expression of stupidity and cowardice".

Benito Mussolini Quotes:

- "Fascism conceives of the State as an absolute, in comparison with which all individuals or groups are relative, only to be conceived in their relation to the State".
- "The Fascist conception of the State is all-embracing; outside of it no human or spiritual values can exist, much less have value. Thus understood, Fascism is totalitarian, and the Fascist State -- a synthesis and a unit inclusive of all values -- interprets, develops, and potentiates the whole life of a people".
- "The corporate State considers that private enterprise in the sphere of production is the most effective and useful instrument in the interest of the nation. In view of the fact that private organization of production is a function of national concern, the organizer of the enterprise is responsible to the State for the direction given to production".
- "Against individualism, the fascist conception is for the State; and it is for the individual in so far as he coincides with the State, which is the conscience and universal will of man".
- "State intervention in economic production arises only when private initiative is lacking or insufficient, or when the political interests of the State are involved. This intervention may take the form of control, assistance or direct management".
- "Fascism should rightly be called Corporatism as it is a merge of state and corporate power".
- "The Fascist State lays claim to rule in the economic field
- "Fascism, the more it considers and observes the future and the development of humanity quite apart from political considerations of the moment, believes neither in the possibility nor the utility of perpetual peace."
- "Fascism is definitely and absolutely opposed to the doctrines of liberalism, both in the political and economic sphere". *(—Here Liberalism means personal liberty – rg)*

- "People are tired of liberty. They have had a surfeit of it. Liberty is no longer a chaste and austere virgin…. Today's youth are moved by other slogans…Order, Hierarchy, Discipline".
  - "It is the State which educates its citizens in civic virtue, gives them a consciousness of their mission, and welds them into unity".
  - "At every hour of every day, I can tell you on which page of which book each school child in Italy is studying".

Any similarity to words or deeds uttered by US politicians today are not coincidental, but based on the historic advancement of Fascism, Socialism, and Socialist theory as a generally accepted fact by the American Education System over past decades.

Such similarity is sadly indicative of just what we are discussing in this book and was the reason for writing it. With my personal avocation for politics, economics, and history, I have been listening to and seeing such glaring similarities for decades because many years ago I studied the writings of *their* Founding Fathers as well as ours. Then, after learning the dialect of socialist language, it became easy to spot Marxist/Statist Propaganda wherever it raises its ugly head.

If you cannot now understand the evil that fascism portends as a political system, there is likely little use in your continued reading. You are sufficiently inoculated against understanding or believing any truth about Socialist/Statist Governments by the US education system and the US Left-Stream Media.

Sad because many people so inoculated never knew what was happening before they were imprisoned, killed, or both by the very Statist Government their silent complicity had helped to install.

Part Two:

If you don't know where you are, how can you know where you're headed?

CHAPTER SIX

Revolution? It couldn't happen here, could it?

A recent Pew Poll reported the following on this subject:

> "Young people -- the collegiate and post-college crowd, who have served as the most visible face of the Occupy Wall Street movement -- might be getting more comfortable with socialism. ... The poll, published (12/28/11), found that while Americans overall tend to oppose socialism by a strong margin -- 60 percent say they have a negative view of it, versus just 31 percent who say they have a positive view -- socialism has more fans than opponents among the 18-29 crowd. Forty-nine percent of people in that age bracket say they have a positive view of socialism; only 43 percent say they have a negative view. ...
>
> Indeed, ... poll also found that just 46 percent of people age 18-29 have positive views of capitalism, and 47 percent have negative views... income inequality ... has received more and more attention in politics and the media since the Occupy movement launched in mid-September. Usage of the term rose dramatically in news coverage following the start of the protests, and politicians from Senate Majority Leader Harry

The Coming Fourth Reich

Reid to President Barack Obama have used the movement's language to describe divisions in the American public." (1)

Where and why did these young people suddenly reverse their own parent-group's opinion (one held, in fact, since the founding of the USA?) The answer is in the first words above, *the collegiate and post-college crowd.*

Universities (especially State-run Universities) have been secretly teaching Marxism as an alternative to capitalism and a viable form of government since the first 'Friends of Lenin' and 'Fellow Travelers' set up cliques and clubs among American professors, and that was concurrent with the formation of the Soviet Union. It has accelerated recently, and shifted into warp speed with the advent of Barack Obama's introduction of class envy, hatred, and violence as acceptable American Virtues. Under his leadership, the rhetoric has become increasingly overt and filled with a specific hatred and venom for Capitalism in general, and for the American System in particular. President Obama even revised American History, while describing as a virtue, the following blatant National Socialist Ideal, in his first campaign speech of the new election year, January 10, 2012:

> *"We are not a country that was built on the idea of survival of the fittest," ... "We were built on the idea that we survive as a nation. We thrive when we work together, all of us."*
>
> Barack Obama (2)

Pure National Socialism! But, his wife had already foreshadowed just such fascist idealism before Obama was elected, in a speech on May 2008; (to those who understood what they were hearing);

> *"Barack knows that we are going to have to make sacrifices; we are going to have to change our conversation; we're going to have to change our traditions, our history; we're going to have to move into a different place as a nation."*
>
> Michelle Obama (3)

If you know where you are, you may figure out where you are going. However, if you follow someone blindly, you had better be certain you can trust them!

The following is my own capsule recap of major historical Marxist Revolutionary tactics.

The ultimate goal of all communists, fascists, and statists of every stripe is to completely subjugate every person in their nation into automatons of national service, whose only duty in life is to enrich the nation/state.

The primary difference between Fascism and Communism is that fascists claim to do it for the 'good' of the 'Nation' (*National* Socialism), and communists claim to do it for the 'good' of the *Proletariat*, Marx's term for the 'Working Class' (i.e., "Dictatorship of the Proletariat"). Both are but the "Skin of a reason, stuffed with a Lie". While there are rhetorical rationalizations for the differences, both are simple Totalitarian Statist Socialism, both bow and worship at the altar of Marxist Socialism, their 'holy grail' is essentially defined as:

> "Everything belongs to the 'Working Poor' or to the 'Nation State', and we, as your betters, have appointed ourselves to govern you for it, and it for you".

Welcome to Socialist Slavery! Both are, or must become Totalitarian Socialist Dictatorships because people are neither ants nor bees. It is humanly impossible that living in a communal society where everyone is shackled to an inferior level of mediocrity can be a normal human condition. Modern fascism historically requires some charismatic "Leader" who then becomes the all-powerful dictator, while communism has either a (Communist) party head who is an all-powerful dictator, or an Oligarchy, an all-powerful group of leaders, i.e., The Communist Central Committee.

Communism concentrates on class hatred to assist class conflict, and, the constant state of revolutions they believe necessary for the "evolution" of mankind into the glory of the final Triumphal Revolution, which creates the fulfilled Communist State, or Utopia.

Fascism concentrates on the constant states of conflict between differing ethnicities or nations as required to achieve the deserved health and shared destiny' of the sacrosanct Nation and its servant people.

Both require common enemies and goals for their people, in order to focus them on 'external' problems rather than realizing that their own government is the one actually enslaving and tyrannizing them.

However, regardless of the socialist's 'holy writ', people are all individuals, with individual likes, talents, and environments, which shaped their personalities (yes, even those raised under socialist tyranny). So while people can eventually give up all hope of ever being an individual under the multiple generational tyranny of socialism's "equality" (actually equal pain, equal misery, and enforced equal mediocrity), the yearning for freedom, and to be who they are, is always alive (even if merely a smoldering ember), in the human breast.

This is what established the greatness of the American Founding Fathers. They not only recognized this fact, they labored and even died, to establish a nation where the dream could live and yes, even flourish.

However, the biggest socialist lie told, that the American People unfortunately swallow, 'hook-line-&-sinker', is the one pitting the 'poor' against the 'rich'. However, wealth in America is *not* a static situation as it was in old Europe and the rest of the world.

Did you know that in some large cities in India there are people who are born, live their complete lives, and die within a few hundred yard square area? Yes, a whole lifetime! That has been true in India and many other nations in the world for millenniums. America was founded to reverse that situation, to let men rise to the greatest they can be through personal freedom. However, today, with active revolutionary pressure in the streets being encouraged and supported by our own President, we are closer to losing that than at any time since our founding.

The truth is that neither affluence nor poverty is a static situation in America, as in much of the world. In America, with the freedoms we have, multitudes of men and women have been born poor only to become successful, famous, and yes, even rich.

Many people in their early adult life, being recently educated in some work skill, recently married, and raising young children, are still finding or advancing in work and skills. They are today's 'poor', but more importantly, most likely they are tomorrow's middle class, comfortable, well off, affluent, or even rich!

While some Americans become wards of the state, completely dependent on government support, the rest of us go through these cycles in our lives. Beginning young and broke, eventually achieving some comfort zone in a level of the middle class which our talent, determination, and work ethic has earned us, then retiring and using up much of our nest-egg enjoying our declining years.

There are also, of course those who are born to wealth. However, we have all watched some of these who used that wealth wisely, who increased it during their lifetime, and we have watched a single generation squander wealth previous generations had built up.

We've also seen a number of people like Steve Jobs and Bill Gates, who had nothing but a dream, and working tirelessly, eventually created a billion dollar business that 'began in a garage'.

There was a time that was the universal American Dream. But today, under the heavy hand of increasingly powerful and onerous State and Federal Governments, piling innumerable and constantly increasing job-killing restrictions, regulations, and taxes, coupled with crony capitalism obviously an acceptable form of business to the current White House, it has become the universal American Nightmare.

The aging totalitarian monarchy as a form of tyranny has been fairly well refuted in today's modern cultures. This happened over a number of centuries, beginning with the Magna Carta, signed in England in 1225, forcing the monarchy to curtail some of its god-like rights, and beginning the long path to the parliamentary form of government they now have.

Even though these first fragile freedoms from monarchial tyranny were assigned only to the upper class (barons, nobles, etc.) it was because these 'landed gentry' were necessary to the King, so they were able, by standing together, to compel him to assign some decent rights to the common people.

While to us, this is unthinkable, before the Magna Carta the King could arbitrarily punish (even to the death) any subject "freeman" without question or rebuke. When I use the term, "god-like powers" I am not fooling.

On the other hand, over the past two centuries, Statist Tyranny, in various forms of Socialism or Marxism has flourished. With Kings out of the way, the people thought they were going to be free. However, there are always plenty of evil people out there, longing to have power over people's lives. These then are always dreaming and scheming how to take control. Unfortunately, telling the people *'we are taking care of you'*, or *'we are doing it for your own good because we know better than you'*, endlessly suckers a majority of people very handily.

Even though it is the basic ploy of the socialist tyranny, which slaughtered over a hundred and fifty million people in the twentieth century, it is amazing to watch a free people accept this proven lie and end up under tyranny repeatedly. There is truly nothing new under the sun.

So now, referring to the Pew Poll at the beginning of this chapter - currently almost half of our youth (ages 18-29) have a positive view of socialism, while a majority holds a negative view of capitalism. Add that to two other groups who also have positive views of socialism, Blacks, who favor socialism fifty-five to thirty-six percent, and liberal Democrats who favor socialism fifty-nine to thirty-nine percent. This is a substantial and growing voting group, as these youth attain voting age and more follow them.

Add to these the seven point nine million unionized public-sector workers and seven point four million private sector union workers, the majority of whom will vote and contribute to keep the socialist candidate who gives them the biggest and most wages and benefits. Add those Welfare recipients whose Social Security, Medicare and unemployment insurance checks make up to thirty five percent of US Wages. Add the farmers (and employees of the huge corporate farms) who live by the subsidy instead of the land. Add those who work in and on the completely subsidized "Alternative Energy" sector now booming in the US, because of environmentalists and their bought and paid for lackeys in power in Washington DC and the State Capitols around the nation. Add how many others who have their own sterling-silver 'nipple' permanently attached to the 'government trough'. Dangerously close to half the population.

It is a wonder America has kept her freedom this long, but now we are now reaching the fifty-one percent 'tipping-point', warned about by Thomas Jefferson at the founding of our nation. We have arrived at the point where those who hate America, or love their sterling silver 'nipple' at the government trough more than they love America are together gaining the voting majority.

We've now reached a point where those who love America, and want to leave it to their grandchildren intact, whose ethics are to *work* for their living, who simply want the government to leave them alone, are quickly becoming the forty nine percent. The minority in our Ill-fated Democracy who are expected to keep working and paying taxes to subsidize the "takers" while being cursed and berated by President Obama, as the USA spirals into revolution in the streets, civil war, and the "Tyranny of the Majority".

Still think it cannot happen here? Dream on!

CHAPTER SEVEN

How did the seeds of Marxism come to the USA?

"Socialism is the doctrine that man has no right to exist for his own sake, that his life and his work do not belong to him, but belong to society, that the only justification of his existence is his service to society, and that society may dispose of him in any way it pleases for the sake of whatever it deems to be its own tribal, collective good."

Ayn Rand

Ayn Rand is a controversial author today. Possibly, because after she lived under Soviet Communism part of her life, and became free after coming to the USA, she dared to write articles and books showing the farce of human tragedy Marxism/Communism is and always has been. Interestingly, that is not a popular opinion to voice in today's America, even though the Soviet "Utopia" collapsed on its own after slaughtering merely tens of millions of its own people. However, for me, even after a lifetime of being an anti-Communist, I found her description/definition of Socialism to be the most vivid, vital, and true description of the Socialist State I had ever read. I guess it was because she had seen its evil face in person instead of merely studying it from a distance.

However, while Fascism is merely a form of Socialism, Marxists do not claim it because it does not recognize the 'rights' of the working class to steal from and murder any other class. Instead, Fascism maintains that the National Government has those rights exclusively, "For the good of the Nation". In addition, because of Adolph Hitler, being openly Fascist is even less acceptable to Americans than Communism has become. However, the "nation" is the "state", and vice-versa, under Socialism. The convoluted reasoning of the rulers bears no difference to those being slaughtered, imprisoned, or merely slaves of whichever brand of socialism they are unfortunate enough under which to live. Either 'brother' is a bloodthirsty and brutal tyrant.

However, because Americans are ignorant of what fascism is, they have readily accepted a large amount of it in their current government, because the foundation of both is socialism. In addition, we presently have a highly Socialized government in our nation. The reason I believe fascism will win over communism in America is that Americans will always want some degree of capitalism. So a charismatic leader who knows how to play the people and use crony capitalism to his advantage will have greater success leading the American People off the 'cliff' into national socialism than into a communist 'dictatorship of the proletariat'.

But those who lust after power over mankind will utilize either or a combination of both, and the end result will still be slaughter and imprisonment for ten to thirty percent of the American population and the tyranny of simple slavery under an NKVD or Gestapo type police force for the rest, and for their progeny.

This discussion of Socialism and Fascism would not be complete without tracing the early arrival of, and the increasing infection of Marxist Socialism into American mainstream thinking. That story follows here with a little background.

Socialism, as described in Marx's Communist Manifesto, is a phase, or a step on the road to Communism. This is troubling, because if we accept from Marx's own writing that socialism is merely a stage in a nation's progression to Communism, we must admit that socialism is increasingly accepted, especially by the youth of the USA as a viable form of government. This indicates that America is already at least (small S) socialist nation, and quite possibly well on its way to becoming a (large S) Socialist Nation, complete with Socialist Tyranny.

Astoundingly, the same 'Marxist, Socialist Religion' by which past Communist and Fascist regimes slaughtered some one hundred fifty million people during the twentieth century, is now accepted by 49 percent of American youth among the 18-29 age group, and by varying percentages among other groups, according to a recent (December 2011) Pew Poll. Of course, most of these brainwashed young people believe "It will be different this time, because we've *"Evolved, and we are smarter now"*.

However, *where* did this come from and how did it happen?

First, remember that socialism is the noun half of the name, National Socialism. Next, remember this: Germany under Hitler, Italy under Mussolini, Spain under Franco, Argentina under Peron, Chile under Pinochet, and Japan under Tojo, all *became a* Fascist Nation during the twentieth century.

Each of these was nations struggling from under some form of socialist, or monarchist and aristocratic tyranny. However, they did not become communist nations, and neither were they originally capitalist nations.

Nevertheless, they certainly ended up with a nationalist "Leader" who then became a dictator, and who transformed their nations into a Dictatorial Fascist Police State. Half of these nations ended up on the "Axis" side during WW II, destroying their own nation in a quest for national expansion or glory. Spain, while ostensibly 'neutral' was sympathetic with the Axis as well. Argentina became a hideout for infamous Nazis eluding capture as war criminals after Germany lost the war and their evil was exposed.

The sad truth is the route to dictatorial, police state socialism is virtually identical for both a Communist and a Fascist takeover.

The Coming Fourth Reich

Miscellaneous details may differ, but the route to revolution follows very similar road signs.

First, a complacent, mentally lazy public, either disinterested, uncaring, or unaware they are drifting and had been brainwashed to believe in socialism as a viable form of government. *Second*, a charismatic leader achieves a position of some power, using demagoguery and populist lies to divide people into opposing factions and groups, normally based on ethnic, political, or economic hatred, greed, and anger. *Third*, a real or created national emergency, utilized as a crisis, may further create discomfort and angst among the population, further dividing them. *Forth*, the leader and his agitators to turn anxiety and division into violence and rioting in the streets carefully escalate discomfort. This can then be carefully exacerbated and manipulated into all-out Civil War. Civil War then causes the people to call out to the leader for control of the situation, which is what he has been waiting for. He can now respond with pre-engineered laws and civil rights, curfews, arrest of opponents, nationalization of the press, and declaration of martial law. Best of all for the "Leader", a "democratic" election can now bring him into complete control, with sweeping new powers that he has already prepared. The opposition party is destroyed, leaving no more detractors, no more bad press or barricades to his becoming dictator. The transition from a free or semi-free people to a dictatorship is complete. Here we have "Democracy, one man, one vote, one time!" That is exactly how Adolph Hitler became Dictator of Germany, in less than two months.

Did you know that Adolph Hitler, a charismatic street agitator supported by union goon thugs, after his party gained only 43.9% of the vote, was appointed Chancellor of Germany by President Hindenburg on January 30, 1933, representing a coalition government? Yet, by March 23, 1933, after several "crises", was able to pass his previously written *Enabling Act* which, combined with his February 28, 1933 *Reichstag Fire Decree*, granted him dictatorship of Germany? You had better know who paved the road you are following!

During the past century, this nauseatingly repetitive situation has brought numerous nations under a socialist dictatorship. It seldom varies to any extent, yet it works repeatedly. As King Solomon said, "There's nothing new under the sun".

PLEASE, please, do not take my word for this! Unlike *every* Socialist and Marxist, I do not want to lie to or brainwash you. I just want you to use your own intelligence a little bit. Go buy some history books (preferably some over 75 or 100 years old – which is before the Progressives began to re-write and re-format history into 'Social Studies'), at least use your computer and 'Google' a few key terms to find pages and pages of information, and read the information for yourself. Of course remember, you will get both right and left sides of every argument, so you will need to do your own careful research to find the truth which lies somewhere between.

Someone once said,"The price of freedom is eternal vigilance". So what do you have to lose except maybe your own freedom? While that might seem a frivolous thought to many Americans today, if freedom is not worth any effort on your part, forget about it, because you are ready for dictatorship. This book was written for the task of trying to awaken the sleeping giant of the American People to the freedom crisis we are facing today. The rest is really up to us (that means each of you, and me, individually and together), but the road to freedom must be paved with the truth, so we each need to find it. The road to serfdom, on the other hand, merely requires what most Americans are already doing.

Author's Note: During the following discussion of European Rulers, which includes those governments, which have ruled the European people since even before the Greek and Roman Empires, and the European Peoples, who were ruled, not always, but in too many cases, by tyrants, we will use labels to identify these groups.

This is not done for re-defining them, but for clarity to the reader, in an attempt to describe varying groups, from varying nations, with simplistic, generic labels, which generally describe them. While there will be many Individual differences between groups, we hope to describe properly by using their relative positions in the 'food-chain'. We understand that it would take a much more refined study to investigate this history in a detailed manner. In this simple exploration of Ruling and Ruled, classes we hope these labels will make the simplified titles easier to follow to the point we are trying to make.

"Monarchs" will logically refer to those who were members of any certain Royal Family, or one of the Family Groups from which the European monarchy were normally chosen.

Because the "Landed-Gentry" consisted at different times and places, of those called, aristocracy, or nobility, and because in most cases those lines of distinction have little meaning to Americans, for whom this book is written, we will here utilize the words *"Aristocrat"* to describe this class.

We will use the term, *"Commoners"* for those who suffered the ignominy of being trampled on and tyrannized as commoners, serfs, vassals, or various other demeaning names by the Monarchy or Aristocracy. There is no stigma intended in any of these terms, but merely an effort to provide clarity and continuity in the context. rg

~~~~~~~~~~~~~~~

The Sad Moment that brought Marxism to the USA was unfortunate, in that a group of immigrants came to America seeking freedom, however they came clinging to their hatred of the systems that had traumatized them and drove them to immigrate. The hatred they carried eventually blinded them to the difference between the US and where they came from. We have already discussed the blood bath that was the French Revolution. It was supposedly a 'small-c' communist revolution because Robespierre and other leaders had the ideals, and the required hatred to perform mass murder on all segments of French Society, but had not yet clearly or scientifically defined Communism.

That task remained for the unstable sociologist-revolutionist, Karl Marx to complete. He was commissioned in 1847, along with Fredrik Engels, in London to write a manifesto organizing and illuminating the communist philosophy, by a group known as the "Communist League". Marx's Communist Manifesto was completed and published in February 1848, during what some have called the "Spring of Nations", in which the worker-class in Europe unsuccessfully tried to throw off the inequity thrust upon them by the industrial revolution.

The industrial revolution had uprooted many people from a millenniums-long agricultural based society and economy into the new industrial economy, under which some were now expected to perform factory work instead of farm work. But because the European system of Government had mostly been either a tyranny of Monarchy or of Aristocracy, and because both were allowed land ownership, which was denied in most cases to Commoners, both tended to treat the people, whether agrarian or industrial, as they did other 'natural resources' on the land they owned and ruled. That is, the Commoner was simply expected to provide all labor required by the landowner for the 'privilege' of living on the land.

While working the farm at least more or less kept the family fed, industrial work depended on wages to feed the family, and these were all too often either insufficient, or not forthcoming at all. This prompted the common people to form Trade, or Workers Unions, which would then present a united front to the King or Landed Aristocrats, requiring sufficient wages to survive.

Being groups of people with a common purpose, and being necessary for the labor they performed, Unions were not so easily threatened as individual Commoners could be. Therefore, Trade Unions became, in newly industrialized Europe, a necessity for those who labored. However, because they had recently been illegal under the tyranny of Monarchy or Aristocracy, they were a hard-won victory for Commoners who desperately needed them for relief from millenniums of tyranny.

The European revolutions of 1848 were a sad chapter detailing the hapless struggle of the peasants and serfs of Europe as they tried, mostly unsuccessfully, to throw off the chains with which centuries of Monarchy and Aristocracy tyranny had bound them. It deserves review, as it illustrates just how brutal those who ruled the European people were, as well as the hopeless state of affairs, and the desperate mindset of the people to whom Marx's Communist Manifesto was published and read.

While a degree of change eventually came to European Aristocracy in a form of democratic election of parliamentary bodies to represent them, those who could be elected to the parliament were still regularly chosen from and by the Aristocracy or other privileged class. These were not, after all going to give more power to the Commoners than they were forced to. The European Commoner's "democratic" deck was as stacked against them at the very beginning as ours here in the USA has become under our current "Two-Party" farce. Our new, self-appointed aristocracy here in the USA chooses today who will be selected for election from both political parties, just as surely as the old Aristocracy of Europe chose those who could be "Democratically" elected to Parliament.

However, regardless of how badly Marxists have tried to relate the American Revolution to European's struggle, the European situation was always completely reversed from the original forming of a free government in America. Our nation was not formed by arguing with and taking what scraps of freedom kings and nobility would give away under duress. The American Colonists had revolted against, and won their independence from the tyranny of the King of England. The Founding Fathers had led that revolt and understood the rule of monarchy and aristocracy they had shed. Freedom here was never founded to be shackled by those same chains.

Nevertheless, beginning in the 1850's European Immigrants came to the USA, carrying an earned hatred and grudge against the European political structure, which was still struggling out from under the tyranny of Monarchy and Aristocracy.

However, these new immigrants carried, like a plague, their undying mistrust of governments, industry, and anyone with authority or affluence, judging all of these through the lens of Marx's Communist Manifesto and with their previous untenable life situations. These were natural emotions, based upon their personal history of survival under Monarchs and Aristocracy, who had ruled Europe on the backs of the Commoners for Millennia. However, that hatred infected an America without those pre-existing conditions, with a new dose of the age-old class hatred and envy shackles that she had shaken off and thrown down only a few decades earlier during the American Revolution, while preparing the foundation of a new nation based on freedom of the individual.

By living and breathing the old class envies and hatreds and by forgetting they had immigrated to America to escape that evil bondage, these immigrants brought their misfortune to a complete circle. By misunderstanding their new homeland, and by mistaking those who had gained affluence in the new, free, American World by entrepreneurship and hard work for their old monarchist and aristocratic tyrants, they infected their adopted land with hatred and envy toward the very people who furnished them work and paid them the wages necessary to begin a new life here.

Nurturing the old hatreds and envy against those who provided them with the wages that granted them survival and a means for gaining affluence in their new-found nation, they began to agitate against them to organize and form trade unions with which to gain control, as the Communists had taught them to do against the European Aristocracy.

Their hatred of their old system had locked them into a prison, from which they ended up escaping, only to re-create their old system by that hatred. Even though they had left behind the class-based European aristocracy, they still engaged in class warfare with those who furnished them work and wages. Thus, they brought, nurtured, and infected America with Marxist class hatred and warfare because they were unable to leave behind their old hatreds. It is a sad story, with an even sadder ending today.

Just over a hundred and fifty years later, we watch sadly as Marxists raise the specter of Socialist Revolution here in America with American Labor Unions overtly and boldly assisting them, just as unions have done on numerous previous occasions in a number of other nations which then fell into socialist tyranny.

CHAPTER EIGHT

How do you create a Socialist revolution?
Part One: Basics

> *"Society will develop a new kind of servitude which covers the surface of society with a network of complicated rules, through which the most original minds and the most energetic characters cannot penetrate. It does not tyrannize but it compresses, enervates, extinguishes, and stupefies a people, till each nation is reduced to nothing better than a flock of timid and industrious animals, of which the government is the shepherd."*

Prophetic words from Alexis de Tocqueville, a Frenchman who studied America and our Revolution during the mid 1800's.

This chapter is divided into parts one and two because it covers so much territory. Unfortunately, my experience with the American People is that too many of them are hopelessly ignorant of this information. That ignorance is certainly not stupidity, but sadly, due to several generations not having studied American and World history, while those who wish to destroy our freedoms and install a tyrannical government are working hard and waiting for my generation to die out so they can proceed. That is *not* a statement of personal pride, but of personal and profound pain that it can be so confidently stated. Why confidently stated, you may ask. The following information from the Pew Poll should give you a hint:

> *"Young people -- the collegiate and post-college crowd, who has served as the most visible face of the Occupy Wall Street movement -- might be getting more comfortable with socialism. ... The poll, published (12/28/11), found that while Americans overall tend to oppose socialism by a strong margin -- 60 percent say they have a negative view of it, versus just 31 percent who say they have a positive view -- socialism has more fans than opponents among the 18-29 crowd. Forty-nine percent of people in that age bracket say they have a positive view of socialism; only 43 percent say they have a negative view. ..., Indeed, the Pew poll also found that just 46 percent of people age 18-29 have positive views of capitalism, and 47 percent have negative views... income inequality ... has received more and more attention in politics and the media since the Occupy movement launched in mid-September. Usage of the term rose dramatically in news coverage ... Senate Majority Leader Harry Reid to President Barack Obama has used the movement's language to describe divisions in the American public."*
>
> Pew Research Center poll. (1)

Question! Where and why did the youth of America people suddenly turn their backs on the freedoms and the Free Nation their forefathers bled and died to give them, reversing even their own parent-group's opinions that have been held for the past 230 years?

Where and how did socialist ideals and beliefs infiltrate the minds of our youth, and how in God's Name could they have believed possibly the biggest lie in history, to the point they essentially pledge their very "lives, fortunes, and sacred honor" to a statist, and tyrannical, form of government? One that can be historically proven to have slaughtered far more than one hundred and fifty million human beings over the past hundred years?

While we slept. How did they create a Socialist Revolution?

It takes a long time to create a socialist revolution in a free society where people are generally well off, happy, industrious-minded, and busy. But because there are always people who would rather take than give, hate than be happy, and steal than earn, as well as evil people who lust for power over what they consider the 'Stupid Masses', there are always ways to generate discontent and anger over real or perceived wrongs and inequalities.

These then, are an infection, which can be fed, fertilized, and eventually metastasized into a national scale class and ethnic hatred. From there they can become strong enough to create an endemic lynch-mob mentality, one capable of 'hanging' an individual (or a whole society), as soon as they have attained the democratic fifty-one percent majority.

And just as the "Big-C" cancer lurks near each of us, awaiting an opening through which to create bondage to itself, decimating and destroying each life it invades, so Statism lurks near every nation's body-politick awaiting an opening to destroy every last vestige of human freedom and subject all to its tyranny.

Historically speaking, the common people who obtained a modicum of freedom from monarchial tyranny beginning eight hundred years ago with the Magna Carta (1215), slowly, and at great personal cost, have increased those miniscule freedoms over the past eight centuries. Now, the game has been changed! They are now being conned and manipulated into the bondage of Statist Socialism, by Leftists utilizing the "tyranny of the majority", the lies of those who sell Democracy as freedom. It is not!

Statism's normal course of tyranny over past millenniums was applied through monarchies and aristocracies. Today however, Statism's weapon of choice is either socialism or fascism, both of which utilize the ages-old dissatisfaction and anger of the common man against monarchist tyranny to manipulate them and gain dictatorial tyranny over every facet of their lives, thereby placing them in absolute bondage. That is sad but true, and while the methods of manipulation have changed, the results of oppression, bondage, and essential slavery remain the same, or possibly worse.

This is happening even though the closest mankind has ever come to true freedom began in 1776 with the American Revolution and culminated with the formation of the United States of America and its constitutionally bound Federal Government. This gave mankind *a rule of laws, not a rule of men*. Yet, today that precious freedom is in jeopardy because complacent Americans, along with the rest of the world are being conned with the Democracy-is-Freedom lie. All too many Americans today even believe that the freedoms paid for in blood and given to Americans *was* a Democracy. That is not, *never* was, and can never be the truth!

Not coincidentally, during the exact same time-frame that freedom was being authored and *gained* in America, Communism (although not yet well defined) was raising its ugly head in Europe, pretending through "Mobocracy" to emulate the freedoms for the common man that had taken root in America.

Socialist Communism, based somewhat on Darwin's evolution of the species, can see no evil in wiping out ten to thirty percent of the population, because they believe they are assisting in the evolution and the collective salvation of mankind. Transforming them into a race of ant-like creatures forever building a colony in which the Socialists rule, as did the Kings of old. Men without freedom, individuality, or personal will, lacking memory or even knowledge of such things, become docile and easily controlled. A brain-dead mankind having no mental ability to question this "Leader's" rights.

The US Government however, was based upon Judeo-Christian principles and a Rule of Law, not a 'Survival-of-the-most-evil-and-hate-filled". Our "Revolution" was fought in self-defense against the soldiers of a foreign tyrant king who was enslaving us. Our Founders knew that the flame of freedom burns eternally in the breast of all mankind, even where crushed to an ember. Whereas, the French Revolution was founded and birthed in class hatred, envy, and thirst for blood. Not only hatred against her own leaders, but additionally some of her own classes. So that when blood flowed it merely exacerbated blood-thirst, leading to more slaughter until no class was left untouched. Communism was off to its blood-soaked start with a stark preview of things to come.

Following is a personal historical recap and view, based on my life-long study of history. Disagree with me if you wish, but base your argument on sound research and study of history, not some Socialist Professor's revisionist version of history. That could never be a true disagreement, only reacting hysterically, i.e., emotionally, to history you do not like but cannot disregard.

Most liberals and all Marxists, tend to either ignore or blindly deny the huge death toll caused by Socialist Revolutions in all their various forms. While death tolls running into the multi-millions among ethnic and cultural classes of people are an undeniable fact of Socialist Revolutions due to their need to exert brutality and force on a people to enslave them, that subject is patently avoided in discussion by those who champion a democratic-socialist form of government. It is just too difficult to explain to other people, whose minds are not ideologically blinded to the evils of Socialism.

Historically, the methods for destroying a free or semi-free people or nation and setting up a Marxist, Statist dictatorship are simple, because people tend to forget or ignore history's lessons. Yet, these methods are so repetitive and predictable it boggles the imagination of anyone who has studied them that an intelligent population can be so thoroughly conned by them, time after time. These tactics are easily researched by anyone with the will to do so, but even a free people tend to think, "it's different this time, or mankind has evolved and gotten smarter, or it won't happen like it did before" (Twilight Zone Theme-song here).

Well, wake up and smell the coffee! Currently we *all* know that many of our youth are involved with drug habits that are lethally decimating both their physical bodies and their mental capabilities.

But unrealized by many adults, they've also been conned and convinced by Marxist propaganda from major Universities and Hollywood and from others, into lethally destroying and overturning the freedoms and wealth they inherited along with the nation which furnished them the freedoms to live their life of selfish decadence as well. Again, "There is nothing new under the sun".

First, if you read the quotations at the beginning of the chapter (please do so); you must realize that some of the strongest arguments *for* a Constitutional Republic and *against* a Democracy were made by our Founding Fathers. However, the chilling thing is that these arguments also showed the enemies of freedom just how the founding of America as a Democracy could have resulted in an untimely collapse.

Therefore, Statists and Socialists have used the Founders very arguments against democracy as the basis of their plan to destroy America, by turning us *into* a Democracy. However, Democracy (or per Thomas Jefferson, the "Tyranny of the Majority"), is only a poison-pill substitute for the freedoms the Founders gifted American Citizens with. Therefore, it was necessary to anesthetize the American People while eroding and destroying the freedoms-providing constitutional structure of the US Government.

As explained in another chapter, the deadly virus of Marxism was carried to America by settlers from Europe who lived and breathed their hatred of anyone who owned anything. These people ignorantly considered Americans who had attained wealth to be members of the Aristocracy. Therefore, awash with their old Marxist instilled hatreds, these settlers considered all who had earned or owned enough to employ them a mortal enemy.

So, beginning with Theodore Roosevelt, our first "Progressive" Socialist President, continuing under Woodrow Wilson, our second Progressive Socialist President, then under Franklin Roosevelt, and continuing to this day, Progressives of both parties have worked insidiously to change the USA from a Constitutional Republic into a Democracy. This is because a democracy with its terminal genetic fault lines, nearly always ends in tyranny or anarchy.

Progressive Educators have done such a con-job that today, most Americans, if asked, will tell you America was *always* a Democracy. That has *never* been the truth, but a lie, which has taken root, becoming a lethal parasitic growth on America's Tree of Liberty.

So, let us review Education in the newly founded United States.

Progressive Educators today would have you believe that every person raised in the USA before 1900 (the beginning of the Progressive era) were cretins, slobs, unmannered, and illiterate, signing an "X" for signatures, etc. That is because these self-appointed elites have a vested interest in trashing American history before they came onto the scene, bringing the enlightenment of their god-figure, Karl Marx.

The truth is dramatically different, and it puts the Marxist morons to shame for the multi-billion dollar sham cum scam that currently passes for education in today's USA.

Has American Education undergone a change in the past hundred or so years? Well, the definition has certainly changed. For instance:

> "<u>Education</u> - The bringing up, as a child, instruction; formation of manners. Education comprehends all that series of instruction and discipline, which is intended to enlighten the understanding, correct the temper, and form the manners and habits of youth, and fit them for usefulness in their future stations. To give children a good education in manners, arts and science, is important; to give them a religious education is indispensable; and an immense responsibility rests on parents and guardians who neglect these duties."
>
> Source: Webster's original dictionary; 1828

Education - "1. the process of educating especially by formal schooling; teaching; training. 2. knowledge, ability, etc. thus developed. 3. a) formal schooling. b) a kind or stage of this: as, a medical education. 4. systematic study of the methods and theories of teaching and learning.
                              Webster's New World Dictionary, 2012

Some people think Webster's original definition is outmoded. Well, it has certainly been denigrated and unused since Woodrow Wilson and the Roosevelt cousins became Presidents and began work to change America into a Progressive (Socialist) Democracy instead of a Constitutional Republic. People of my (and previous) generation(s) were still educated under the first definition, but even my younger brother suffered serious reading problems as a subject of the experimentation by the "New, or Modern", post-war 'education' establishment. Thankfully, a caring mother who taught him reading by the phonics method, so he is quite literate today and overcame his problems. However, how many did not?

Today many US educated children can spout Darwin, ecological fantasy, "social" studies, and Marxist Mantras, stage shut-outs or sit-ins, but can't read the instructions on a package of instant food, or balance a checkbook. Yet we average one hundred to a hundred thirty thousand dollars per high school graduates, many of whom are functional illiterates. What is going on, anyway?

What is going on is simple. The Progressive Socialists have inserted their European Marxist philosophy into our once-free national scene, even as the trade union people did. They bring broader learning capabilities to those who seek education, while at the same time opening ever-wider scope and latitude of opportunity to those professors who choose to shape, indoctrinate, and manipulate the next generation of Americans into Marxism.

So now, let us take a closer look at American Education from the mid-1600 to the mid-1800.

During this period in America, there were NO public schools, as we currently know them. Private education for the Colonial American population consisted of many forms, but was primarily home, Church, private, or free-market based. Mothers or fathers normally taught their children alphabet, numbers, and reading at home. Church-based, community-based (funded by the users, churches or private benefactors), apprenticeships and private studies, combined with fixed and circulating libraries provided a wide range of books for further chosen education. Additionally, the Bible was the basic reading book found in almost every home. Morality and values were widely based on learning to read using the Bible as a textbook. (*Progressives were frantic to stop that!*).

Mothers usually taught the youngsters reading and numbers, while fathers taught basic agronomy and survival skills, but both mother and father were apt to be reading, either the Bible or some book from a circulating library during the evenings, especially in winter.

I read, as a grade-schooler, how Young Abe Lincoln studied by firelight in his parents log cabin, utilizing splinters of charcoal from the fire to write upon the hearth. In the years before progressives began writing the curriculum, such a story was inspiring. Today with Progressives in charge, these are scorned if taught at all. Yet Abe Lincoln had more greatness and humanity in his little finger nail than the whole lot of American Progressive "Education Elites" stacked in a pile!

Modern 'elites' will tell you this simply can't work, because parents aren't trained in teaching skills. Yet the fact remains that those two centuries produced generations of highly skilled and literate men and women. People who not only laid the foundation for the greatest and most prosperous nation the earth has ever known to date, but who became the entrepreneurs and leaders who created an economy which set the basis for economic growth in the world for over a hundred years. So do not tell me that the American "Experiment" of Freedom for the Individual was a failure and required to be "corrected" by a group of megalomaniac Progressive Marxists.

While this is intended to be a comparison, not a history text to educate you to what you were never taught, or were miss-taught, I did find an excellent article on this subject. (2)

Actually today's literacy rates stink to high heaven when compared to early America's. A study conducted by DuPont de Nemours in 1800 indicated that only 0.04 percent of Americans were unable to read and to write legibly. That is *four in one thousand*! An article in USA Today, dated January 8, 2009 indicates, "an estimated thirty two million adults in the USA, or nearly *one in seven*— are saddled with such low literacy skills it would be tough for them to read anything more challenging than a children's picture book or to understand a medication's side effects listed on a pill bottle". (3)(4)

Well! Guess the 'Elitist-Qualified' teachers, psychiatrists, psychologists, and 'bureau-cretins' aren't good as they'd have you to believe, especially with a current national *average* annual cost per student in U.S. public school of $8,626 for *failing* students! (5)

The average education received and the annual cost is so disgusting, that they try to tell you, "Well, the annual cost is minimal, when compared to the average annual cost of $29,000 per prison inmate per year. In other words, some educators and schools are so hard pressed to show you *any* positive results, they have to stoop to saying, "well, it's better than prison" (6). That should totally insult and disgust every American. What a low-life Con-Job!

Now let us explore education since the advent of Progressive Socialists attaining the US Presidency, circa 1900.

President Wilson and both of the Roosevelt cousins fancied themselves to be "more intelligent than the Stupid Masses", "Intellectuals" and therefore "Leaders" of the American Aristocracy, as well as a vanguard for re-building the American Dream into a Socialist Utopia. They longed in the early 1900's for an "effective" government, structured after Benito Mussolini's Fascist Italy or Lenin's Soviet Union (read your history). They were not alone in this wish. Check out photos of Rockefeller Center on the internet for relief sculptures obviously praising the 'glorious-job' Mussolini was doing in Italy. See the concrete and granite tribute to the praise of Fascism by the self-appointed and self-important 'Progressive' Elites. Their argument, then as now, was that our Constitutional Republic was not an efficient form of government, and our Constitution was problematical because it forbid and bound them from making "Democratic" changes in US government to make it "more efficient".

Barak Obama is not the first Socialist President to whine that our Constitution is a "charter of negative liberties" because it tied his hands in redistributing the wealth of the country to certain groups he favored. Well, neither does it allow such blatantly Marxist redistribution of wealth to *any* group, for *any* reason whatever! Marxist Redistribution qualifies as theft of one man's goods given it to someone *Barak* feels to be more deserving. Statist Marxist's do that with the power of the government behind him. If you or I do the same thing, it is properly called theft. It is when they do it too!

So, race and class envy, redistribution of wealth, and abrogating the checks and balances of the federal and state governments were completely forbidden in favor of individual freedoms and property rights by the US Constitution. No wonder Obama gagged taking his oath of office to "Preserve, protect and defend the Constitution of the United States". I do not believe he meant a word of that!

Remember Robin Hood? Well, in "Jolly old England", circa the Magna Carta, he stole from Monarchs and Aristocrats, under whom the Commoners survived in tyranny, and gave to the Commoners so they could survive, making him a folk hero. However, he never stole from those who had just enough to eat to give it to the 'collective' as Socialists do. That would not have made him a folk hero, but a simple thief or maybe he might have become a Lenin, Stalin, or Mao and murdered people for fun as they did.

Nevertheless, each of these American Socialist Presidents frantically believed they needed greater power vested in the executive branch in order to perform their Marxist shenanigans efficiently. Wilson himself called our form of government with its *"Pre-Modern (i.e.,*

*Pre-Marxism), c*umbersome, *Constitution, in which the ... intricate systems of checks and balance ... were "the problem".* (7)

In other words, our Constitutional Checks and balances against Statist Tyranny was the serious *problem* that kept him from acting as an 'efficient' dictator, therefore he could not immediately change America into the "Efficient" fascist nation he longed to rule.

Nevertheless, Wilson's statement is similar to the whining of our current President, Barack Hussein Obama, who has agitated several times that he might have to leave Congress out of the loop in order to "Fix" the economy. Well, that exactly the type of "Fix" and "Fixer" against which our Founders guarded in the Constitution, because it is a substantial step to setting up dictatorship.

Again, read your history, understand what is going on today is a continuation, *not* a new thing, – remember, the first President who wished to turn America into a fascist nation was in office over a hundred years ago! Therefore, while this is not new, our current President has the advantage of a hundred years of socialist laws, regulations, education, and propaganda experience to work with.

Remember this also. America was protected *carefully and purposefully* by such "problematic" and intricate checks and balances for the express purpose of restraining potential tyrants from "Fundamentally Transforming" our government into an 'efficient' tool for tyrants. Remember the Founders "Tyranny of the Majority" arguments? That's why it took a century long continuum of self-appointed American 'aristo-cretins' to so corrupt and pollute the American Governmental system that only now are we finally beginning to resemble the corrupt Monarchy and Aristocracy manipulated parliamentary tyrannized "democracies" of Europe.

Returning to the field of education, Marxist re-education of a nation's next generation has always specifically required removing children at the youngest possible age from their parent's influence, in order to begin indoctrinate and manipulate them with the state-controlled curriculum.

Removal from parents influence is a hugely necessary first step because parents tend to (or at least used to)model and teach their children to follow personal religious beliefs, and values, to warn and protect their children from the silly, and many times dangerous mistakes youth fall victim to. That was exactly why Hitler removed his specially bred, "Master-Race" children from their parents at birth. Eventually however, these specially bred and trained examples of "Nazi Super Men" turned out so completely ruthless and uncontrollable they were unable to live in German society after the fall of the Third Reich required return to civilized behavior.

In the case of secretly subverting a Constitutional Republic into a socialist leaning Democracy, it is especially necessary to avoid the children learning parental guidance at home. Because a child who is able to read before they go to school has not only learned other truths than those taught in today's indoctrination factories, but also is able to read alternate literature from that furnished by the Regime, causing Marxists no end of re-education problems.

Such alternate texts might even include the much-feared (by Statists) original US History, instead of the 'airbrushed', carefully edited, falsified and re-focused Social Studies of recent decades. They might even include the Statist's fiercely despised Bible, which teaches black and white Judeo-Christian values system upon which the American Constitutional Republic was based. Socialists are more afraid of people who know these truths than they are of guns and bombs, thus the intense hatred shown by Barak Obama toward Americans who "...*Bitterly cling to their guns and religion...*".

So, any State-run education System prefers, not only to physically separate young children from their parental environment and values, but also to completely pre-empt parents from instilling morality, values, or self-learned warnings and cautions about life experiences that parents know to be dangerous. That is because the state then has to 'erase' these values from the children's minds.

"Progressives" answer to this American 'heresy' is to take children into 'Public' School younger and younger. K-12, then Kindergarten, now "Pre-School". Remember, Hitler had his 'Especially Bred'

Aryans raised in nurseries and day-care centers that were like laboratories. In this State-Run atmosphere, Using Marxism and Social Studies instead of history and economics, carefully 'airbrushed' and re-focused history is taught to reflect the Progressive's "Brave New World" vision. A vision with its ultimate vision of mankind as unemotional automatons, industriously expending their lives for the ultimate 'good of the Nation-State, while the self-appointed 'masters' rule the people and live lives of plenty. Does it sound like we have reached "Utopia" yet? Well we are on that path, and will arrive soon, if Progressives get their way.

Each generation is now being taught in our State-Controlled School System that only our self-appointed Progressive leaders can reach that Utopia, with different outcomes than previous human history if only the youth will listen to and join them. I seem to recall that Albert Einstein said the definition of insanity was doing the same thing repeatedly and expecting a different outcome each time. Of course, Einstein was a true genius, not a self-appointed one.

While American Universities (especially State-run Universities) have stealthily taught Marxism as a viable form of government, even before Lenin's first 'Fellow Travelers' set up cliques and clubs among professors; it accelerated rapidly beginning with and immediately following the Soviet Revolution in 1916-17. I remember as a young anti-communist in the Fifties, reviewing transcripts of Editorials from the Seattle Times in 1916 and 17 era, in great praise of Lenin and the great progress he was making. How he was bringing human rights and freedom to the people of the new "Soviet Union". They expressed great hopes that the US would not be slow to follow him into such historical greatness.

Of course, even though the Marxist-slanted media suppressed reporting, some Americans learned about the Kulak Genocide, just as we eventually learned of the Ovens at the end of WW II. The stench of mass-death is difficult to cover, even with a helpful, complicit press.

So, we know how that book (and the movie) turned out after 70 years, don't we? The Russian people are still suffering, even under their 'new-found freedom'. A people with seventy years of cradle to grave Communist tyranny controlling every thought and action have become unable to think in the terms of freedom. For example, they keep asking when the *Government* will instigate 'Free-Enterprise'. The answer is *never*! Such a hope is doomed to be stillborn.

If it isn't driven from the people up, statist politicians will *never* allow the population true freedom any more than Monarchs or Aristocrats have historically done. They sometimes loosen the reins of control as necessary, but *never* relinquish them. In a case where Communist brutality has micro-managed every thought process for generations, the Russian people have become incapable of independent thinking, unfortunately becoming completely dependent on Government to take care of them. How terribly sad!

However, nature abhors a vacuum, and unfortunately, for the Russian People, someone evil and powerful will come along soon enough to precisely define the 'freedom' he is willing to give them in return for their giving *him* power to control their lives.

Much the same as a man who had been in prison most of his life trying to live free of constant detailed direction. This can become bewildering, so the man commits a crime for the sole purpose of getting back into jail, where he can be comfortable again. Unfortunately, I believe the Russian People will once again fall into or accept a tyrannical form of government, just to regain a comfort zone in tyranny. Unfortunately, for those who still fan and nourish the 'longing to be free' flame, that is a simple death sentence.

What kind of a lesson can we take from this situation? Does it help us understand how Commoners remained Commoners for millennia? Does it give us fear for our future if we fall under socialist tyranny? Could it possibly make us look questioningly at our "Welfare-State" Government? Could Americans become this mind-numbed and helpless after seventy or a hundred years of Cradle to Grave Welfare? On the other hand, and even more horrifying, could America even become a part of the new "Fourth Reich"?

From my study of history, being a "Little-Bit" Socialist is similar to being a "Little-Bit" pregnant, or like starting just a "Little-Bit" of fire in your house (or in the forest). Both are a living organism, and both will continue to grow unless aborted. I am personally Pro-Life when it comes to Human Beings, and opposed to human abortion. However, in the case of house fires, forest fires, and Socialist Movements, I am in strong favor of aborting them. The unfortunate alternative is "delivery", consisting of the complete loss of the house (or forest), or, more valuable yet, Personal Freedom.

> *"We have met the enemy, and he is us!"*
> Pogo Comic Strip.

As an introduction to this education section, the following are Four Items from *"Communism's 45 Steps"* dealing with American education, as read into the Congressional Record, Appendix, pp. A34-A35, January 10, 1963: (8)

- *Get control of the schools. Use them as transmission belts for socialism and current Communist propaganda. Soften the curriculum. Get control of teachers' associations. Put the party line in textbooks.*
- *Gain control of all student newspapers.*
- *Use student riots to foment public protests against programs or organizations which are under Communist attack.*
- *Support any socialist movement to give centralized control over any part of the culture–education, social agencies, welfare programs, mental health clinics, etc.*

Does any of that sound familiar? Notice the date, it is important too. It was the Sixties Radicals who picked up carried forward the foundational work of those who, from 1912 to 1940 attempted to lure America into following Russia into the darkness of Marxist Communism that had fallen on that nation.

That work was at the same time compromised and slowed by the World Tragedy of National Socialism and the Second World War. Still, America and England aided Russia by joining with Stalin to beat back the Nazis and paid him for needing their help, then allowed him to enslave millions in eastern European areas, which had temporarily been under Hitler's Control.

State-Run Education has been transformed to corrupt and prepare the minds of American youth with Marxist Socialism by teaching:

- Marxist invented Social Studies instead of history,
- the irreligious religion of Gaia (earth worship), to further environmentalist interests instead of the moral values that created our nation,
- 'diversity' (worshiping our differences) instead of "E pluribus Unum", (from many, one),
- distrust of the Judeo-Christian laws of American society, while embracing anything to replace that standard,
- equalized mediocrity instead of healthy competition, i.e., curve grading, no grades, or everyone passes with an 'A', so losers win too, and there is no use working hard – or even at all!
- elevating mediocrity as the new normal, i.e., cheaters can win too, working hard is for dummies, a crucifix in a gallon jar of urine is 'Art' worthy of federal grants, but a painting in which you can identify something (unless it's grotesque or some sexual symbol) is passé ...

What has modern State-Run Education given us that is not filled with the ugly, the grotesque, and the profane? Everything they have given us is excruciatingly expensive, while at the same time deleterious to our societal best interests and destructive of our national interests, while at the same time they extort an ever-higher wages for destroying our nation.

Disagree with my opinion if you will, but not by giving answers based on statistics from the same bunch of hooligans who have conned the American people that Marxism equates to education!

So, under disguise of 'Education', Marxist indoctrination has continued in America. Generation after generation of American parents wondered why they could not communicate with their children after a college education (and by today, even some high schools). These parents were labeled 'old-fashioned', 'out-of-touch', 'reactionaries', and 'bourgeoisie', among kinder terms. Unless they were also Statists, they lost intimate contact with their children. That was the Marxist's plan too. Divide to Conquer.

However, to the dismay of the Progressives, many young people who went to college or university actually did want to learn how to make money, so the Marxist Fellow Traveler "Educators" concentrated primarily on the children of upper-middle class and wealthy families. Those who would have trust funds, or other lifetime incomes making them able to dedicate themselves to Marxist-invented "Social-Work", and concentrate on dozens of useless degrees in fields utilized only in a socialist society (which we are not – not quite yet anyway)!

However, those who would likely never want, or have to perform a useful, productive day's work in their lives, proved a more fertile ground. After all, what sounds more fulfilling? A life dedicated to making 'evil' money, or a life dedicated to Society in say, "Social Services" or "Social Engineering", which ostensibly make life easier for those who have less. Unfortunately, the truth is such programs simply migrate generations of people into dependency on government, robbing them of personal pride, freedom, and independence, and creating a definite burden on society.

Try this! Go to any national park. The signs will say, *"Don't feed the animals; it makes them dependent on humans and unable to live on their own"*. Well, Duh! Federal Welfare programs don't do the same thing to human beings? Have you forgotten the plight of the "Free" Russians who now whine, "When will the Government set up Free Enterprise for us so we can become wealthy and comfortable?"

All these things were carefully planned by the Progressive Marxists, and are currently being carried out, as they have been for a hundred years. Therefore, by now the breach in our protective wall is large and further eroding.

Then came the "Children of the Sixties"

The children of the Sixties had watched their parents win the Second World War, come home, and become comfortable middle class citizens. They grew up during the most affluent and safe period in American History. They were sent off to the best colleges and universities available. They were actually coddled by their parents, who had literally faced death and survived, and who now wanted to create the very best world for their children.

Nevertheless, something went terribly wrong! These parents, who were so busy celebrating their victory and the peace it earned, who were working just as hard now to become comfortable middle class Americans as they had to win the war, they somehow failed to instill in their children the moral values which created the American Might necessary to win the war. They became complacent concerning the teaching of values that they had learned from their forebears. Thus, in their love and concern in the good life for their children, they created a moral vacuum.

The Progressive Marxists were ecstatic to fill that moral vacuum with their own Marxist, Statist morality. To create a generation bathed in Marxist values had been their dream since 1900 and they did not fail the mission!

So, the values the Sixties generation were taught when they went off to colleges and universities were the same values of those who caused the recently won war, Statist Socialism. The same values which had soaked the ground of Russia, Germany, Eastern Europe, and China with the blood of more than a hundred million "enemies of the State", who couldn't understand how Communism had created Utopia.

Nevertheless, the Sixties generation did not see it that way. The old saying, *"Those who believe in nothing will believe anything"* fits here. While the origin of the saying is clouded, its proven truth could never be. Moreover, the moral vacuum in the 'Sixties' generation, raised in a land of personal freedoms was filled by disciples of the worst tyranny the world has ever known.

The Sixties Generation became an especially rebellious and radical group. It was difficult for them to understand why their parents had not already seen the light and accepted Marxism. They were incredulous that their parents had won WW II, and then came home to enjoy the fruits of peace rather than 'going forth to win the 'world-peace' the Marxists had seduced them with. However, they were determined to perform the duty they believed their parents had failed, so they sought Marxist 'peace', never understanding that it was merely the other arm of the same ugly, evil, creature of darkness their parents had fought WW II to terminate.

The Sixties Generation rebelled and rioted nationally. Their personal "Badge of Honor" was the hurling of paper bags filled with human urine and feces at the police officers in Chicago during the week of the Democratic National Convention in 1968. (9) After all, they believed they were salvaging not only the United States, but the whole world, and with that, bringing about the "Collective Salvation" of all of humankind. To these rebels the Chicago Police and the Democratic Convention they were guarding were worse than the SS or Gestapo of Hitler; they were performing the same duty. Throwing feces at them was a sign of the rebel's utter disrespect and hatred for what they represented.

These then, are the ones who, when this act which they considered perfectly rational, failed to gain the ends they sought, were stunned and appalled, in complete disbelief at its' failure. How could the people of the United States be so stupid as to call *them* "Commies" as if that were a curse word, and stand with the despised police?

Therefore, because they could not understand why their world had not become a Marxist world yet, they were willing to destroy what they could not understand and had been taught to hate, in order to bring on their own "Brave New World".

And so, they rebelled. They rebelled against God, and anything to do with God or morality, against the federal government, the state and local governments, against the police, against drug laws, against schools and universities, against soap and water, and even against personal and mental hygiene. They rebelled against every basic principle that had given them the wealth and freedom they inherited, but especially against the Judeo-Christian Morality with which people have created civil societies for millenniums. Instead, they fought to destroy all those things and instead, work toward the Marxist-Communist version of "Peace", which is the state of being in which all resistance to Communism has ceased, whether by acclaim, by cessation, by exhaustion, or by death.

In their self-deluded rebellion against what they had been brainwashed to believe was an 'unjust system', they used that system while rejecting everything that system had given them. Instead, they welcomed and championed the system that had created the darkness, which had ruled the nations where a hundred fifty million people were slaughtered during the twentieth century. In their rebellion, they accepted the opposites of the freedoms they had inherited and then rebelled against.

Consider Woodstock, (10) the Icon of the Sixties Children, which was anarchy, violence, hatred, vulgar language and behavior, rape, robbery and murder, sex with everyone and anyone who would submit (or not), rolling in the gutter, life in a sewer. What evil didn't they have there? They would have gone out to find that one too!

Maybe you don't, but I remember that time and their disgusting actions well. It made me sick then and still does now.

So, the Children of the Sixties went back to their professors and the coffee house crowds, to the knees of the masters where they had learned Marxism. They seemingly disappeared over the next few years. But they were more dedicated than anyone could have believed. Many of them being the affluent children of middle and upper class families, they simply returned to the Universities and Colleges where they had learned Marxism to begin with. They had lost their youthful arrogance of winning immediately, but they determined to continue the battle inside the system they hated, and so earned degrees in political science, law, and other social and legal areas.

Finally, armed with Master and Doctorate degrees, and totally steeped in Marxist Statism, they became politically active. They ran for elective office, they joined and formed law firms; they became involved in all different levels of bureaucracy, community organizing, social work etc. They became Marx's Moles, as he had directed them.

Today they are State and Federal Legislators, Attorneys, Judges, Bureaucrats, and Professional Organizers and Agitators. And they are very busy, actively destroying with their new-found power the American nation they couldn't destroy in 1968 with their brown-paper bag 'Missiles' and their "Radical Pose".

They have been and are today an extremely effective group of saboteurs. They learned how to legislate Marxist tyranny into US Law, and to implement it by lawsuit, and then they win such suits because many of them became judges to insure such enforcement. It was then taken it to the streets by those who became community organizers and street agitators. They have set up quasi-governmental Marxist, 'Societal' agitation organizations and associations, most of which are partially or fully funded by federal dollars, whether directly or through grants. They are hard at work dividing the American people into racial, ethnic, class, and economic factions, who preach the gospel of Marx as the only salvation (your tax dollars at work bringing Marxism to your neighborhood!). The list could go on for pages, but you get the idea.

CHAPTER NINE

How do you create a Socialist revolution?
Part Two: Uncovering termites, moles, and rats.

"The third rule of ethics of means and ends is that in war the end justifies almost any means...."

"An organizer working in and for an open society is in an ideological dilemma to begin with, he does not have a fixed truth -- truth to him is relative and changing; everything to him is relative and changing.... To the extent that he is free from the shackles of dogma, he can respond to the realities of the widely different situations. ..."

From "Rules for Radicals", by Saul Alinsky

Over the past several years, and especially today, since Barack Obama introduced Class and Racial hatred, along with Violent rhetoric as American Democratic Virtues, the national discussion has become increasingly filled with overt venom and outspoken hatred of Capitalism in general, and of the American System of Free Enterprise specifically. This is true, although most current problems were caused the federal government's intervention within the American System, That is, the majority of them were caused by manipulation, redundant legislation, over-regulation, and just-plain meddling by idiotic bureaucrats.

State-Run-Education is a government bureaucracy (as well as a monopoly), and as such has been specifically fashioned to teach and glorify socialism to the youth of America. How else could it be that 49% of the youth of America, mentioned above, consider Socialism a viable and acceptable form of government? They certainly didn't learn that at home (except from the TV or Hollywood), and they certainly didn't learn it by studying history, unless you are brainwashed enough to consider the Social Studies invented by Karl Marx, and the Ethnic and Diversity Studies invented by his disciples to actually be historically enlightening study, which they certainly are not. They are blatantly anti-American Marxist Propaganda, pure and simple.

So here we are. Class Envy, Greed, and Racial Hatred were winning campaign slogans for the last presidential election, and today, the rhetoric and volume of hatred and violence steadily increases as we move toward the next election. Remembering the President's positive remarks and actions, he has already granted approval to the Occupy Wall Street Movement, the New Black Panthers Jack-Booted Voter Intimidation Squad, and other Marxist or Racist groups to perform violence in the streets. Additionally, his statement that the "Police acted stupidly" before he even had the facts, served as a stern warning to police and everyone just whose side he is on, by giving encouragement for Anarchy in the streets.

Constitutional Rights are currently being re-interpreted by American Marxists with Executive Level approval, giving essential license to vandalize and steal from anyone who has (or might have) more than you do, or simply something you want. Right and wrong are turned upside down by both elected and appointed officials, governmental agencies, judges, juries, and, of course, major media. Anti-Semitism is currently on the rise, being spoken of and acted out with lack of caution for the first time since the Third Reich.

Violent and lawless groups such as the Occupy Wall Street Movement, the leaders of who are admitted Communists, Socialists and Anarchists, are openly doing this. Socialism is chosen over Capitalism by the (soon to be) fifty one percent of the voting population who seek a Democracy instead of a Rule of Law so they may blatantly steal what they want from whoever they want to. Additionally, Occupy Wall Street (OWS) is now demanding re-writing of the US Constitution making it more closely mirror the Constitution of the Soviet Union. How many of you were even aware of that?

Do you see anything even slightly alarming about this type of thing? Well, it has been going on under the surface for some time, is now openly flaunted in America's face? Certainly, you can be any of the above and demonstrate freely as a US Citizen, but not during my lifetime have Communists, Socialists, and Anarchists been so blatantly "In-your-face" with the hatred and anger they are showing.

The reason must to be obvious to any thinking person. Barak Obama's own words and deeds, first as a candidate, and then as President, let them believe they now have not only a 'friend', but also a mentor in the White House. One who speaks their language with authority, one who has never cautioned or chided them, let alone told them to stop. Obama acts and speaks in the Radical Marxist, Saul Alinsky language they themselves use.

After all, their friend Obama worked four years for a Chicago community-organizing group based on Saul Alinsky's model and methods. He was later a paid director for three years, along with his friend and mentor Bill Ayers, a convicted terrorist, co-founder of the home-grown terrorist group, *"Weather Underground"*, and writer of such self-admitted Communist books as "Prairie Fire", the text of which states it is **based on the belief that the "duty of a revolutionary is to make revolution".** (Emphasis added)

Why should they not believe Obama is their ally in ending capitalism and bringing forth a communist government in the United States? What has he done except give them tacit or open approval?

So, how will they perform this task? Sadly, all they have to do is complete the task. So much has been done before them by Progressives from Teddy Roosevelt and Woodrow Wilson to FDR, LBJ, and Jimmy Carter, as well as a number of Republican Presidents who have stealthily paved the road to Socialism while we thought we were between radical socialist ones.

Key tools used for the subjugation of a free people.
Here, let us review the three proven strategic tools of subjugation used by Statists and evil people of all stripe. They are:
- a) Manipulation,
- b) Intimidation,
- c) Domination.

These key tools are effective within any facet of government, business, private life, or virtually anywhere else. Utilizing these tools to manipulate and control people is the absolute essence of evil. However, of course, Saul Alinsky cleared that for them, with, *"The third rule of ethics of means and ends is that in war the end justifies almost any means…."*. That is to say, Marxists accept no rules or moral values to impede them, because they believe they must war against the free will of mankind to achieve the "Collective Salvation" of Humanity. How noble of them! What puffed up Hypocrites!

Therefore, in a number of industrialized nations, these three methods have been useful in implementing the following programs, with which to install Socialist Tyranny over free men:

1) Corruption and re-organization of trade unions and other organized groups into Socialist Action Groups. A Socialists tool called, "Organize the Organized!"
2) 'Nudging' each generation closer to Marxism in the classrooms of State Run Education.
3) Continual passage of repetitive, oppressive and redundant legislation and regulation with which to control industry and discourage even the most independent and law-abiding citizens.

This pattern is a well-worn path. Whenever deemed necessary, the people are first *manipulated* into some crisis position whereby they can feel exposed and become afraid, i.e., *intimidated*. This situation is then allowed or manipulated sufficiently to become or appear serious, then the people will happily allow the government additional powers, believing the propaganda that "something must be done". At this point, the government is able to utilize their newfound power to *dominate* this area of life, and immediately install or further expand tyrannical control where there once was freedom. This has been done in so many nations, so many times studying it will make you dizzy. Read your history

If this makes you think about Barak Obama's Presidency and the repeated mantras like, "Never let a serious crisis go to waste", or "You don't want to waste a serious crisis", etc., maybe you're beginning to wake up. This tactic evolved from Marx to Saul Alinsky, the 'god-father' of modern Communist tactics. Moreover, Obama has definitely never let a crisis, *whether real or a created,* go to waste!

1) *Trade Union corruption and re-organization*
To show I am not making this up, and that it is nothing new, consider the following quotation. This quote is attributed to Dietrich Bonhoeffer (1906-1945), German Lutheran Pastor and Theologian, whose tacit involvement in a plot to overthrow Adolph Hitler led to his imprisonment and eventual execution by Hitler's SS when the allies had reached within 15 miles of Flossenbürg concentration camp where he was imprisoned.

However, Martin Niemueller evidently spoke and used this same terminology previously in various addresses even before the war in Germany, giving him a chronological claim.

To me, because both men were Protestant German Pastors resisting Hitler, I doubt either would fight to claim credit. It is my personal belief that the saying mostly came into worldwide knowledge through the explicit, and widely read prison writings smuggled out of Bonhoeffer's cell before he was executed.

The Coming Fourth Reich

In any case, it thoroughly indicates the guilt suffered by those who felt they had been tacitly complicit with what happened to Germany and the world for not speaking up when the evil that Hitler represented first made itself known. The quotation follows:

> "First they came for the Communists, but I was not a Communist so I did not speak out. Then they came for the Socialists **and the Trade Unionists,** but I was neither, so I did not speak out. Then they came for the Jews, but I was not a Jew so I did not speak out. And when they came for me, there was no one left to speak out for me." (1)
>
>   Niemoeller or Bonhoeffer? Both used it.

So, Trade Unions were named by someone who personally witnessed and suffered under the Nazi Regime, as one of the many groups *destroyed* by the Nazi's, yet Hitler's first successful step into politics was when he joined the tiny German Worker's Party (Deutche Arbeitpartei) in 1919. He took charge of the party's propaganda wing in 1920, and renamed it the *NationalSozialistiche* Deutche Arbeitpartei (*National Socialist* German Worker's Party), nicknamed the Nazi Party, which title he kept that after destroying the group.

As Hitler gained in power and authority, he recruited a gang of union and street thugs to be his 'bodyguards' and 'sergeants-at-arms' (head-thumpers) during political meetings and rallies. These became known officially as the Sturm Abteilung (Storm Dept.). They were also later known as the SA or, Hitler's Brown Shirts, and actually Hitler's 'Goon-Squad', who by 1923 became his own private army. (2)

The Brown Shirts enforced order by brute force as Hitler gained political power as a Street-Agitator (Hmmm, Street Agitator, and Community Organizer? What is the difference?). However, Hitler turned on both of these groups after he attained the Chancellorship of Germany. He murdered their leader and crushed them in a trade for the support of the much more respectable German National Army and Navy to support him for President when Hindenburg retired.

The SA had served its purpose, and was no longer being necessary. In fact, now they had become a liability, because they had dirtied their hands assisting Hitler get thus far. That too, is an often-repeated pattern of life and death for those who assist Socialist Tyrants gain power.

This strategy Progressives call, 'Organize the Organized' is a shrewd way to get the 'biggest bang for their buck', by using an existing organized group and simply buying out or corrupting a few in its top echelons, thus redirecting a large group of people and their funding with relatively minimal effort and cost. Again, that is their normal tactic. Progressives sneak around like cockroaches, mostly hiding in dim or dark places, necessarily stealing their sustenance because they have no talent to create, only to destroy.

Of Lenin, Hitler, and Mao, only Mao did not use Trade Unions, simply because the prevalent Monarchist and Aristocratic Chinese system of government had never allowed unions to be formed at that time. However, in Europe, Unions had been formed to protect the Common man from the Monarchy or Aristocracy after the Magna Carta and Industrial Revolution.

Trade Unions were corrupted by, and taken over as a shill for Marxists in order to sell that same Common man back into Slavery under a Statist, Socialist Government, but the unions were then tossed aside like used toilet paper when the Statist gained the control he wanted. But ever since the industrial revolution, predatory parasites who wish to overturn freedom in order to install tyrannical government have used unions in industrialized nations to form a populist and financial base for their revolution.

This works because it is an easy sell to create labor unrest with a few well-trained agitators and disaffected workers who convince other workers their wages and working conditions are an insult for the work they perform, and that their 'bosses' are evil men. Actually, even if that were true, trading that situation for socialism is like trading an itching rash for cancer. In the end, after gaining power, the Socialist-Statist Tyrants end up destroying the unions, because like any other totalitarian tyrant, they cannot, and will not stand for union workers continuing demands for better conditions after they have once served their purpose. However, it works.

The supreme irony of using the trade unions is a double-edged blade, it cuts both ways. While almost never voiced, the most glaring and tragic irony of Socialists-Statists using Unions as organs to help create a revolution and help install their form of government instead of free enterprise, is that organized labor's continued freedom is possible *only* in a free or semi-free society with free or semi free-enterprise. They would be virtually impossible to organize under *any* form of statist government, including Monarchy, Socialism, or Fascism.

Stop and think about that a moment. Certainly, no totalitarian monarch, nor any statist, socialist, communist, or fascist dictator would *ever* let anyone own a business enterprise except a relative, a friend, or an ally, and these would then be total monopolies, paying tribute to the leader, and making monies on the backs of the people (subjects) or simply by robbing them. There would be no recourse by forming a union, as such a group would be outside the law, and because the Leader has the power of life or death over all subjects. That is basic human nature as revealed by any objective study of history.

This certainly does *not* mean that every union member, legislator, or teacher is complicit, or even aware of being used, *far from it*! In most all cases these keys and strategies for control are kept within the echelons of the 'sell-outs' subverting their union to the socialists. However, they are buried in 'feel-good' propaganda (the skin of a reason, stuffed with a poisonous lie) for the 'rank-and-file', because even in today's much more liberal (much less freedom) nation, most Americans still have a natural suspicion of too powerful, 'Big Brother Government'.

2) 'Nudging' each generation closer to Marxism in the classrooms of state run education,

If you have not noticed this, you have not been paying attention. If you do not believe it, denial is not just a river in Egypt. This has been going on since the 1920's, but it shifted into overdrive when Jimmy Carter authorized the US Dept. of Education. In doing so, he federalized control over another area of local government, giving federal bureaucratic appointees power to dictate curriculums over the state and local school boards, generally thumbing his nose at local control, which kept America free. See Video (3). American Education has since lurched violently to the left over the following 23 years, upholding Darwinian Socialism as a viable form of Government, and the worship of Gaia, Mother Earth, and Environmentalism as the religion of the future. Of the people, by the people, and for the people, my foot!

But that's nothing new, did you know the Nazi's were the first "Green," or environmentalist regime, as well as pushing government education, government healthcare, healthy eating, and anti-smoking campaigns, for the better health of the "Master" Race? Nothing new under the sun. (4)(5)

Neither is student rebellion a new thing, being recorded as far back as ancient Greece. Again, like unions, it could only happen in free or semi-free nations. Under tyranny, it would be crushed by the military might of Tyranny. Only in America, can the children of middle class and wealthy families wage student rebellion. It would never be tolerated in a Statist Regime, yet Statist Regimes historically use these 'Useful Idiots' to assist them to power.

From the fall of the Roman Empire until Charlemagne, educational institutions were much on the decline. While the Catholic Church provided education for some, education was essentially a religious school providing teaching of reading and writing, necessary for education in Christianity, basic arithmetic and possibly simple geography might be added as well. The 'palace' school was also available for the children of royalty or aristocracy. By the Thirteenth Century, the University of Paris had been established, providing theology, law, medicine, and liberal arts education, but it was still essentially a school for the children of the privileged. While the Renaissance did bring some increase in education for Commoners by the mid 16th Century, most Commoners' children were able only to receive free or affordable education from religious schools, which were financed by the Church.

Education of Commoners in Europe continued to gain ground, but was unfortunately used primarily for indoctrination of children to become patriotic subjects, steering them either into a trade or into the military, depending on their talents and the national needs. While the Catholic Church operated schools primarily to teach Christianity, the governments frequently allowed them to exist because only The Church provided Commoner's children education without cost to the government.

As a rule, Europe has used education variously to satisfy the whim or fancy of its succession of tyrants and revolutionary governments. Today, even Commoners have been allowed education, and over the past couple of centuries, many European people have attained some freedoms from State-run tyranny.

But in free and semi-free Europe, beginning in the nineteenth century, institutions of higher learning finally began receiving students from a wider spectrum of the population (at last! *even* the Commoners). This has brought broader learning opportunities and capabilities to those who seek to learn, yet at the same time opening ever-wider scope and latitude of opportunity to *those who wish only to shape, steer, manipulate, and indoctrinate the next generation*.

Unfortunately, that is still the primary purpose of education in much of Eastern Europe, The Middle East, and Asia. Whatever progress toward freedom for the common man was conceived during the nineteenth century, was aborted and its feeble dying body thrown in the trash to die, as Lenin, Stalin, Mao, and a gaggle of Marxist Socialists achieved power and murdered freedom along with a hundred million and more souls.

From Finland across to the North Pacific Coast of Siberia, down the Pacific Rim to South East Asia, then westward across the southern border of the old Soviet Union to Eastern Europe and back to Finland, the evil spirit of Karl Marx and his disciples have slaughtered millions. They have saturated the ground with the blood of those who were the wrong race, who resisted, or maybe just got in the way. When people of this stripe control education, you had better know that their goal is not freedom.

While I can find no confirming research today, it has been my long-held understanding that the reason for Lenin's remark that, *"the United States will fall into our hand like a ripe plum."* was because he had faith that the Marxist-leaning American Professors he called, "Fellow-Travelers" would one day indoctrinate enough Americans to tip our nation into Communism. I have read that somewhere in the past. I have not been able to find it recently, but I also know the Progressives have been slowly airbrushing, erasing, and re-writing history to favor their own propaganda world-view and to hide their continuing sabotage for the past 50 to 75 years.

That is no surprise, because neither can I readily re-find internet sources and articles from even three to five years ago. I believe the day is coming when only hard copies will still be in existence, and those will have to be either hidden or lost to 'censors' (yes, the Nazi's burned books with German efficiency). Moreover, today, the Leftists, American and International, are quietly erasing and airbrushing massive historical libraries from the internet, and. I have no doubt that some of the large internet service providers are working with them, as are some percentage of all major US businesses. That is the definition of crony-capitalism.

Speaking of Crony-Capitalism and Government Graft, I spent many years working and travelling in the third world where government corruption is so rife it is taken for granted (even though it's illegal there too). No business completes or accomplishes anything without paying off one or more officials at the proper levels. In Saudi Arabia when I worked there in the late 70's, almost all personal and local business dealing were handled with cash. If you were paid by check, you were expected to give a bank officer a percentage of the check for the privilege of cashing it. The more the value of the check, the higher level of the officer (and the percentage!). I knew of one American Company who was forced to wait several months to cash a several hundred million dollar contract progress payment check from the Saudi Government, because the Bank Manager who should necessarily get the "percentage" for cashing the check was out of the country on extended vacation. With interest 15-18% at the time (Carter Administration), just think of several months interest on several hundred million dollars at that rate and you will get an idea how much that company lost. A number of American companies eventually closed their American businesses out and re-incorporated in Switzerland or other nations who allowed business to be conducted inside the rules of the Nation where they worked.

To do otherwise put American businesses at a distinct disadvantage. When I first went to Saudi in 1977, America was Number One in worldwide Construction. When I left in 1981, we were Thirteenth! Other nations assisted their construction companies in competition and winning of projects. The American government always made things harder for American Companies. That is why I ended up working for Local Contractors most of my time there. Unless an American Company was huge, it had no chance.

I also knew of an official in a Korean Company working in Saudi Arabia, who was targeted by the Saudi Government to make him an 'example'. He brought in a suitcase or two, carrying the amount of the "baksheesh" he had agreed to pay for winning a contract, and was immediately arrested for breaking Saudi law.

In Saudi prisons, all men are locked in a single room with a steel door containing a small door through which to pass food and small items, a half inch iron pipe with a faucet protruding from the floor or wall in one corner, near a four inch hole into the sewer. That combination is the drinking fountain, the sink, and the toilet all in one. In addition, there's no law inside the cell, after you're thrown inside that door, the strong and evil rule brutally, stealing food and cigarettes, and ravenous for sex. The last word I heard about that Korean was that he was begging his company to give him a pill so he could kill himself. I will let you imagine why.

In my experience, that kind of what the Saudi's call "baksheesh" business dealing has a certain 'smell' to it, and over the past couple decades, our federal government reeks of it. Oh, by the way, Corporatism is Mussolini's term for the 'partnership' of Business and the (Fascist) Government. . The age of crony capitalism did not begin with Obama, but as I watch, he and his sycophants are proving to be every bit adept at it as were either Mussolini or Hitler.

Don't believe me? Do some research and study your own history. That may be the price you pay for keeping your freedom.

The best sources of American History today are books written from seventy-five to one hundred fifty years (or more) ago. If found, these books recorded history as eye witness accounts well before the revisionists who wish to turn America into a one-man-one-vote, (one time) democracy got their hands in the 'cookie jar'. History recorded truthfully is a deadly enemy of the Socialist Statist. He fears it will show you where you came from, so you might be able to figure out where you are, and where he is leading you.

Hint! He is leading you to death or a state even worse than death for a human being. Whether Communism or Fascism, both are just a form of Socialist Statism and complete Tyranny.

3) Continual, passage of petty, repetitive, and redundant legislation and regulation.
The Statist is constantly pushing for more and more petty and redundant legislation and regulation to be passed, year after year, until like Gulliver in the Land of Lilliput, the thousands of threads tying the giant (a.k.a. the American people) down, create a prison, wherefrom the people, like Gulliver can no longer rise. Did you never wonder why legislatures (both State and Federal) are constantly bombarded and lobbied by (mostly) Leftist Special Interest Groups to pass new, 'necessary', or 'emergency' laws or regulations encompassing every micro-aspect of life, until no one can even breathe without breaking a law somewhere?

Why do we need tens of thousands of laws, many of them incredibly idiotic and ridiculous restrictions on personal liberty, to enforce Ten Commandments? Because the Leftist Progressive Socialists need to chain the people with thousands of 'thread-like' laws and regulations, because like Gulliver, someone binding him with full-size chains or ropes would have awakened the sleeping giant. However, the tiny additions of thread-like laws allow him to slumber on, unconscious to the fact they create a web, making him a sleeping prisoner. Besides, such idiocy creates disregard for the complete law because no one can obey them all anyway. Most Americans are unconscious that the real reason is to control them completely.

With thousands of these laws in place, if 'Big Brother' wants to arrest you, he can easily find a law that you have broken somewhere. You have little or no chance to survive unless you bow to those in authority and kiss their 'ring', which is exactly the supine behavior they lust for. That gives (or will eventually give) a tyrannical government a huge hammer for keeping the citizenry 'under control'. Fascism is the perfect example of a government, which wishes to control every micro-facet of human life. A fully regimented people are the stock in trade of Fascism.

Did you hear the news announcements that as of January 1, 2012, Forty Thousand *new* pieces of legislation took effect across the USA? These are merely those passed during last year, which were *scheduled* to take effect the first of 2012.

Do any of you know how many *more* laws were passed last year by our out-of-control government that went into effect on a different schedule? The ObamaDoesn'tCare Law itself contained some 2700 pages, containing how many laws, how many regulations? Two years later we are still discovering them, yet *nobody still* knows exactly how many. Moreover, our legislators call that Government of the People, by the People, and for the People? What a bunch of liars!

Who can doubt this is but petty, repetitive, and redundant legislation and regulation being passed with the precise goal of indoctrinating, intimidating, and disciplining the American People to live their lives under the regimentation of a fascist state, humbly subservient to arrogant bureaucratic fools. If I'm paranoid about this, then so were the Founding Fathers, who wrote many pages on this subject, and who wrote the Bill of Rights and Constitution to restrict, not entitle the federal government for this exact reason.

Now, we have reviewed American Education, both the first two hundred years, and the past hundred years in Chapter Ten. Now let us go back to the Marx cum Alinsky revolution-creating scenario.

Operation: Revolution in the Streets.
Carefully cultivated and inflamed civil unrest and discontent among the working class and the dissatisfied, timed and coordinated with a serious economic or other civil crisis may easily be used to foment severe civil unrest and anger.

From this point, using a small, planted minority of disaffected union workers and leftist leaning "useful idiots", followed with continually growing rhetoric and left-slanted media coverage to stoke greater discontent and anger, the *"Peoples Revolution"* can begin.

This "People's Revolution" may then be followed by openly shown rebellion and hatred for leaders, law enforcement and/or military, as well as the always suspect 'rich' groups (bankers, industrialists, Jews, etc.).

The level of street protests and violence may then be ratcheted up if not curbed by the government to protect the balance of the population. If it *is* curbed by the government, that is considered a bonus, and the violence and demonstrations are immediately be ratcheted up several levels, because now the government has become the "enemy" as well. Such violence in the streets causes increasing government intervention, in turn causing creating more violence, etc., ad infinitum.

At this point two things can happen. Those in the government who are in favor of a statist takeover can begin to work from the inside for a new "People's Democratic Movement", while allowing acceleration of civil disobedience and demonstrations until the situation deteriorates into civil war. Based on history, Socialist-Statists are willing to gamble that the outcome of such a civil war will usher in a new socialist government of "One man, One vote, One time". Remember the Lynch Mob democracy example?

So, by creating this plan of attack to instill anger, dissatisfaction, and class hatred, among the 'poor', working and middle class (including unions), while 'nudging' each generation closer to being leftists through slanted education, the seeds of an ultimate revolution have already been sown. All that is currently required is a 'crisis situation', or 'perfect storm' to provide nourishing 'rain' for the crop of revolution to grow. Oh, I know! We have that too; it is called the "Obama Recession cum Depression cum Economic Collapse Crises". That will work! It was created to order, in fact!

With small variations to the major theme, it happened that way in France, Russia, Germany, China, and Cuba, to mention a few better-known nations. It happened a little differently in Muslim Iran, where a so-called "Man in the Street" revolution installed a Radical Imam, who had been in exile in Paris for years, with Jimmy Carter's blessings. Next, a radical, Hitler 'wanna-be' was installed as president, a terrorist who was likely involved in the Iran Hostage Crisis, and who treats his people worse than slaves. A man who may even now have nuclear capability with which he candidly states he wants to wipe Israel off the Middle Eastern map. Therefore, a previous Progressive President assisted also in installation of radical, Anti-American Muslim leadership, replacing one open to dealing with the United States. What is going on here? Are you still napping?

Modern developments.
Early in 2011, the so-called Muslim Street Revolution fomented a 'Democracy' movement across North Africa, named "Arab Spring".

Even though experts immediately identified the Muslim Brotherhood (MB) as the power behind the so-called spontaneous uprising, the Director of National Intelligence testified to the American People that the organization has "pursued social ends" and a "betterment of the political order". Although the Administration further muddied the truth with weasel words, that was what all average Americans heard on the subject. However, those who had studied history knew different about the MB.

The CIA's website lists the MB as a "religious-based" party, and sixty seconds of Google searching "the Muslim Brotherhood is a secular group" would have turned up over nine million hits on information, both pro and con. Most Americans do not know the following Truths (Emphasis mine - rg:)

- MB originated in Egypt in 1928 as a social and religious organization. It has branches in 70 countries
- The MB motto is "Allah is our objective. The Prophet is our leader. Qur'an is our law. Jihad is our way. *Dying in the way of Allah is our highest hope.*"
- MB founder, Hassan al-Banna, was a *devout admirer of Adolf Hitler and the Nazi regime*. During the 1930s, al-Banna and the MB became a *secret arm of Nazi intelligence.*
- Hitler's ODESSA network, helped *thousands of high profile Nazi's flee to safe havens* assisted by MB's Al-Husseini.
- Husseini received *ten thousand dollars monthly by Hitler*, actively engaged in Nazi activities, broadcasting radio programs urging Arabs to resist Allies, and calling for a *jihad against Jews*.
- The (Nazi) New Egypt Party and MB installed Nassar as Prime Minister of Egypt; Nasser created the Fedayeen Arab terrorist squads to attack Israel, and then merged them with MB activist Yasser Arafat, a nephew of Al-Husseini, to form the PLO.
- In retaliation for his *assassination attempt* on Nasser, Al-Banna was killed and MB was banned in Egypt in 1949.
- *Sadat was also assassinated* by the MB, in retaliation for his Treaty with Israel.
- MB agreed to making it a *religious obligation of Muslims to abduct and kill U.S. citizens in Iraq*
- Today, Russia insists the *MB is the key to Chechen terrorism*.
- Muhammad Badi', of the MB said in 2010, "... the improvement and change that the [Muslim] nation seeks can only be attained through jihad and sacrifice and by *raising a jihadi generation that pursues death, just as the enemies pursue life.*" (6)

This list just points to a few of the high (or low?) points in the 'family' history of the Muslim Brotherhood.

Regardless of that, the 'Arab Spring' movement was encouraged and cheered-on by, among others, the President of the United States, giving instant credibility to another "One man, one vote, one time" democracy. Similarly, Jimmy Carter gave instant international political credibility to Imam Khomeini, who led the revolution in Iran and to the Sandinista (Communist) revolution and takeover of Nicaragua by granting them "Diplomatic Recognition". Is a pattern detectable here?

In April 2012, while Egypt's Leaders played "Mind-Games" with the US by detaining American Citizens, the Secretary of State smilingly agreed to waive human rights concerns and sign off on more than 1.3 billion dollars of foreign aid to Egypt's rulers. Then, Surprise! Surprise! The Muslim Brotherhood, the old and well-known terrorist organization with a taproot that reaches back into the Third Reich, suddenly won almost 75% control of the Egyptian Government, and now claim the Presidency. Now, well financed with American Tax dollars, coupled with its other victories across the area, the MB has suddenly become the dominant political power in North Africa and the Middle East. Well interesting, I wonder just how that happened.

So, during a short spring campaign, requiring only minimum funding to incite and inflame street riots, by utilizing disaffected and angry Muslim street people and other 'Useful Idiots", and with positive recognition by the President of the United States, the MB coasted to an easy win in their revolution. By the way, did you know the MB insiders called people like Mohammed El Baradei, "hamir al-thawra, "or "donkeys of the revolution"- How Leninesque of them!).

That win, coupled with a US President's diplomatic boost and "Wedding" gift of 1.3 Billion Dollars of American Taxpayer money, suddenly tilts the machine to favor the Muslim Brotherhood to dominate *in the whole of North Africa* and to make an Iran-Style takeover, with all that portends for Southern Europe, the Mediterranean, Israel, the United States, and world-wide Muslim terrorism. No longer do we have Mid-East Leaders who, while Muslim, had become accustomed to dealing with the United States (for a price), and tacitly letting Israel live in semi-peace. Those have now been relegated to the history books in favor of Radical Muslim Terrorism. Does anyone see a pattern here? Well, at least, it has certainly been "Hope and Change" to the better for Radical Islam.

Oh, but wait, more to come! The Ayatollah of Iran recently stated that last year was the year of the "Dictators', next is the year of the 'Kings'. Could he possibly mean that the Kings of Jordan Saudi Arabia have already been targeted for next spring?

That appears likely. After all, they have been American allies for some generations, not acceptable to Radical Islam. Turning those nations over to the Nazi-embracing Muslim Brotherhood will accomplish a number of purposes, all huge trouble for the Western World, just as the MB presence in Chechnya has been for Russia. It would also be a gigantic victory for the MB to tumble the two -pro-western monarchies in the Middle East and take control of their land, people, and resources:

- It would at once send a message to the rest of Islam the MB is in their ascension.
- It would give MB the riches of the largest oil-bearing nation in the region, placing them in charge of OPEC.
- It would give MB ownership of Mecca, the holiest site for Islam.
- It would certainly either strangle or triple the price of Saudi Oil to the US, assisting Obama in making fossil energy so expensive America can be forced to embrace his idiotic Green "Alternate Energy" Plans to cut our standard of living to a third-world level.
- It would completely isolate Israel, who, according to Obama is actually the real problem festering the Middle East anyway.

It is a huge plum, likely only to be picked in the same manner as was Egypt and the rest of North Africa. This means with tacit permission and approval from the U.S. President!

However, if they have reviewed Obama's previous actions in North Africa, how could the MB or the American People have any doubt as to his position and actions toward this next one?

So today, for the first time in decades, the power structure in the Middle East is heavily tilted, and sliding rapidly toward the Radical Muslim Brotherhood. The MB with a historical active and overt alliance to the Fascist Nazi's during WW II, who helped hide Nazi war criminals post war, and who admittedly hate Israel and "The Great Satan" (the United States) more than they love their life.

However, in fact, our President appears to be their ally in conquest. However, reading his book, "Audacity of Hope", Obama already stated,

> "I will stand with them (Muslims) should the
> political winds shift in an ugly direction."

Therefore, today, we have the Anti-American Muslim Brotherhood and the anti-Capitalism Occupy Wall Street groups, both with either tacit or open blessings from our President. Does it not then make sense that they share a common their goal, which is the "Erasing" of Israel, and the ultimate destruction of the "Great Satan", the United States? How could he possibly be on the side of the United States in this battle with his past statements and present actions? What other rational decision can we reach?

Today, instead of asking how to create a Socialist Revolution, you should be asking how to **stop** one!

Additional items to accelerate the weakening of America
America is a huge prize for the Socialist Tyrants, but it has been a long-term battle. In America Socialist-Statists have added to the first three strategic tools, a fourth and a fifth to further weaken free enterprise and bring a crisis of hopelessness upon the people. These are Government Subsidies, and Environmental Regulation.

4) Government Subsidies. The fourth strategic tool is a double-edged sword, subsidies and taxation. Most Americans know that the power to tax is the power to destroy. They have also heard the old saying, "If you want more of a thing subsidize it, if you want less of a thing, tax it." That is because it is not simply a saying, but without argument, a truth. Of course, a "heavy progressive or graduated income tax" is also the second item in Marx's 10 Pillars of Communism as well, adding to its importance.

Under Woodrow Wilson, the Farm Loan Act of 1916 provided low-cost long-term mortgages for American Farmers to begin their dependence upon the Federal Government. (7) Then FDR's New Deal passed the Agricultural Adjustment Act of 1933, and with agriculture trade barriers already in place, it gave the US Federal Government more power over agriculture than the *farmers themselves* had with their own land and crops. Yes, even in the thirties (8).

Then, a 'Perfect Storm' Crisis occurred, created by a depression turned into a 'Great' Depression by Republican President Herbert Hoover's *Progressive* meddling, followed by Franklin D. Roosevelt being elected and veering even farther to the Left. FDR then commenced to use that crisis to further manipulate, intimidate, and enslave the US, including the farm community, with myriads of new 'social' (Socialist) programs, legislation, and regulations.

In order to showcase his power to enforce the federal government's usurpation of private property and the rights of property owners, he used the power of the federal government to make a national example of one small farmer named Roscoe Filburn. In 1938 the morons in congress (no, the morons there today don't have any corner on that title or attribute), had passed the Agricultural Adjustment Act, utilizing Interstate Commerce as authority for the Feds to intervene in private business. The ludicrous purpose of this act was to control the sometimes-violent swings in the world price of wheat by setting maximums of wheat production on American Farmers. Yet today is little different, the morons in Congress still CREATE wild swings in commodity prices by manipulating the markets with Taxation, Subsidization, Regulation, or just plain Greed! Today farmers have come to *count on* being subsidized. Again, there is nothing new under the sun.

Mr. Filburn was "given" a federal "allowance" to plant only eleven point one acres of his own property so he might grow wheat. However, because Mr. Filburn wanted to raise some wheat to feed his own chickens, he planted the federal law-breaking acreage of twenty-three acres, intending to use the excess on his own property, to feed his own animals, stating that because it was for use on his own property, Interstate Commerce rules did not apply.

Of course, no tyrant of any consequence could allow some simple farmer to get away with such a dastardly thing as disobeying the tyrant-king's orders. Of course, by then FDR had enough time in office to "Stack" the Supreme Court with judges of his own political stripe (Self-Appointed Rulers of the 'Stupid Masses). So, his Secretary of Agriculture, one Mr. Wicklund, took Mr. Filburn to court for refusing to destroy his crop and pay the assessed fine (9) Similar to burning down your house to reduce fire insurance payments, or like getting paid not to produce farm products!

Using the full power of the federal government and ending up all the way to FDR's 'Stacked' Supreme Court, the Tyrant King won his case against the Serf who dared to refuse him.

Guess it is a good thing Mr. Filburn had his American Citizenship and 'Unhandy' Constitutional rights handy. In any totally Socialist or Monarchist nation, he would likely have been hung (or under the current Administration, possibly killed by a Drone Missile, as decided by some invisible committee), and his property (and crop) would have become the property of the self-appointed ruling class to spend on furtherance of the Revolution. Nevertheless, FDR had succeeded in his goal; he had begun the intimidation and subjugation of the American Farmer, which continues today.

Since then, of course the federal government has made farmers dependent on their subsidies and insurance to survive, and thereby subservient to federal rules and guidelines to keep their subsidy payments.

This of course has decimated the Family Farmer and Family Farm to the point that they have become an endangered species in the USA.

But it allows huge Corporations to gobble up Farms, land, and subsidies, without care for land, peoples, or crops. Guided by banks of corporate lawyers whose only dedication is to wringing the last dollar of crony-capitalist subsidy from their 'friends and allies' in high federal places.

It is hard to believe how well this has worked for the self-appointed Elites who were elected to power. A percentage of this stolen tax money *always* ends up as campaign contributions to them, to keep them in power. How handy for the revolution! How destructive to the American Farmer and Farm Family! What a Fascist Example!

Today, the cost of corn subsidies in the US alone, have from 1995 thru 2010, added $80.6 Billion dollars to the price of corn, due to corn's being subsidized with tax dollars drawn from the rest of the public. Moreover, that does not even include the cost of trade barriers in place or the tax-swindling boondoggle of using food to create fuel (ethanol) (10).

At the first Centennial of the Founding of the United States, Ralph Waldo Emerson's Poem for the occasion, *The Concord Hymn*, read:
> *By the rude bridge that arched the flood,*
> *Their flag to April's breeze unfurled,*
> *Here once the embattled farmers stood,*
> *And fired the shot heard round the world.*

However, those once brave, 'embattled farmers' have today, by accepting, and becoming dependent on federal subsidies, been "Broke-to-Lead" into accepting government tyranny virtually equal to what the King of England and his Redcoats once represented.

They now timidly obey, *or even look forward* to obeying the federal "Kings Men" who direct the use of their private property and their lives from Washington DC. How tragic, how sad, that these who were once some of the most independent and proud people on earth have now been "Broke-to-Lead" by a federal government out-of-control with self-appointed Elites, who manipulated, intimidated, and dominated them into virtual serfdom.

5) Environmental Regulation. The fifth strategic tool progressives have added to destroy America is Environmental Regulation. It is the not-very-new religion of those who believe, "the enemy of my enemy is my friend" (And I will take care of *you* after we have destroyed our stronger enemy together).

Why can't America become energy independent? Why can't America use her own natural resources to become free from dependency on other nations? America has as many or more natural resources than almost any nation on earth. Where is the problem, and why can it not be solved.

The simple, and uncomplicated reason is Environmental Regulation, placed on the backs of, and stolen from the pockets of the American People by Congressmen, Senators, Presidents, and State Governors and Legislators, who have been bought and paid for by a small, but very powerful group/cult, whose religion of choice is Statism, and whose goddess is Gaia, or Mother Earth.

By the way, did *you* realize that this environmental fraud is a second-hand one? One used by the leaders of that sterling "Utopia" know as *Nazi Germany?* See if the following programs, put into practice by the Nazis to assist in the regimentation and control of the German People sound vaguely familiar:

> *"The Nazis created nature preserves, championed sustainable forestry, curbed air pollution, and designed the autobahn highway network as a way of bringing Germans closer to nature."*
>
> How Green Were the Nazis" by Franz-Josef Bruggemeier

Hitler launched this "Feel-Good" Program within months after he gained dictatorial power. He sold out his prior terrorist army, the Sturm Abteilung, a.k.a. the SA, or Brown Shirts, because he realized that he could not continue to operate the whole nation with head-busting terrorist tactics alone, without a public backlash.

So, to calm the people into giving him personal loyalty, to mask his past terrorist connection, and look to him as a benevolent leader, he gave them the "Beauty of Labor", and later, the 'Reich Nature

Protection Law' program, and enacted laws to control air pollution, and so on (sound familiar yet?).

These programs gave the people productive work building the Auto-Bahn (to benefit his future war plans), as well as national forest work, and beautification projects to give workers a "pleasant workspace". It also kept their hands and minds occupied, gave them an income, kept them physically fit for the pre-planned conflict, and at the same time created a web of laws, rules, and regulations with which to tax and control the people for both current government expenditures and future war funding.

Of course, his biggest supporters immediately came from environmental groups, who will always trade freedoms of the hated humanity for environmental gains, which they call 'the greater good'. They just do not say for whom.

So, back to the current Environmental Groups and the politicians whose souls they have purchased.

Just as all not all Christians are Catholic, not all environmental worshippers are Gaia followers. However, from where I sit, the majority of those who worship their "mother earth" believe that man is like a virus on the earth, which needs eradication, or at least his population kept below six hundred million, or however many Gaia Lovers there happen to be at any exact moment in time. The rest of us need to kind of 'disappear' for the old girl's best interests. Therefore, they do not believe a human should use any natural resources, except maybe grave spaces.

Therefore, of course it is up to them, as self-appointed saviors of Gaia (who by the way, is all-powerful, but cannot take care of herself), to legislate and regulate mankind off their favored planet. As far as being like all the 'other' self-righteous, self-appointed Statists, Yogi Berra would have described them by saying,

'They're kinda like Deja-vu all over again'.

If their statist policies and regulations cause mass starvation, place Communist or Fascist Dictators in power to cause wars, or to cause any other forms of human death, they are ecstatic, because after all, their idea is to reduce the population of the viral mankind on the planet they revere.

Of course, it makes those who lust after being Communist or Fascist Dictators happy to recruit these flakey environmentalist wing nuts and bathe in their love and cash donations while regulating the common man out of freedom and into slavery. It is both amazing and terrifying how well these two work together for the destruction of the human race.

So, we can't drill for oil, use natural gas, fish in the ocean or lakes and streams for food, we have to leave all natural resources (except grave spaces) for the select few Gaia Lovers who want to be the only human population left on earth.

I only hope the Senators, Legislators, Presidents, and state governors who are selling us out to these wing nuts are aware that they are in for a short ride they're in for.

Only those on the very top like an 'Adolph' will be able to tell them to shut up or die before he brings upon his nation or possibly the whole world a cataclysm that will come close to destroying both mankind, and the earth in the process.

However, the Socialist-Statists will be happy. At least those who chance to survive their own holocaust will.

CHAPTER TEN

Who were the Kulaks, and why do we care about them?

"One death is a tragedy, one million is a statistic."

Joseph Stalin

How many Americans know who the Kulaks were? How many have *even heard* of them? Do *you* know the history of the Genocide of the Kulaks, and its importance to America and America's continuing freedom?

Those of you who love freedom and want your children to live free should know about what happened to these people the Kulaks, because as Santayana said,

"Those who refuse to learn from history are doomed to repeat it".

Here is a capsule history of who the Kulaks were, and why likely very few people know of them. The Kulaks were simply land-owning peasants who provided an object for Bolshevic hatred, and a terrifying example to all Russians who had any hope of escaping the tyranny of Communism under Lenin or Stalin. In this role, the Kulaks became the victims of genocide. They essentially ceased to exist, except as an example of Communist brutality during the Communist

Revolution and the creation of the Soviet Union, even though the Kulaks were neither a racial, ethnic, nor a political group.

First, let us recap of how this happened under Marxist Tyranny, and how it can easily happen again.

As previously mentioned, Statist/Socialist Tyrants don't merely just want, they desperately NEED to have "enemies of the people" toward which the anger and hatred they feed and stir into their crowds of "disaffected" followers can be aimed and channeled. Before a tyrant gains full control of his own population, it is much safer for him to have an internal group or class, from inside his own nation unless there is a national history of animosity with some outside group. Toward this group (or groups), his venomous and hateful rhetoric can aim his followers anger and hatred like a machine-gun (and don't forget the useful idiots, who stupidly swell his ranks)! Only after he gains control over his own population can the Statist Tyrant safely expand his list of enemies beyond his own nation's borders.

For example, the French Revolution targeted the widely hated, tyrannical Monarchy that had ruled France for centuries, along with the Aristocrats, and the Authoritarianism of the State Church, with which the French People had become weary. Using enlightenment stemming from both the Magna Carta and the founding of America, yet poisoned with more hatred of the tyrants than true concern for French Citizenry, the French Revolution destroyed the Monarchy, Aristocracy, and Religious Authority. However then, its thirst for blood turned into a taste for blood, and turned inward, even slaughtering many common people who only took part in the first place to gain freedom from tyranny.

So, the French revolution destroyed the tyranny it so hated, but having been founded in vengeful hatred and blood-lust, it ended with a bloodbath of innocent citizens, and eventually with Napoleon Bonaparte, who was a member of the much-hated Nobility (Aristocracy), and a Revolutionary General himself in numerous battles, using his revolutionary position to become Emperor. The rest, as they say, is "History". (1)

After the French Revolution, in 1847, the "Communist League" met in London and commissioned Marx and Engels to write a manifesto, which would become *The* Communist Manifesto. Shortly after, the European rebellions of the 1848 era began. Communism had now come into its own as a Karl Marx defined tool to foment revolution and civil war, but was still untested at a national governing level. It took the evil cunning and moral bankruptcy of one Vladimir Lenin, followed by the ruthlessness of the soul-less Josef Stalin to bring it to a level of national government performing the slaughter and inhumane economic and political experiments necessary to transform a paranoid, hate-driven philosophy into an *absolute* totalitarian tyranny. Bringing a level of tyranny and slaughter such as few Monarchs or Aristocrats could ever have even dreamt, because at least their commoners were considered a 'resource'. (2)

The Communist takeover in Russia resulted in brutal government-committed barbarism, and atrocities committed in the *name* of the common man *upon* the common man. That *"fundamental" transformation* happened at the cost of tens of millions of human beings slaughtered, tortured, starved, imprisoned, or simply worked to death in slave labor camps. Now, that's *really* Fundamental!

No one knows will ever know how many people were murdered or died because of Soviet Communism, but it set the evil 'norm' for subsequent Communist Revolutions and takeovers. The historic human toll for communist takeover of a nation ranges from ten to thirty percent of the population. The long-term toll is unknowable, as murderers are close-mouthed, and leftist Journalists from all nations conspired by reporting only the 'glorious' things about a communist government, not its horrific death tolls (3).

I personally have been in a crowd of tourists in the Moscow Subway. Most were admiring the beautiful artwork, both ceramic tiles and paintings. The place resembled a Cathedral in aesthetic beauty. However, it was empty and cold to me, because for years I had studied the human tragedy through which Lenin and Stalin had created the Soviet Union. Human suffering both enjoyed inflicting, if you had read your history. The funds to create this 'Cathedral' had come from forced (slave) labor, or executions followed by confiscation of private property, purposefully inflicted pain and suffering upon the people, and the ultimate death of the Russian People's spirits.

I could never see the beauty; only feel the sick feeling in my stomach because I knew what it had cost in human suffering and blood. The only pleasure I found there was in giving out small Russian language Bibles to children, with a dollar bill folded inside (which equaled a full day's wages at the time), then moving away and hearing the children squeal in delight as they found the cash. However, I digress.

To illustrate the point and usefulness of "Enemies of the People", toward which a tyrant can direct the (real or imagined) anger of his goons and street rabble, consider the following. The French Revolution had Monarchs, Aristocrats, and the Church as targets. Lenin and Stalin had the Tsars (Monarchy), and the Bourgeoisie (Aristocracy), who were all people of wealth or property ownership. In Lenin's eyes unless you were a Bolshevic Revolutionary, if you had enough to eat or a shack to live in, you were Bourgeoisie and need to be killed, if you were Religious or merely Educated, you were a potential enemy and must be re-educated. Hitler had the Jews and the Communists to begin with as the Monarchy and Aristocracy were already been partially eliminated. Later he used the Catholics and Protestants who could not believe he was a force for good and not evil. Mao had the authoritarian Monarchist and Aristocratic Chinese system, the religious seemed no problem except for the Christians, whom he persecuted and imprisoned. Almost every self-appointed elitist communist revolutionary since the French Revolution has had, or simply invented similar "Enemies of the People". By these men's morally depraved Marxist/Socialist rationale, any and all who did not agree with them and their revolution were either enemies of the revolution or might someday become it's enemy, *and therefore must be either re-educated, or eradicated i.e., Killed!* Remember that sentiment. It will come up again in the discussion of Socialism.

Vladimir Lenin, the Russian Marxist/Communist 'Elitist' did not believe in waiting for the 'Proletariat' to bring about the Communist Revolution he sought, like other Russian Communists. Like the too-hungry vulture in the desert, he believed he had to kill something to survive. Because of his impatience, he believed in assisting the Revolution to birth by armed struggle, combining terrorism, assassinations, and robbery, of wealthy individuals, government, and official institutions by Communist (Proletarian) Revolutionaries, in order to provide funding for their own revolutionary actions and the ultimate goal of Civil War. But rather than rot in the Tsar's prisons he, being a self-appointed elite, and more important than the 'proletarian soldiers' hid in exile in Switzerland between 1914 and 1917 watching others do the dirty work while he was plotting uprisings and revolution, both in his homeland Russia, and the land of his exile. (4)

While he had no particular success in Switzerland, the February (1917) Russian Revolution caused Nicolas II's abdication and imprisonment, thereby opening the door for Lenin's return to Russia. Incidentally, the February Revolution also ushered in our old friend, a 'Democratic' Government – you know by now, "One man, one vote, one time".

Actually, this one did not even get to the one vote one time stage, because democracy was not enough for Lenin and the Bolshevics. They wanted complete Communism. So, after he returned and the Bolsheviks had won the October (1917) Revolution, Lenin took over leadership of the Party to become the first full-fledged Socialist Communist national leader and butcher in history. Together they would create a police state filled with such death and destruction wreaked upon Russia and its people that it would last over seven decades. It gave the world a preview of just how mercilessly any following Communist Socialist Revolutions would treat citizens who could or would not bow to Communism.

Today various internationalist and/or anti-American groups and movements scattered across our nation and the world have coalesced into a movement that is not only visible to those who can identify it, but is visibly moving toward a common goal. This movement then, and direction it is moving, plays an eerily familiar tune to those who recognize it, and have no wish to see it repeat in another incarnation.

I firmly believe the current US Administration has the goal of using and fusing each one of these groups and movements into an irresistible force, with a mutual goal of the "Fundamental Transformation" of America, as Lenin did in Russia. I certainly know that for the past one hundred years Progressive Socialist-Statists have labored to transform the United States from a Constitutional Republic, into a Democracy. We have discussed that and the historical fact that democracies *always* collapse into either anarchy or tyranny. This truth is clearly visible to all who wish to research and identify it.

For those understanding the difference, it is frighteningly obvious that America today not only has *become* a democracy, but that most of its citizens are so ignorant of their history that they believe it was *founded* that way Therefore, the next step for the United States, according to the Socialists/Statists, is to implode, either into Anarchy or Tyranny. In my history-based opinion, Anarchy will likely happen first, incited through lawlessness and rioting in the streets, setting the 'Perfect Storm' stage for a Tyrant to take power.

The current United States recession/depression may easily cause the collapse of the US Dollar as the world's "Reserve Currency" (the one in which the Worldwide petroleum price is denominated). Coupled with the imminent collapse of the European "PIIGS' (Portugal, Ireland, Italy, Greece, and Spain), this then creates incredible pressure on the Euro and the European economy, setting the stage or just such a "Perfect Storm" scenario.

In such a scenario, groups like the Congressional Progressive Caucus, whose goals are based in Socialism (whether communist or fascist, who cares, there's really little difference unless you're the ones in power), and can assist in creating a collapse of law and order in the United States through civil disobedience and riots. These would be similar to those currently happening in Greece, and bring us to the brink of Civil War through Anarchy. At such a time, Progressives currently in power in our federal government can readily step in to "save" the nation by imposing martial law, likely leading to dictatorship. Don't believe such people are in elective office? Simply do an internet search for "Congressional Progressive Congress" to find out there are currently over 80 members between the House and the Senate. Then look at their agenda. (5)

Such a scenario has played itself out in numerous nations that ended up under communist or fascist tyranny over the past hundred years. To disbelieve its possibility for the United States is to bury your head in the sand and shout, "It can't happen here?" If you really think that, may God help you and your progeny!

So, who were the Kulaks?
In 1906, under Tzar Nicholas II, an Agrarian Reform Experiment in the Ukrainian Region of Russia had dissolved peasant communes and purchased land from the nobility, turning ownership over to the local peasant farmers. This experiment increased efficiency and food production in this area, known as the 'Bread-Basket' of Russia by 40%, proving the theory that ownership of both their own land and the fruit of their own labors increased productivity.

Unfortunately, this lesson was completely lost on the ideology-blinded and hatred driven Communist Tyrant Lenin. I recall that as late as the 1980's it was well known that Russia's 'Collective Farms' produced less than 50% of the food consumed in the Soviet Union, while peasant's 'back-yard' gardens produced over fifty percent of their food, without which the people would have starved.

The particular group of Russian Peasants who received land in 1906 was generically known as the "Kulaks". Unfortunately, as proud and prosperous property owners, they readily became targets of opportunity for the paranoid and hate-filled Bolsheviks, who ultimately resorted to essential genocide, first under the deranged Lenin, and continuing under the soul-less Stalin, in order to destroy the Kulaks as a group, and absorb their farms into the all important (to a communist tyrant) collective farms.

The Kulaks with good reason, had supported the Russian Government's "White" Army in the Civil War, knowing the Bolsheviks would re-collectivize their land. Unfortunately for the Kulaks, the Bolsheviks won the Civil War.

After the Bolsheviks won the Russian Civil War and Lenin, as Party Leader became virtual dictator of Russia, famine broke out due to both war and communist collectivist policies. War then continued in the Ukraine and other western regions several years longer, as Lenin attempted to reclaim all areas formerly controlled by the Tzars for his Communist Empire.

With a combination of war and border agreements, Lenin accomplished this by 1921, and began shipping grain to the hungry Russians in Moscow and other high population areas. However, drought concurrently came to the Ukraine that year, choking grain production in the already war-torn area. These two situations, compounded by Lenin's targeting of the Kulaks for death and destruction when the grain he confiscated from them and other farmers failed to be sufficient for Russia's needs, along with the inefficiency of his ideologue driven enforced collectivization of farmland created widespread famine and anti-Bolshevic sentiment across Russia.

At this point Lenin and his Bolshevik Party could not afford to have the Russian people starving, and with a growing sentiment in the streets that the Communists could not feed their people. However, neither could he afford to purchase grain from abroad to feed them.

Therefore, Lenin resorted to confiscating *more* grain from the peasant classes, including the Kulaks. Because of the war and drought conditions coupled the failure of collective farms, there was not enough grain available to collect. And, because Lenin 'needed' a group toward whom the Proletariat might direct their 'rage', and of whom he could make a terror-filled example, he ordered seizure of not only the Kulak's personal grain-food stock, but additionally all the seed grain they had stored to plant for next year. Then, when there was still not enough grain, Lenin upped the ante again.

Clearly illustrating the evil inherent in Communism, Lenin declared *"Merciless war against the Kulaks! Death to them"*. In so doing, Lenin immediately worsened the national famine situation, but being a dedicated Communist, who believed communism would better develop as the ideology of a group of armed terrorists, he "Doubled-Down' and sent his proletarian troops to make examples or the Kulaks.

The Kulaks were specifically targeted for destruction as a class. It is impossible to know if they were all destroyed, as they were not an ethnic people but merely a group of peasants who owned small parcels of land when the Bolshevics came to power. Nevertheless, Kulaks eventually ceased to exist, except as a scapegoat name for anyone who did not perform exactly as expected by Lenin or any of the goons in his Army or Checka.

Lenin sent out countless orders to harass and generally terrorize and destroy the Kulaks. Quoted here is a message to the Central Executive Committee of Penza soviet, from the website article, Darwinist Dictators

> *"Comrades! The kulak uprising in your five districts must be crushed without pity. The interests of the whole revolution demand such actions, for the final struggle with the kulaks has now begun. You must make an example of these people. Hang (I mean hang publicly, so that people see it) at least 100 kulaks, rich bastards, and known blood-suckers. Publish their names. Seize all their grain...Do all this so that for miles around people see it all, understand it, tremble...Reply saying you have received and carried out these instructions.   Yours, Lenin".* (6)

In Lenin's Communist "Utopia" being called out of a crowd as a "Kulak" was normally an immediate prison or more likely, a death sentence. Sometimes complete families or groups were put into boxcars and exiled to 'Settlements' in Siberia, which normally meant being thrown off the train hundreds of miles from any civilization and left to survive or die. No one knows how many people perished this way. (7) I personally travelled two-thirds of the Trans-Siberian Railway, from Moscow to Irkutsk. Believe me, even today there are hundreds of miles of nothing but poplar trees and brush. Moreover, I travelled it in early September, not in winter.

Lenin's (and later Stalin's) campaign was so successful in terrorizing and destroying any though of private ownership amongst the people in the Soviet Union, that when they ran out of true Kulaks, they simply 'invented' them. While Kulaks were originally wealthy peasant land owners, as they became scarce, being defined as a "Kulak" might be for any of the following reasons, or for none!:

- ownership of property or business,
- use of hired labor, even a farmer employing his own son,
- renting out of land or facilities,
- having any source of non-labor income,
- a family having a metal roof on their house,
- those who sided with kulaks opposing collectivation,
- having enough food to sell some surplus,
- simply having personal possessions deemed "excessive",

One Soviet politician said, "We are fond of describing any peasant who has *enough to eat* as a Kulak". Essentially, anyone who had or did anything that pissed-off some Cheka, Army, or Bureaucrat goon could be called a Kulak. To make matters worse, local officials were tasked with finding and identifying minimum quotas of Kulaks, so many times they simply 'Pointed out a Kulak' to meet their quotas. However, the Bolshevic militants were by this time, well versed in and well prepared for terrorism and torture, as well as murder. I shall not here describe the gruesome methods of killing Kulaks I have reviewed, but it is my belief that even battle-hardened Viet Nam, Iraq, or Afghanistan veterans would be sickened to read them.

"Dictatorship of the Proletariat", to Lenin meant *full, and total dictatorship*. It also meant *full and total tyranny by the Bolshevics,* to insure that all life, all property, and everyone's lifestyle was dictated by the "Soviet" (defined as *the elected government in a Communist country*, which is the *first* big lie!) Elected by whom? Communism's entrance into Russia had begun with Lenin's armed goons and gangs, using robbery, sedition, kidnapping, and murder, liberally sprinkled with terrorism as might be necessary to begin a civil war. During that civil war, the Bolshevics never hesitated to perform the most unimaginable crimes, including torture and murder of their opponents.

Then, after winning the civil war, these seasoned and trusted terrorists became leaders in the army and the Checka (precursor to the NKVD & KGB) to insure the tyranny of terrorism continued. In this way, Lenin could strangle and destroy all opposition, all private property, all personal liberty, and ensure the total society advanced toward his *Tyrannical Communist Utopia.* The alternative was to die, maybe with a small caliber bullet in your head, maybe suffering some exotic type of crucifixion or other extremely painful type of death, quite likely after watching your family die first. Yes, Lenin and Stalin founded a true Communist "Utopia"! One not advertised by its adherents here in the Free World.

If you do not believe me, check out *"The Black Book of Communism"* (8), by Harvard University Press. The picture it paints is dramatically more bleak and evil than I have described here, because it was written using released archives from the Soviet Union's Secret Police after its collapse. The most 'controversial' thing about *"The Black Book of Communism"*, was that the author indicated that both Stalinism and Nazism were political systems relying on violence and terrorism. I believe him.

While my life-long study has always indicated this, and it makes me happy by adding validity to my own observations, it makes Communists and Socialists *'squeal like a pig stuck under a gate'* to have an authoritative book, based on Communism's own records compare them with their Nazi brothers. Those who were exposed to the world as the thugs and goons they are! However, remember, Communists and the Nazis *are* as similar, like non-identical twins. Nevertheless, they are always brothers, forget that at your own peril!

Unfortunately, Hitler crossed the line, creating such evil press that the Progressive Socialists could no longer publicly defend it. His worst offense to American Progressives had been when he attacked the Communists while attaining power. Like brothers, remember? Targeting the Jews in the 30's was no sin, but pretty much 'Business as Usual' for the self-appointed elites in Europe, *and* the USA. It was never really a problem for Progressive/Socialists, then or now, but at the end of WW II, they could not stop Hitler from getting a black eye in front of the world for his "Final Solution" to the Jews. After the grotesque death-camps, the ovens and the mass graves were seen by hundreds of our GI's, the sights were too graphic for any man who experienced them to forget during his entire lifetime.

> General Eisenhower stated these atrocities were, *"beyond the American mind to comprehend."* … *"I never dreamed that such cruelty, bestiality, and savagery could really exist in this world."*(9)

For these reasons he ordered that all the civilian news media and military combat camera units be required to visit the camps and record their observations in print, pictures and film. As he explained to General Marshall:

> *"I made the visit deliberately, in order to be in a position to give first-hand evidence of these things if ever, in the future, there develops a tendency to charge these allegations merely to 'propaganda.'"*(10)

But while the Russian Communist 'Pogroms' against the Jews had gone unreported and therefore virtually un-noticed thanks to a purposeful blackout of coverage by the European and even US Media, they had also been complicit with and done the same for Hitler during the late 30's and early 40's. Progressives, who were well imbedded in both Western Governments and Western Media were obviously 'Brothers' to all other stripes of Socialists as well.

However, there is no historical proof that Hitler was any more evil or terroristic than Lenin or Stalin, Hitler was merely a German, with the Germanic fetish for efficiency. Anyone who believes Lenin or Stalin wouldn't have used the Zyclon B and the ovens as a final solution for the Kulaks and the Cossacks is simply brain-dead! Lenin and Stalin were obviously neither smart nor efficient enough to perform what they did with the efficiency of a Hitler. However, that does not make them any less evil or bloodthirsty, only less mechanically efficient. The difference between the Soviets and the Nazi's death-toll was mostly technical, but Progressives necessarily shunned the Nazi's after the Holocaust to hide from their own guilt. Nevertheless, they have non-reported, and even covered up for the Soviet murders, atrocities, and bloodthirsty activities since 1917. They still do, it is who they are.

Actually, while I had always considered Stalin to be the most soul-less and bloodthirsty of the two, research done for this volume has made me realize that Lenin only murdered less people because he didn't live as long in power. Research indicates he was at least as bloodthirsty and terroristic a tyrant as Stalin, he simply died before he could kill as many people as Stalin eventually did.

So, these were the Kulaks. Now why should we care about them?
First, let us do a little background history.

I have studied and involved myself in US and world politics, as they affected the US, my whole life. I well remember blackouts after Pearl Harbor, WW II and having all the adult males gone to fight for Freedom, watching planes fly over Eastern Washington bound to Alaska and points west, the Balloon booby-traps, Rationing, FDR's death, VE Day, VJ Day, listening to the explosion of an Atomic Bomb on the radio in 1945, the 'Holocaust discovery, my father's return from the Pacific, the Dewey beats Truman headline, Korea, "I Like Ike", etc., all of which happened before I was an adult.

Around fifteen or twenty years ago, based on my lifelong personal studies and observation in economics, politics, and history, I formed an observation that the people of the United States were going through a 'Sea Change' in their societal personality, which would likely end in their election and adulation of an "American Hitler". The passage of time has confirmed this opinion.

While anyone may freely argue with my opinion, no one who tries can ever be successful without demonstrating my studies are suspect, or flawed, thus making my opinion flawed as well. While I was fully comfortable in my original opinion, the research I performed for this book, to demonstrate the viewpoint logically, has served to harden my original opinion. The only revisions I have found necessary after current research strengthen my resolve that the original observation was actually more correct than I could have realized years ago.

And so, the nation that worked together and won WW II came home from that cataclysm to enjoy the fruits of their labors, but forces already at work to undermine the strength and wealth of the USA had been advancing as well. These forces, made up of people who openly admired Hitler and Mussolini for the 'efficient' operation of their national governments before the war, or who had longed for the US to follow the Soviet Union into Communist "Utopia" had been hard at work. Unfortunately, Hitler had betrayed Socialism along with them with his unbelievably brutal and efficient "Final Solution", thus making his and Mussolini's Fascist governing model a horror to the average American.

So, to perform damage control, and maintain invisibility from the American People, the Progressives first shifted gears, becoming 'Anti-Fascists', instead glorifying our 'ally' it's 'benevolent' Soviet Union Utopia. Ignoring and excusing the terroristic, genocidal brutality Lenin and Stalin showed the Kulaks, the Cossacks and the total body-count of Russians who would not become 'good' communists. Retreating necessarily because Fascism, anti-Semitism, and hatred of the Judeo Christian Rule-of-Law, all pillars of Progressive's 'Faith' had been so thoroughly sullied by Hitler they must to be relegated to the back burner, until the generation who fought and won against Fascism had died off.

Only when the current 'Greatest Generation', those who remember the horrors of Fascism and Communism were passed, and another generation came to maturity could Socialists proceed again toward the revolution they desired. That task called for a generation who had been taught a "new and different US and World "history". A Generation fearlessly and openly glorified the 'Great Strides Forward' of the Soviet Union and the 'Glories' of various "Peoples Revolutions". A Generation who would fully appreciate the wonderful 'Utopia' formed by Mao's 'Cultural Revolution', and the many "Social Justice" victories by Totalitarian Socialist Regimes. Only then could Socialist Marxism in *all* its ugly forms again be resurrected. Today they are so close to success, they smell blood.

So the Progressives have necessarily waited, if somewhat impatiently, until those who still remembered the names and the evil deeds of Lenin, Stalin, Hitler, Mussolini, and Mao Tse Tung, are dead and can no longer raise a warning flag.

Only now can their 'New Revolution' begin, bringing Marxist "Social Justice", to the whole world destroying the Rule of Law with a New World-Wide Government. Without fail, this Revolution must erase the power and strength of the United States, so a new Federal World Government forms under the Marxist/Socialist model, which previously enslaved and slaughtered hundreds of millions of people during the twentieth century.

Only then, But *then* may already be *now*! Because today, the 'Greatest Generation' *is* almost gone, and there are only a few 'in-betweeners' like me left. Those who independently studied world history and economics, keeping the values our upbringing taught. Those who learned to read before they started school, who are not intimidated by Marxist Progressive's "Neutral-Value" which teaches grey on grey, not Black and White Values. Those who still remember WW II and *why* we fought it, those who brought up with the Original American value system, which preceded the Progressive Socialists editing of, and re-defining of, both US and World History to "dumb-down" the next American generation so they would accept bondage in the name of security.

However, today, we have the Sixties Generation. Those who in their youthful vigor could not 'Save the World for Socialism' by hurling human feces in paper bags at the police in '68, but who went back to their adopted 'family' of Marxist Socialist Professors, studying and working hard to become the movers and shakers of today's Marxist-Socialist-Statist organizations. Those who become entrenched and imbedded in the American social, legal, and governmental systems, so they could be guarantee being financed by our tax dollars as they worked to destroy our Constitutional Republic and the Rule of Law they despised so much.

A video featuring an FBI Confidential informant from a 1982 Documentary *"No Place to Hide"*, tells of sitting in a meeting with Bill Ayer's and some 25 members of *"Weather Underground"* discussing logistics for "After the Revolution". Many of these 'Weatherman' had graduate degrees from Columbia and other well-known Universities. He asked the question, "what is going to happen to those we can't re-educate, that are diehard capitalists?" The response was that they would have to be 'eliminated'. When pursued, the response was that they estimated some 25 million people from these re-education centers would need to be eliminated. Ayres added, when I say "eliminate", I mean "kill". (11)

For those of you who don't remember or never even knew, Bill Ayers and his wife, Bernardine Dorhne were members of the radical's radical Students for a Democratic Society (SDS) (12)who formed the off-shoot Weather Underground. They were involved in sedition and murder, and are unrepentant to this day. Ayers is today a "highly-respected" (by Communists and other America-haters) faculty member at the University of Illinois at Chicago. His front room is where Barak Obama reputedly launched his political career. According to Wikipedia, Ayers upon hearing of the FBI informant's charge retorted that "everyone knows the FBI was built on lies.". Isn't it funny how every felon is "Not Guilty", even with blood still on their hands? But of course, the detractors of *every* Communist Revolution were also lying if you listen to a lying Communist. And if you read Ayres' and his wife's book, "Prairie Fires" named after a saying by the 'honored'" Chairman Mao", in what appears to be the Foreword, they state:

> *PRAIRIE FIRE is written to Communist minded people, independent organizers and anti-imperialists who carry the traditions and lessons of the struggles of the last decade,"* ... *"PRAIRIE FIRE is based on the belief that the duty of the revolutionary is to make the revolution". (13)*

So, Ayers and his wife, as the book's authors are admitted Communist Revolutionaries, whom the 'feces-hurlers' looked up to and listened to. I can also smell feces in their words and actions, mixed with the blood on their hands, no matter how highly they are considered by the corrupt Chicago Political Machine that spawned and nourishes them.

Oh, by the way, their book is dedicated, among other Marxist "Comrades", to Sirhan Sirhan, assassin of Robert F. Kennedy. It must make you proud to know in whose front room Obama launched into Politics!

Like Lenin, Stalin, Mao, and Castro before them, the Sixties Marxist Generation's hatred extends to almost everyone with property or wealth, to anyone who is an intellectual, or even has capabilities, unless they are bearing the Marxist torch. Undeniable signs today indicate that these people are loading their paper bags again. However, this time with an even more vile form of excrement, the excrement from Lenin, Stalin, and Mao's, Revolution, slaughter, and Totalitarian Socialism. These Revolutionaries are commencing now, to exploit Marxism's hate-filled class, racial, ethnic, and economic divisions or any other possible division in American society. They will then utilize these divisions, with the chaos, anarchy, and disaster they bring, to destroy and enslave America.

Those who cannot be re-educated will "eliminated", either be killed outright or 'utilized to death' in some form slave labor for the "Good of the Nation". This includes people who guard against those willing to destroy and enslave our much-loved United States, those who believe in or yearn for individual liberty, and those who know and dare to speak the truth of the murderous and blood-drenched history of Lenin, Stalin, and Mao, their Marxist Heroes.

However, this time these 60's sack hurlers will be *directing* the police, *they* will be *sitting as judges, lawyers, and lawmakers*. This time *they* believe they're going to win, and if they win, a pall of great darkness will fall on the United States and the whole world, because they fully believe it will be necessary to re-educate or slaughter tens of millions of Americans who will not accept a Marxist, Statist Government. People like Ayers are fully prepared to perform the task, as Lenin, Stalin, Hitler, Mao, and so many Statist Socialists before them did. Survivors in America (and the World) will be disenfranchised of freedom and enslaved under Marxism. Which are the lucky ones? Remembering the Kulaks, it is very hard to know. Is death better than slavery? Well, never fear, whichever form of Marxism people end up with, either are freely distributed by the tyrants in charge.

Today, in concert with various anti-American and internationalist groups and movements scattered throughout our nation and the world, those who believe in Marxist/Statist government have coalesced into a worldwide movement, visible to those who are aware, who have studied and understand Marxist dialectic. It is a movement becoming more transparent every day, because they believe that *today* is their best chance.

Today, using the philosophy that "The enemy of my enemy is my friend", Radical Islam has again joined forces with them, even as they joined forces with Hitler because he also hated the Jews. This noxious amalgam of America-Haters is visibly moving toward their common goal of Marxist Revolution. They are hidden only from those who are blindly complacent, complicit, or who purposefully keep their eyes closed. However, this movement, and the direction it is moving, plays a painfully hideous and familiar melody to those who can identify it from history, and have no wish to see such history repeat. It is a chant from the dank caverns of hell itself.

I firmly believe the present scenario, which is clearly visible to anyone who wishes to look for it, has the goal of using and fusing all of these "Hate-America" groups and movements into an irresistible Force. The goal of such a "Force" is the 'Fundamental Transformation" and collapse of American military and economic leadership in the world. American World Leadership must be absolutely destroyed because only after a total collapse of American power and the final submission of the US, can the One-World Socialist or Fascist Marxist "Utopia" successfully be formed.

I also understand that for the past one hundred years Progressive Socialist-Statists have labored to transform the United States from a Constitutional Republic into a Democracy. We have discussed that and the proven history that democracies always collapse into either anarchy or tyranny within 200 years or less.

For those who know the difference, it is obvious that America today has not only *become* a democracy, but that most of its citizens are so ignorant of U.S. history that they believe we were *founded* as a democracy. Therefore, if you actually buy that, our next step is to implode as democracies always do, into either Anarchy or Tyranny. Most likely the Anarchy will come, setting the stage for a Tyrant to take power.

The current near-collapse of both the United States and the European economies and currency, has set the world stage for a "Perfect Storm" crises scenario. One in which those groups whose goals are based in Socialism (either communist or fascist), can potentially create a collapse of law and order in the United States through civil disobedience and riots, bringing us to the brink of Civil War. At that time, the Progressives currently in power in the federal government can step in to "save" the nation by imposing a martial law, leading to dictatorship. This scenario has played itself out historically in numerous democracies that ended up under communist or fascist tyranny. To disbelieve it is a possibility for the United States is to bury your head in the sand and whistle. If you really think that, you have failed to understand history.

So, how did we get here?

Although Marxist Socialism/Communism began in France, became a defined movement Europe in 1847, and a specific form of Statist Tyranny in Russia in 1917, Marxist Socialism historically commenced in the United States in 1901 with the election of Theodore Roosevelt as President. Roosevelt was an admitted Socialist and great admirer of European Social Programs and leaders. It was then greatly furthered as Roosevelt undermined the Republican Party, running as a third, "Bull Moose-Progressive Party", splitting the American vote and essentially electing the elitist, racist, Socialist, Southern Democrat, Woodrow Wilson as President. Wilson's policies and legislation during the ensuing 8 years seriously commenced the downward spiral of our Constitutional Republic into a democracy, which will ultimately destroy our nation. As well, the anti-negro racism of Wilson, with his deep-southern staff and cabinet choices, set US racial relations back almost to the civil war. He was an anti-black bigot! Look it up, I have no reason to lie!

Also, please do not make the mistake of thinking this is a Republican book or argument. Actually, if Republicans would assist, the task of taking back our 'Republic' would be much easier. Today the greatest threat to the continuation of our Constitutional Republic resides in the White House, but that is because of who *he* is, or what his *belief system is*. It is *not* because he is an elected Democrat (notice the Party is, and never was the *Democratic* Party). But then neither is today's Republican Party hierarchy a staunch guardian of America's Constitutional *Republic*.

Progressives at the beginning of the twentieth century were as many in the Republican Party as in the Democrat Party. The defeat of TR's 'Bull Moose' Party isolated and angered the Progressives within the Republican Party so they mostly kept their distance until Franklin Delano Roosevelt ran for President, when many of them abandoned the Republicans and joined the campaign for the Socialist Democrat, FDR, who was the 'Second-Coming' for Progressives. Progressives have never cared which party they inhabited, it was only a costume to wear while they worked out of sight of the 'too-curious' eyes of the American People (It was Karl

Marx himself who compared the revolutionary struggle to the work of a mole working beneath the ground so he leaves no sign of his work on the surface).

So, from TR's "Square-Deal" to Wilson's "New Freedom" to FDR's "New Deal", and Lyndon Johnson's "Great Society" the American Constitutional Republic was gradually and methodically degraded into a Democracy-based clone of Mussolini's Fascist State. It took this long because the American people had to be conned into believing in Social and Industrial "Justice" and "New Nationalism" (TR), the "New Freedom" (WW), the "New Deal" (FDR) and the "Great Society" (LBJ).

But each of these programs was just evolutionary states of Statist Socialism. But such tyranny was thoroughly maligned, and warned about by the Founders, it was subject to suspicion by most Americans. Therefore it must be crushed into tiny fragments and mixed with 'sugar, spices, and alcohol', like old time "Snake-Oil" to make it palatable. Even then, it required a gifted orator, or even better, an actual lying demagogue with the power to hypnotize the masses with the sound of his voice, to sell it in quantity.

But, little by little, the American people swallowed bits of it. Little by little, some became addicted to it. Little by little, others became used to it, and, as always, a few loved and became addicted to it immediately. But the seeds of Socialism, planted originally in the Republican Party, were merely a different variety, not a crop failure.

Fabian Socialists.
Due to of our nearly complete ignorance of Statism/Socialism, it is doubtful many Americans are aware of what *Fabian* Socialism is, although we have lived under an incrementally increasing form of it for a century.

The Fabian Society, formed in Britain and dating to the late nineteenth century, is a socialist movement which believes the principals socialism should be advanced, but through an evolutionary movement rather than through a revolution. It was named for the Roman general Fabius Maximus, and emulated his tactics of small victories and wearing away of the enemy instead of full-on battle, until 'just the right moment' to take him out.

Here is an example of the much extolled, "Genteel" Fabian Socialist George Bernard Shaw, who applauded and glorified Hitler, Mussolini, and Stalin in numerous articles. The same George Bernard Shaw, who said the following:

> *"You all must know a half dozen people, at least, who are no use in this world. Who are more trouble than they are worth. Just put them there and say, 'Sir, or Madam, now will you be just kind enough to justify your existence? If you can't justify your existence. If you're not pulling your weight in the social boat, if you're not producing as much as you consume, or perhaps a little bit more, then clearly we can't use the big organization of our society for keeping you alive, because your life doesn't benefit us, and it can't be of much use to yourself."*

And later, in 1934;

> *I appeal to the chemists to discover a humane gas that will kill instantly and painlessly. Deadly by all means, but humane, not cruel. (14)*

Of course when Adolph Eichmann admitted to killing Jews "Painlessly" with Zyclon B in 1944 and 45, Shaw was 'troubled and confused', because his statements were meant only for getting rid of the useless, imbecilic, and others he considered 'dead-beats, like those who "didn't pull their weight". He defended his intent for the humane but 'Deadly Gas' was simply to 'better the human race, *not* practice racial genocide'. As a Socialist, Shaw had no moral values or conscience unless trapped in uncomfortable and untenable position that might damage his cause.

Can you imagine the Jewish People worried about Shaw's confusion as they watched the horrifying Zyclon-B gas fog through the vents, and began struggling "Painlessly" and "Humanely" for their lives and the lives of their families in the chambers, for Hitler's *'betterment of the human race'*? The Nazis were simply using

Shaw's idea for their own version of *'societal betterment'*. Could it have made any difference to the millions who were slaughtered like insects, and robbed of their possessions, later used to finance the war and protect those who ran the "Slaughter-House"? Or was it just Socialists (National Socialists in this case) just doing what hard-core Socialists whether Fascist or Communist have historically done, i.e., slaughter millions of people with abandon? You tell me!

The Progressives who control the Republican Party apparatus have, since the early 1900's has been closer to Fabian Socialism than to Revolutionary Socialism, but like Shaw, they are still Socialists with a Socialist morality. Those currently in control appear to be a mixture of both Fabian and Revolutionary socialists. Current Republican federal candidates are obviously vetted by that Socialist Leadership, and unless they have a huge grass-roots movement behind them as Ronald Reagan did, those who are not socialists are kept from becoming candidates. Looking backward today, I cannot name one successful Republican Presidential Candidate other than Reagan who ran *against* the Republican Socialist Establishment and *for* America and the American People and won. However, the Republican Establishment worked to derail his candidacy for years.

Just look at the Republican Presidential Candidates this year. The only two who had the full blessings of the Establishment were not just miles, but a galaxy away from believing in America as a Constitutional Republic. They are instead Fabian (evolutionary) Socialists, who believe with Shaw, in greasing America's slide into a democracy with "Bite-Sized" pieces of Socialism, or better yet, as a flavored powder, mixed into some "Snake-Oil" potion, so we do not gag on it. While their method is different from Barack Obama's *"Stuff Socialism down their throats whether they like it or not"*, Socialist Tyranny and Slavery for America will still be the result. Wake up and read your history!

No, this book *definitely is not* a book touting the Republican Party. That party no longer exists to serve or protect America as a Constitutional Republic. At this point I am convinced that the Republicans 'gradual', Fabian approach to United States Socialism over the past hundred years quietly and efficiently followed Fabian Socialism between the more radical Socialist Democrat terms, creating the road down which Socialist Democrat Presidents advanced their Panzer Tanks!

Barak Obama is merely the latest, most radical, and most openly Marxist revolutionary of these. In addition, while not all Democrat Presidents were Revolutionary Socialist Ideologues like Wilson, the Roosevelt's, and Lyndon Johnson, still the weaker ones, in obedience to the long-time Democrat Party's Socialist Leadership, performed 'trail-breaking' tasks for those ideologues that would follow them.

No, actually this book is *very* Non-Partisan when it comes to American Political Parties! In fact, my current opinion is that America today merely has a right and a left wing of what should more properly be called *The Socialist Party, USA*. Both Republicans and Democrats are *intentionally* taking us down the garden path into Socialism, merely at different velocities. Somehow, the American People have equated this varying speed with being at odds on the outcome. If you carefully review leadership and legislation differences in the two parties, it becomes tragically obvious that neither Party truly supports governing America by the Constitutional Government and Rule-of-Law under which we were formed.

I have studied and watched with increasing horror and disgust through my lifetime as this scene progressed, "two steps forward, then one step back" in Socialist Jargon. However, notice there is always a forward gain. With few exceptions, the American People have remained sound asleep to the freedom-destroying Socialist taxation, regulation, and legislation the American government is legislating.

Yet everything Socialist-Statists do is carefully programmed, meticulously done, inherently destructive of Freedom, and above all, is completely predictable. Everything they do is for the sole purpose of destroying the wealth and strength of the United States, and creating a One-World Socialist Government under which the total planet will be ruled by a dozen or so self-appointed, self-important tyrants who consider themselves "Elites", and "More Highly Intelligent than the ignorant masses", no different than Lenin, Stalin, Hitler, and Mao. Are you ready to live in that Utopia? Or to *die* in it?

The 'Masses' of the world will then experience life as have all the peoples in the major historical Communist or Fascist ruled nations. First, there will be slaughter on a massive scale as the "Revolution" asserts its power and ideology. Those who refuse to be 'transformed' into the new 'utopian' society will experience "Re-Education Camps". Those who cannot be re-educated will simply be killed, by bullet, torture, or slave labor, whichever is deemed best for "Society" (Remember the Kulaks?). Eventually, after ten to thirty percent of the population is "pacified", the mass killings will taper off. Of course, it will always be necessary for the Secret Police and Government Spies to be observing people's lives and reporting all signs of individuality or 'Dereliction to Socialism'. These will need "re-education", imprisonment, and or death, in order to keep people terrified, and under control. The better to "Guard the Revolution".

And, considering that the majority of Socialist Elitists adore and praise historical leaders such as Marx, Engels, Lenin, Stalin, Hitler, and Mao Tse Tung, as being exemplary socialist leaders and Heroes of the Revolution (and therefore the political evolution of mankind), we can only expect the "New" Socialist, Statist Utopia to remain historically indistinguishable from earlier ones. As always, they are long on promises, and extremely short on the public's utopian expectations. In fact, what today's Socialists call Utopia, is exactly what I refer to as *"The Coming Fourth Reich"*.

"Equality", was always a hallmark of Revolutionary Socialism. if we define equality in historical Socialism, it will mean *equal* government-assigned work tasks (some may be more "equal" than others), *equal* mediocrity, *equal* indoctrination into Socialism (beginning with pre-school or nursery), *equal* run-down government housing, *equal* shortages of food and necessities, *equal*

misery, *equal* 'free' healthcare offered by a run-down, inefficient, overworked and uncaring state medical systems, *equality* of all be spied upon, *equality* of all to have your door broken down at midnight and be arrested by armed government thugs, as well as *equality* of all to face imprisonment, slave labor, or death for thinking they can work a little harder to better themselves, or to escape from their Socialist Masters, or even just "thinking" without government approval. This then, is the "*Social, or Equal Justice*" under which people have historically existed under both Communist and Fascist Totalitarianism. Are you ready for such "Equality"?

After winning the "Revolution" even if those in power are different people than Lenin, Stalin, Mao, or Hitler, expect them to be worse and more bloodthirsty, not less. That is because Socialism, while natural for ants and bees, is an unnatural state for the humankind. Mankind has a mind, he reasons, he wants. Even an evil and lazy man wishes to improve his condition. The poor wish to become wealthy, the slave wishes to become free, the weak wish to become strong, those imprisoned wish for open space, ad infinitum. The earthbound human wishes to fly, and why should he not? Totalitarianism can imprison or kill, and crush some spirits, but there are always men and women whose minds cannot be bound, either with chains or by utopian ideals. These are the ones against whom the Revolution must guard, and eliminate to maintain their so-called 'Socialist Utopia', lest they infect others.

The World Federation of Nations envisioned by Socialists would be ruled (not governed), either by a supreme dictator or an oligarchy of party leaders. In such a world, the tenets of Statist Marxism would be the law, which would necessarily be enforced with a combination of Leninist/Stalinist brutality, but with the ruthless efficiency of an Adolph Hitler and modern technology. No escape!

History indicates such a government could likely end up being the "Thousand Year Reign" sought by Adolph Hitler. That is because if the United States strength and influence is destroyed and in captivity, there would exist no earthly force capable of overthrowing it, nor of championing such an overthrow.

The Coming Fourth Reich

History indicates there might never again be another truly free nation like the USA to light a torch for Liberty, saying:

> *"Give me your tired, your poor,*
> *Your huddled masses yearning to breathe free,*
> *The wretched refuse of your teeming shore.*
> *Send these, the homeless, tempest-tos't to me,*
> *I lift my lamp beside the golden door!"*
>
> Poem on the Statue of Liberty

Oh yes, I can hear the outcry from those Leftists who are blindly addicted the Socialist Revolution: *'Please! Believe us; Socialist Tyrants will become kinder and gentler! We will be different this time, we promise!'*

Sorry! But if you believe that I'm certain some guy has a bridge or a swamp or two he'll sell you at bargain prices. Can you now understand why we all need to know about the Kulaks and understand what happened to them under Lenin's Utopian Socialist Marxist Regime? Death lies at the door! Let it in at your own peril!

Being convinced of this situation and its potential for evil through a life-time of study and research, I sometimes want to scream, "Look out!!!" to the American People who are paying so little attention they may be walking in front of a speeding 18-wheeler! But, many obviously don't care, aren't interested, just can't believe it could happen here, or simply don't want to hear any warning at all, because it might interrupt how well they think they're doing.

Concerning the seriousness of the potential outcome, that makes me extremely sad.

Part Three:

If you know who blazed the trail you're following, you can see where you're going.

CHAPTER ELEVEN

Some people *do* know where they came from.

> *As the Twig is bent, so is the Tree inclined.*
> Early 18th century proverb.

Beginning in the summer of 2008, a practically unknown US Senator, with feather-light credentials for any position, ran for President of the United States. From the very beginning the wildly enthusiastic acclaim given by adoring crowds, coupled with his obviously questionable resume, his recognizable Marxist rhetoric, and his, shall we say different perspective of history caught my interest?

I began immediately to research and study this man, because with his Press coverage, I truly believed he would win the election and become President of the United States. And so he did.

Barak Obama began his run for office in 2008 with the promise of bringing "Unity" instead of division and, armed with a nebulous and undefined mantra called "Hope and Change". However, his speeches, especially to semi-private groups, soon began to use familiar terminology, historically used by Marxists worldwide to create racial, economic, class, and political division, leading to open rebellion and civil war. It is a well-worn road. It was certainly not the old boring, disgusting, and well-worn American Leftist political clichés, but in many cases unmistakably, if somewhat indirectly stated, "Marxist-speak", recognizable to anyone who has read or studied the writings of Karl Marx and his numerous flakey disciples since. This divisive rhetoric was immediately picked up by the Left-Stream US Media, and quickly accelerated into regular Marxist class warfare news shows and group 'chants' as the campaign continued.

Well before the election, I had listened to him, reviewed his record light though it was, and discovered that his, and his wife's political histories were both deeply grounded in the most corrupt, and evil institution in the United States, the Chicago Political Machine. Besides being corruption defined, that Machine has taproots reaching back into both the Capone Mafia and the twenties and thirties Communist eras. What could be found of his family history was available but not without diligent search. Chillingly, there was sufficient information in these areas to indicate strongly that this man might possibly be the first committed Anti-American, Marxist/Socialist in history to become President of the USA.

Obama's education, family history, political record, political connections, supporters, rhetoric, chosen friends and cohorts, and his nearly invisible but very sufficient financial funding for living and attendance at exclusive Law Schools, and immediate prominence within the inner circles of the hugely corrupt Chicago Political Machine was sufficient for me to draw my own conclusions. However, too many Americans were either ambivalent or charmed by his phony Marxist unity rhetoric.

Although what he exposed of himself while campaigning was miniscule, and even that carefully crafted, if you had studied Marxism, its current idioms, the history of the Communist Party USA (CPUSA) during the Twentieth Century, and the writings of Saul Alinsky, the alarm bells could not be silenced! Unfortunately, very few Americans other than those complicit in working to bring about a Marxist United States had done so, and those were all laughing up their sleeves because the people of America, either ignorantly or stupidly did not understand the Marxist Socialist code words Obama was reading from his teleprompter.

Then suddenly appearing, like cockroaches in the dark, a new breed of fiercely dedicated political activists sprang into action to laud, defend, and champion Obama. Suddenly money began flowing into his campaign, from Wall Street, from widely scattered and suspect 'grass-roots' organizations and 527 groups, from the Marxist roots of organized labor, from bankers and crony capitalists. From all who smelled money and power with this man as President, including Soros-style internationalists who despised the wealth and power of the United States and wished to destroy it.

Websites and Political Action groups appeared, disappeared, changed names, and re-appeared. Obviously, their main goal in life was to 'protect and elect' Obama from the 'Smears' of those who raised questions as to his true anti-American, socialist ethics, or anything else. Extreme, and out of control or context Political Correctness reared its fascist, anti-free speech head, and with anger, hatred, and venom spurting from all of the above, viciously attacked anyone who dared to question Obama. His pastor Wright's Marxist-Communist Liberation Theology (Google search "Liberation Theology, Definition") and "G*d D*mn America" and "America's chickens came home to roost on 911" comments. These Leftists came out of the 'woodwork' to protect or hide Obama's extended Marxist Socialist family, friends, and cohorts overt Marxist beliefs, his Socialist ideals, his pro-Muslim anti-Semitism, and anti white statements. Additionally the fact he launched his political career in the home of Bill Ayers and Bernadette Dorne, unrepentant seditionists, writers of acknowledged communist literature, and well-known, self admitted Communist terrorists who 'felt they hadn't done enough'(sedition and murder?), however much that is!

To obscure Obama's wife's generational ties to and his own un-questioned acceptance into leadership circles of the Chicago Political Machine, which is the resounding definition of political corruption and scandal, or his internationalist stance, is to deny light and darkness. These Marxist-Socialist groups showed immediate amnesia for (or more likely laughed about) the American Left's previous "Bush-Derangement Syndrome". They had for eight years regularly gloried in the American Left-Stream Medias and numerous "prominent" Journalists and Politicians orgasmic lauding of "Prize-Winning" 'docudramas', plays, books, articles, or "News" Commentaries, fantasizing of the death or assassination of George W. Bush, referring to him as Hitler, an international criminal, or if possible something worse. That and whatever else such hatred-darkened souls could conjure up indicating their hatred of, and lack of respect for the American People, and their elected President, even the one who spent eight years paving the road to Marxism down which their hero, Obama would blitz his Panzer Tanks. However, of course, if your Ideal leader is Marx, Lenin, Stalin, or Mao, why should anyone expect you to revere anything about America except its destruction? However, where were the average Americans? Asleep or in Love with Obama's smile, I must suppose.

I remember some of my Catholic friends admitted being "troubled" that Obama's major victory, as an Illinois legislator was to essentially establish an altar for the worship of Abortion, because one of the few bills he showed up to vote more than 'Present' for, was a law guaranteeing any baby who somehow survived an abortion in Illinois must be summarily thrown in the trash and *must* die with the rest of the garbage! Yet they assured me the 'good' he would do bringing about Marxist "Social Justice" was more important than his signature legislation, legalizing infanticide.

I will never understand how Christian People can believe in Obama's "Hope and Change" while ignoring the words of their own Christ who said, *"By their fruit you will recognize them. Do people pick grapes from thorn bushes, or figs from thistles?"* In my considered opinion, the human compassion Obama demonstrated in his signature Illinois legislation easily compares to that shown by any Lenin, Stalin, or Hitler, i.e., government mandated death for innocent human beings as a means to power! Who could be more deserving of a chance to live than a child who just survived a botched abortion attempt? But Obama's hatred wouldn't even give a baby that tiny advantage to live! His is a Nazi culture of Death! (1)

Another Marxist Obama sycophant, SEIU President Andrew Stern bragged he had raised $60.7 million for Obama's election, thus netting SEIU two Cabinet appointees, Health and Human Services Secretary Kathleen Sebelius and Labor Secretary Hilda Solis, and for Stern himself, status as the most frequent visitor to the White House during the first two years of the Obama Administration. (2) Unfortunately, this upcoming hero of the Revolution abruptly 'stepped in it' and resigned during a federal corruption probe. Like Van Jones, he had become a liability. But of course, Marxists take care of their foot-soldiers, and Stern will merely be shifted to another well-paid position where his blatant radical socialist, global-government history is no liability to Marxist 'progress'.

And, in spite of all this Anti-American mess, for the coming 2012 elections organized labor is still expected to match or slightly exceed the estimated $400 million unions spent to help elect Barak Obama and congressional Democrats in 2008. From Harry Bridges and 'Uncle' Frank Marshall Davis, to the current Richard Trumpka and Andrew Stern, it is handy to have morality-free Marxist Friends in positions of power if your name is Barak Obama! Google it!

Family, Friends, and ideologues.
Show me your family and friends, and I will tell you who you are.

> *Author's Note: The following portion of this book has been researched as carefully as possible in order to determine how young Obama's life and ideology were affected and shaped by those who raised him without whitewashing it as his official sites do, or damning with broad strokes as others do. Any broken home has enough pain and heartache, and while I am in total disagreement with Obama's political ideology, I'm not a troll who would create pain in others to sell a book. However, Truth, like Sunlight, dispels darkness and lies. rg*

Obama's mother was born and raised it Kansas and finished High School in Seattle. Stories vary. One is that her father moved to the Seattle area for a furniture salesman job. Another is that he took the job so she could be educated at what we in Washington State knew of and called "The Little Red Schoolhouse", because of its reputation as a "Commie-School". However, the School Board Chairman there *did* testify before the House Un-American Activities Subcommittee that he *had been* a member of the Communist Party. There were also one or more '"controversial" teachers.

While I recall "The Little Red Schoolhouse" as a scandalous thing in 1950's Washington State, it was a badge of honor to the collection of Marxists in King County and nationwide, who longed for the USA to follow Russia's example in 1917. It was also important to the CPUSA, as it was a finger stuck into America's eye. Also, I seem to remember that in the middle '50's it was illegal to be a Communist!

However, either way, in this "Little Red Schoolhouse" (3), she would have become well versed in Leftism, Cultural if not actual Revolutionary Marxism, and many other Leftist, anti-American, anti-Capitalism, ideals. I personally remember a seventh grade teacher in the early 1950's we called "Commie", particularly because of his lectures on the great fairness of the Soviet Union, and his defense of Julius and Ethyl Rosenberg, who were later executed for espionage and giving nuclear secrets to the Soviets. In spite of later being honored for this act of treason in Khrushchev's Posthumous Memoirs, where he gave them credit for the Soviet Union having achieved atomic bombs, the execution of these "Innocent" spies are, to this day, a cause Célèbre to Liberals, Lefties, and Communists alike.

Having myself grown up in Washington State in the 40's and 50's, it is completely logical to me that Obama's mother would likely have been chided, scorned, or described by acquaintances as a "Fellow Traveler" while attending a Marxist ideology driven school like "The Little Red Schoolhouse". Especially with her with parents also being members of the(Unitarian) "Little Red Church on the hill". (4)

Most likely, she would at the very least been called a Communist Sympathizer ("Com-Symp" in the vernacular of the day) and roundly suspect as being a member of the Young Communist's League as well, except by those in similar circles of hatred and rebellion against America and American values. I remember the post-war years well. Communists were *not* popular with average Americans outside of their own cells and their own circles of friends, although the Seattle Times always gave them good press. This would be especially true if she were, in fact outspoken concerning Leftist ideals. Americans in those days recognized Marxism for what it was and most did not favor it. It remained for decades of gradually increasing leftist teaching in public schools and universities to anesthetize and brainwash younger generations of Americans into believing in Marxism as a viable alternative to Freedom and Capitalism. However, the USA certainly reached that point with the election of Barak Obama.

I also recall that in the mid-fifties, you had to have dedication to be outspoken and called a Communist. It was *not* popular with the majority of the American People. Only hardened Communists from the '30's and idealistic young people on a University or College Campus did so, and even some of them 'hid' in plain sight, as "Marx's Moles", because it made lurking around easier while engaging in the covert sabotage of the nation that nurtured them.

After the Dunham family moved to Honolulu in 1960, she attended the University of Hawaii, and met Obama's father. Barak was born in 1961.

Then, after Obama Sr. completed his studies at the University of Hawaii, he left to continue his studies at Harvard without his wife and son. He later returned to Kenya upon completing on studies. Obama's mother filed for divorce in 1964 and remarried two years later. Young Obama then lived four years with his mother and second husband in Indonesia before he she returned him to Hawaii, where she left him in the care of his grandparents while his mother eventually completed her PhD in Anthropology and returned to Indonesia, assisting impoverished women.

Therefore, Obama's mother obviously influenced his personal ideology during his formative years. He himself credited her in an interview as *"the dominant figure in my formative years..."*. (5)

Obama's Grandparents became his surrogate parents during his adolescent years, in addition to his grandfather's friend, whom Obama identified in his book only as "Uncle Frank".

It is difficult to trace exactly what the politics of the Dunham family were, except for several specific historical indicators. First, of course, was the "Little Red Schoolhouse and Church" era, previously discussed. Second, and actually more indicative of lasting Marxist inclination, was (Grandfather) Stanley Dunham's friendship with, and trusting the mentoring of young Obama to "Uncle Frank". "Uncle Frank" was a name I instantly knew when I heard his full name, from my life-long studies of Communism in America. 'Uncle' Frank was Frank Marshall Davis, well-known American Communist!

Frank Marshall Davis was a well known America-hating Communist in the late 1940's and 50's when I was only beginning to study the workings of the Communist International, called the *Comintern*, and its wholly owned subsidiary, The Communist Party USA (CPUSA). Founded as soon as Lenin had gained some degree of control in his Russian bloodletting, he established the Comintern to foster and assist Communisms spread internationally as the name implies. The Comintern established the CPUSA within months, with explicit directions and funding, of sometimes more than a million dollars a year, spanning the life of the blood-soaked Soviet Union.

In 1935, one William Schneiderman (agent of the Soviet NKVD, and later head of the Communist Party of California) directed the CPUSA to establish a presence in what was then the American Territory of Hawaii, with the intention to drive the presence of the war deterrent US Fleet out of Pearl Harbor, among other things. (6)

Eventually, well known Communist and Union Organizer Harry Bridges moved (or was dispatched) to Hawaii where organized the International Long-shore Workers (ILWU) and other projects to bring Communism to the (by now the coming US State of) Hawaii, although he still denied membership in the CPUSA, but it was later proven. (7)

In 1948 Frank Marshall Davis, American Communist, journalist, and poet, emigrated (or was dispatched) to Hawaii with letters of recommendation from both Bridges and from Davis' long-time friend, Actor and Singer Paul Robeson. Although Robeson denied membership in the CPUSA and took the fifth amendment, he was not only identified under oath as a member by others, but later identified and glorified as, "a revolutionary, a Communist, and a 20th Century giant" by CPUSA Chairman Gus Hall (8) in a pamphlet and in the CPUSA newspaper. Ooooops! So, like the rest of the CPUSA Members, these 'Freedom-Fighters' were fighting for the 'freedom' of the American people to be enslaved under Marxist, Leninist, and Stalinist tyranny and death, just as the Kulaks were. That is what passes for freedom and equality under Communism!

For whatever reason, "Uncle Frank", with his acceptance by, and recommendations from both the CPUSA and the corrupt Political Cesspool in Chicago, was chosen by his Grandfather to be young Obama's 'Mentor' throughout his teen years. Davis, exposing his hatred of whites, taught him this gem on race relations;

> *"What I'm trying to tell you is, your grandmother has every right to be scared. ... She understands that black people have a reason to hate. That's just how it is. For your sake, I wish it were otherwise. But it's not. So you might as well get used to it." (9)*

Davis then steered him to Chicago, obviously with proper introductions, instructions, and sources for funding opportunities, further education, and political allies. Again, in keeping with the Marxist "Mole" theory, such allies, with Uncle Frank's introduction, 'Understood' just what kind of help this young man would need, and just which items would need to be kept 'out of sight' of those who might not approve of the CPUSA and other radical revolutionary connections Obama had.

Yet another huge influence, according to Obama's *"Dreams from my Father"* was Obama Senior. Information about Barak Obama Senior that excludes the sensational or the strictly partisan is not easy to find. I have drawn on the following snippets of information, concentrating only on areas that would have formed young Obama's ideological beliefs.

Obama Senior appears to have been a charismatic and self-confident person, which traits his son obviously inherited. However, ideologies are taught and formed by environment and experiences, not inherited, and that is what we are researching here, beginning with Obama's paternal Grandfather

Obama's paternal grandfather Hussein Onyango Obama, a Kenyan of the Luo tribe had a horrific experience in 1949, during what we Americans know as the Mau Mau Uprising. Details vary, but as the British routinely destroyed official records after six years, we have mostly word-of-mouth and remembered accounts of exactly what happened. Certainly terrible things happen during revolutions and freedom-movements, normally both sides have a list of grievances or there would not be a 'divorce' happening.

But the one certain thing we can draw from the incident with Onyango is that he, and likely his whole family, would have developed a sincere and deep-seated anger and hatred toward the (white) British, who subjected him to what the family stated was severe torture. This anger and hatred is then a life-experience, which would affect more than one generation, forming a part of the environment, which creates someone's lifetime ideology. Knowing this, it is easy to understand why Obama returned the bust of Churchill to England early in his presidency. It was a reminder of his grandfather's unfortunate incident

Barak Obama Senior was obviously intelligent and a quick study who reportedly had problems with discipline. However, he managed to achieve a secondary school certificate and applied to US universities. In 1958 Cabinet Minister Tom Mboya, potential successor to Prime Minister Jomo Kenyatta and founder of the socialist, Nairobi People's Congress Party handpicked him to come to the United States for study preparatory to Kenya's independence, utilizing an American sponsored scholarship in economics to the University of Hawaii at Manoa. A number of promising Kenyan youth were afforded similar education grants to provide a source of western education toward the future governing of the nation of Kenya.

Obama Senior evidently had great plans for his future after his acceptance to the University of Hawaii and then Harvard. However, he left with a Master's Degree in Economics, not the PhD he had sought. He never completed his Ph D, but his US education gained him a senior economist position with the Kenyatta government. However, in completing his Harvard education and returning to Kenya, Obama Senior left young Barak and his mother behind. She divorced him and remarried. Other than a month trip to Hawaii in 1971, Obama Senior apparently never saw his son again.

Obama Senior was against Kenya keeping close ties with the West. His 1969 Paper advocated communal ownership of land, forced confiscation of privately controlled land, nationalization of "European" and "Asian" owned enterprises, and dramatically increasing taxation on "the rich" even up to the 100% level, i.e., Communism. Although Senior's viewpoint agreed with "Uncle" Frank's, it placed him at odds with Tom Mboya, the mentor who chose him to receive a US education

Because Mboya's choice of the US for education, his ties to Kenyatta, and his pro-Western economic proposals were known as the "Third Way", his 'socialism' appears to be closer to what we would call 'Democratic Socialism', more in line with other African Socialist Governments forming into newly independent African nations at that time. However, Mboya's policy paper, *"African Socialism and it's applicability to planning in Kenya"* suffered what was called *"a cutting attack from the left"*. In the book, *"The Risks of Knowledge"* by Odhiambo and Cohen. (10) This "cutting attack" was written by none other than Barak Obama Senior, and published in the East African Journal, in July 1965. (11)

I have a copy of this paper and I have studied it. I personally find it little more than a typically standard Marxist-Stalinist diatribe. These always make my eyes cross with boredom. Most could have been pre-printed with "fill in the nation or ethnic group and place" blanks for any time or place a Marxist Government was to be installed without a civil war or revolution. It is an excellent example of Communist "Group-Think"! This paper is a direct repudiation of the Democratic Socialism proffered the Kenyan People by Obama Senior's mentor, Tom Mboya. However, those who believe in "Scientific" Marxism have Comrades, not friends.

Mboya evidently remained a friend and mentor to Obama, but after Mboya's assassination in 1969, Kenyatta himself eventually fired Obama Senior and told him he would never work for the Kenyan government again. Obama Senior died in an auto accident a few years later. One telling Marxist point Obama Senior made in his 1969 paper was inherited by President Obama today, i.e.:

> *"Theoretically, there is nothing that can stop the government from taxing 100 per cent of income so long as the people benefits from the government commensurate with their income which is taxed."*

That can only be described as "Scientific" Communism! Phrased into "Capitalist" terms, it would say, *"The government which can give you everything you want or need, is powerful enough to take away everything you have!"* That is the difference between Freedom and Tyranny, and Obama Senior's paper clearly advocated installation of Marxist Tyranny upon the people of Kenya. Like father, like son!

As was popular in those days, first the University of Hawaii, and then Harvard taught Obama Sr. and other students the theories of Scientific Communism, but withheld the blood-soaked history of how its installation and maintenance. However, the truth remains; "Those who refuse to learn from history are doomed to repeat it"!

About the time of the 2008 election, I told friends, "I expect Obama to be elected, and I expect him to do about as much good for

America as Robert Mugabe has done for Zimbabwe". Well, today he is President, and Transforming America. If he gets a second term, I predict USA will stand for "Socialist States of Amerika".

Actually, Obama Senior's paper also sounds eerily similar to the "Fundamental Transformation" that young Obama is currently making in the United States. While not word for word (he has to win the 2012 election), his endgame is the same. If you understood Obama Senior's writing, a Marxist United States is indubitably the "Dream" Obama the younger inherited from his father.

Neither his father nor mother spent much time with him during their lives, making him an odd type of orphan, making it a painful, difficult, and heavy life-burden to bear. Nevertheless, the truth is, Barak was raised mostly by his grandparents, and "Uncle Frank".

Therefore, if your mother's parents guaranteed her schooling in the "Little Red Schoolhouse" and attended the "Little Red Church on the Hill" in the Fifties, If your mother and father both abandoned you in your tender years to further their own interests, and left you with grandparents while they helped other people in socialist nations. If your grandfather's good friend was a member and a stalwart of the Communist Party USA, whom he chose to mentor you during your fragile teen years. If your father was such an aggressive communist who he could not even hold a job in a newly formed socialist nation, whose leadership had originally chosen him, who, and what might you become if not angry and spiteful?

However, if you know where you came from, you *can* know where you are, and where you are going. Was it a difficult situation for Barak Obama to become president of a nation whose history he despised thoroughly? Or was it the fulfillment and culmination of his life-long dreams, to assume a position of power from which he could bankrupt America and redistribute its wealth, thereby avenging all the actual and perceived grievances brought upon "his" black race by the despised whites who had founded America?

It is my own personal considered and researched opinion that Obama's presidency, in fact his whole life's goal, was always about the second option. I do not consider that lightly or frivolously. It is based totally on what I found about his upbringing, environment, how young Obama utilized his background, and who mentored him after he reached maturity.

Still, as a Stalinist Marxist, Obama's hatred of whites overcame his first choice of Communism for *National* Socialism as the following quote indicates:

> *"Desperate times called for desperate measures, and for many blacks, times were chronically desperate. If* **nationalism** *could create a strong and effective insularity, deliver on its promise of self-respect, then the hurt it might well cause well-meaning whites, or the inner turmoil it caused people like me, would be of little consequence."*   *(Emphasis mine - rg).*
> Barak Obama, "Dreams From My Father"

Have no doubt Obama knows exactly where he came from. If his growing up years cast a shadow of Marxist Socialism upon him, such things were largely outside of his control, as are the environment of any young person. However, what Obama made of that background after maturity is the indicator of who that man is today.

I base this opinion upon research, study, and comparison to previous historical happenings and events and their outcome, the same yardstick with which I have measured world happenings and politics my entire life. I firmly believe today that Obama wishes to destroy and humble the United States of America, which he sees as evil.

While I freely admit my opinion was already formed before I commenced writing this book, the research necessary to document it for the reader has further confirmed my opinion and hardened it into concrete!

CHAPTER TWELVE

Fundamental Transformation was *never* Hope, *only* Change!

Fundamental: *of or relating to the foundation or base; elementary, forming or serving as an essential component of a system or structure; central, of great significance or entailing major change.* www.thefreedictionary.com

Transformation: *change, conversion, alteration, metamorphosis, transmutation, renewal, revolution, radical change, makeover, sea change, revolutionary change.*
www.thefreedictionary.com

Speaking on October 30, 2008, while obviously glorying in his populist popularity and polls, Barack Hussein Obama stated,

> "We are five days away from fundamentally transforming the United States of America." (1)

Moreover, most certainly, after his election the Fundamental Transformation of America did commence, *and in-Spades!*

Based on what I have previously written, you must know that I was never surprised at the leftward lurch into classic Marxism Barak Obama's *"Fundamental Transformation"* has wrought, and is continually wreaking on our nation during his Presidency.

However the critically important question to America today is:

Exactly what does his statement mean, and what are its effects, implications, and ramifications upon our own lives, the lives of our children, and their children?

The answer to that question can only be found in Barak Obama himself, and in his Presidential performance. To find out whether Barak Obama is a Marxist to the extent of being a danger to the freedoms of the American People, or merely a leftist ideologue, we must investigate and draw our own conclusions by observing not just his words, but also his actions as President.

We know that young Obama must have suffered powerful trauma from rejection as a youth. From his paternal grandfather's suffering at the hands of the (white) British, to own father's abandonment of him as a babe, and even his own mother's essential abandonment, leaving him with her parents to be raised, even though he mistrusted them because they were 'typical' white folk.

Experiences such as these suffered by Obama or any child could have made his youthful feelings of rejection difficult, or even suffocating. Therefore, when he experienced acceptance and tutelage from a new major male role model, Frank Marshall Davis in his pre- teen or early teen years, he also found a hero, mentor, and, father figure. One who's strong Marxist and racist influence would likely have become an anchor in the pitching seas of his young life to that point. Given such a powerful Marxist influence, it would be curious if the adult Obama did *not* become a Marxist.

Obama's education and broken family life situation is in no way unique in modern America. However, his writings, his open door, welcome-mat acceptance into the Marxist Chicago Mafioso cum Political Family, and substantial gratis College and University funding, all led to well-paid positions on Boards instead of working jobs. Then, his immediate acceptance and the prestige he received from numerous Anti-American, Pro-Marxist groups, all strongly indicate that his acceptance into that political spectrum came through the recommendation of someone who was a trusted friend or ally of the American hard-Left.

Moreover, because Obama's written and spoken ideology so closely mirrors that of his mentor and role model, Communist Frank Marshall Davis, Davis himself likely provided that recommendation.

However, while Davis' credentials as an America hater and active member of the Communist Party USA were eminently acceptable to the insiders of Chicago Political family, they would also immediately indict Obama in the eyes of Americans who do not want America to become a Marxist Socialist nation. Moreover, such a Marxist-Stalinist America is precisely the goal Frank Marshall Davis spent many years working to create. Why should we then believe his protégé is *not* working toward the same goal?

Obama's writing in *Dreams of My Father* definitely reflects Davis' ideological, as well as his racial influence, i.e.:

> "I ceased to advertise my mother's race at the age of twelve or thirteen, when I began to suspect that by doing so I was ingratiating myself to whites."

> "I found a solace in nursing a pervasive sense of grievance and animosity against my mother's race."

> "There was something about him that made me wary, a little too sure of himself, maybe. And white."

> "It remained necessary to prove which side you were on, to show your loyalty to the black masses, to strike out and name names."

> "I never emulate white men and brown men whose fates didn't speak to my own. It was into my father's image, the black man, son of Africa, that I'd packed all the attributes I sought in myself, the attributes of Martin and Malcolm, Dubois and Mandela."

Quotations from *"Dreams of My Father"*

Therefore, brightly lighted signs were there for any who understood Marxism and the Communist Party USA to read. Obama and the Democrat Party he represents also laid it out clearly, defining their exact course during the presidential election campaign to anyone who could understand their language. To those of us familiar with world history, the course Obama pointed to was previously well defined by Karl Marx in the *"Communist Manifesto",* and enacted in the histories of Lenin, Stalin, Hitler, Mao, and other Marxist-Socialists.

Adult Barak Obama was always a Marxist-Socialist, judging by his own words and actions, even though he downplayed that early in his campaign and Presidential term, because Americans have a natural aversion to Socialism. However, today, so many revolutionary street agitators and known Socialist, Communist, and anti-American organizations have praised him and his actions, he jokes about it, essentially daring the right to state openly that Socialism is wrong.

This is a calculated Alinskyite move on his part. By creating dissention, he creates feedback, from which he can identify his friends, his detractors, and those who are paying no attention at all, allowing him to know where to apply the Alinskyite pressure of isolation and ridicule, who not to worry about, and where to back up. He is not afraid, because he has tremendously empowered his loyal followers during his three years in office, with either public support or tacit approval for their radical actions. This opens the door for them to receive funding from radical Marxist sources.

Obviously, Obama has studied all Marxist Tyrants who went before him. He learned their ideologies, their strategies, their propaganda, their inflammatory and demagogic language and dialect. That he is naturally a charismatic demagogue is simply another strong point to his advantage. It is my considered opinion that Obama uses a teleprompter, not because he's a poor speaker, but because he's not yet ready to allow the general American Public hear him launch into a Demagogic Rant, although a few of his speeches to 'friendly' audiences have given a glimpse of that 'talent'.

Therefore, the signs were all there, but all along the American People could not, *or would not* read them. Obama may have played a coy Socialist, possibly because of what his father suffered under Kenyatta for his obtuse, Stalinist political views. But coy or not, Obama's family, his school, his male-role model cum mentor, his book writings, and his working and political histories all loudly scream, "Marxist", to anyone who understands that ideology. The only question remaining to be answered is whether he is an evolutionary or a revolutionary Marxist, i.e., a Fabian Socialist or a Stalinist-Socialist.

Of course, that Obama's course of action is perfectly defined and described in Saul Alinsky in the book, *"Rules .for Radicals", is* another large indicator of that answer. *'Rules'* was specifically written to revise, refine, and modernize Stalinist-Marxist Revolutionary techniques into "new and better", Twentieth Century tactics than the "feces in paper-sack throwing crowd" from the Sixties used.

At this point, we have mentioned and quoted Alinsky, but have not yet introduced him. So, let us explore Alinsky's political leanings.

Saul Alinsky and Obama were from different generations and never met. Yet, while Obama plays it coy about Alinsky's role in his education, David Alinsky, Saul's son, offered a different opinion. Speaking of Obama's handling of the Democrat Convention in 2008, Alinsky wrote:

> *"It (the Alinsky-style Organization of the Democratic National Convention) is an amazingly powerful format, and the method of my late father always works to get the message out and get the supporters on board. When executed meticulously and thoughtfully, it is a powerful strategy for initiating change and making it really happen. Obama learned his lesson well. ... I am proud to see that my father's model for organizing is being applied successfully beyond local community organizing to affect the Democratic campaign in 2008. It is a fine tribute to Saul Alinsky as we approach his 100th birthday ..."* 9/1/2008 Boston Globe (2)

According to an article in New York Daily News (no longer on web), Obama was 'struggling to find himself' after graduating from Columbia University in New York, when he found work in Chicago as a community organizer. We also know that Saul Alinsky was the Chicago-based philosopher cum "Art of Warfare" Architect for modern day Communist-Socialist Revolutionaries, who dedicated his *"Rules for Radicals"* to none other than *Lucifer*, the god of darkness, or Satan, as follows:

> *"Lest we forget at least an over-the-shoulder acknowledgment to the very first radical: from all our legends, mythology, and history... the first radical known to man who rebelled against the establishment and did it so effectively that he at least won his own kingdom - Lucifer."*
>
> Saul Alinsky, Rules for Radicals (3)

While the *"Communist Manifesto"* was the original game plan under which Socialist Tyranny was to rule the world, the lesser well-known Saul Alinsky's *"Rules for Radicals"* is a Twentieth Century update of that plan. "Rules" was written especially to assist American Radicals undermine and overthrow the Constitutional Republic of the United States and turn it into a Stalinist "Utopia". This is critically important for Americans to understand, because while Alinsky's language is familiar, being written in the American vernacular and lifestyle, it is still a loyal interpretation of classic Marxism, updated and filled with modern tactical refinements aimed precisely at America's heart. (4)

Alinsky's plan was borne of and based on Alinsky's admitted love affair with what he called Communism and I call Totalitarian Socialism, even though he claimed he never joined the Communist Party. But of course if "the means justify *any* ends-"(an Alinsky quotation) who could possibly know how true that might be?

In "Rules", Alinsky details his accrued knowledge of how to create, irritate, infect, and abscess, class and ethnic hatreds. Whether those feeling are real, created, or imagined disenfranchisement, or merely disillusionment with Life, they are important tools with which to organize, and prepare for power with which to create a Communist Revolution.

For a period, there were two Communist groups in the USA, Stalinist Communists and Alinsky Communists. These were at odds with, and somewhat suspicious of each other, however, today, after the fall of the Soviet Union; the Alinskyites have pretty much gained the ascendency. Alinsky's plan is currently being used nationwide by both covert and overt Socialists, Fascists, Communists, and Anarchists, as well as most generic forms of America-haters, for the sole purpose of creating a Socialist Revolutionary Army and a Socialist Revolution.

This Army is comprised of "useful idiots" lead by a dedicated and motivated group of Marx and Alinsky trained Socialists. They are people who can be whipped into an instant lynch mob on a moment's notice (remember democracy in action). Such mobs and the street violence they create are necessary programs to create anarchy and revolution in America, for the end purpose of enabling a Socialist takeover.

"Rules for Radicals" was especially written as a guide to assist and encourage the rebellious Sixties paper sack throwing youth movements into 'changing their radical ways for the satisfaction of their radical ends'. Instead, Alinsky encouraged them to go into the universities where they could be better educated in socialist ideology, then go to work, and to assimilate into society, creating a fifth column of elected officials, bureaucrats, and community organizers (street agitators in Hitler's time), capable of bringing a revolutionary army into being. This army is Alinsky-trained to not fall victim to the errors, which cost success to earlier generations of Stalinist Marxists in America.

I find it fascinating, that although Alinsky, being Jewish stated he was anti-fascist, the tactics he encourages in "Rules" are based *as much or more* on Hitler's successful methods in Germany as on any of Lenin's or Mao's. Hitler came to power by beginning as a Socialist Street Agitator (Community Organizer?) who worked to infiltrate and corrupt the government with his sycophant friends (Goebbels,

Himmler, et al), while raising populist support with his street meetings. During those meetings, he used union and street thugs as 'security and crowd control'. Almost comically in my opinion, Alinsky and his followers express an undying love for Stalinist Communism, all the while emulating and practicing Hitler's National Socialist (Nazi) organizing and infiltration principles on an equal or greater basis. Remember, Lenin was more overt and brutal.

However, whether Proletarian Socialism or National Socialism, they are merely two slightly differing forms of Totalitarian Socialism. From the view of the "man-in-the-street" (most likely, laying on his back in the street, staring up through blood) one Socialist looks just like the other. Whether NKVD with a Tokarev, or Gestapo with a Lugar, whether you are Kulak in the Ukraine, Jews and Gypsies in Germany, or a formerly free American, the view is dim and blurry, and either one will cold-bloodedly kill you or drag you into the life destroying slavery of the concentration or labor camps that define Totalitarian Socialism. The Marxist form of 'E Pluribus Unum' is obviously, "Many Bodies, One Mass Grave".

Because the majority of Americans have a generational, almost in-bred suspicion of too much, and too powerful government, the new Alinsky cum Obama Army needed to invent a new routine, one which would refine the embittered, America-hating' 'police-hating', 'rabid Communist', 'Hippy', tactics *(never their goals, only their tactics)*. So they must *not* appear to be Communists or Socialists, but *'good, liberal Americans'*, gagging on the title American, but needing it to disguise the road to tyranny they are paving. They must appear to be 'helping the poor and needy', or some other such 'feel-good' 'con-job' to deceiving decent, moral people into supporting and voting for them, even though it is still a total (and deadly) 'con-game'.

These 'neo' communists, Alinsky realized, must learn new techniques to succeed in 'suckering' the American people into accepting Socialist Communism. Creating, refining, and teaching these new techniques were Alinsky's reason for writing "Rules for Radicals".

Alinsky, in his Lucifer-skewed logic must do more to change their appearance than re-name themselves "Progressive". The 'new'-communists must now learn to be succors, providing assistance and relief to the 'poor', the 'downtrodden', the 'disenfranchised', etc. Instead of openly deriding and blaspheming the American society they despised, they must blend into it; become a 'better citizens' than its own true supporters. They must become friends of the 'victims' of the oppressive society, and organize to assist them by working *inside* the societal system, and in doing so gaining the power of organization and numbers to create their revolution.

Having accomplished some organization and power, they can more effectively continue infecting and stoking them with anger, hatred and rage, with which to gain more numbers, and through those organized numbers, more and more power, ad infinitum. Rage and anger in the streets without organization afforded little power, and Alinsky was always, and totally addicted to gaining power.

So, they must blend into the society they despised, to help society's 'victims'. They must support multitudes of legislation and regulations for the 'Children', or the 'Environment', or for 'Less Pollution', or for 'Honest Government', or 'Fair Treatment', and for, of course, their favorite new key-phrase, 'Social Justice'. And then, with Obama as President, activate massive 'redistribution of wealth, in other words, tyranny wearing a three-piece suit instead of a 'hop-head' with a scraggly beard and dreadlocks!

But always remember one thing! They were never interested in helping humanity, only in gaining power to be used for destroying existing society, and bringing about Marxist Utopia. So, *whatever* the issue, the issue was *never* the Issue. *The Revolution was the Issue*, the only reason for all the work was, *The Revolution!* This way they may be for everything that works for them and ignore or be against what doesn't, because there is *always only one Issue!*

One excellent example of an Alinsky principle in action was the self-admitted Communist Van Jones. Jones started out looking and sounding like a thousand other America-hating communist revolutionary hippies, ragged dreadlocks, scruffy beard, and raised on 'mothers-milk' of anger, hatred and obscenity. But after finding and following Alinsky's principles of 'change to infiltrate to destroy', he ended up clean-cut, wearing a suit and tie, and being appointed as Obama's Green Jobs Czar. Wow, *that's* working inside the system!

Unfortunately, some of his earlier taped remarks surfaced, in which he admitted to being a Communist. Then another tape surfaced, where he essentially stated, *'I'm willing to forgo the cheap satisfaction of the radical pose for the deep satisfaction of the radical ends'*. When these tapes became widely broadcast, they created a situation whereby President Obama might be openly questioned as to why he had appointed a self-admitted Communist.

Obviously, that was more than Obama wanted America to know at that time, so Jones quietly resigned over a weekend and went to work for the Soros funded Communist (oh excuse me), "Progressive" think-tank, *'Center for American Progress'*. Remember, Progressives always make sure either their key people stay in high-paying, government or private think-tank positions, funded by American taxpayers or anti-American Internationalists like George Soros. Leftist take care of 'family'. Naturally, they also destroy defectors. Check out what happened to Malcolm X, or others who have disappeared.

Jones situation and statement make a classic example from Alinsky's training manual, i.e., become a part of the establishment in order to undermine and destroy it. Mask the radical pose, dress, foul language, rhetoric, and everything that marked the Sixties Radicals hatred and contempt for America, instead become a bureaucrat, a social worker, a community organizer, or a union boss, etc., in order to work hidden inside the structure of American society. Like a mole to undermine, like a termite to weaken the structure, like a disease to bring sickness and decay to the body, and like a maggot feeding on the death caused by their own revolutionaries. Beautiful people, these Socialists!

Key among his Communist Activist talents, Alinsky became the national 'Father' of US Community Organizing, and "Rules for Radicals" became its primary textbook.

Curiously, Alinsky like Obama had a near father-figure mentor named Frank. In this case Alinsky's 'Frank' was Al Capone's "Enforcer, Frank Nitti (you know, the guy who 'takes you out' if you fall out of favor with Capone). Nitti was also the man who took over running the Chicago mob when Elliot Ness sent Capone to prison on a tax charge.

They became good friends. Alinsky, an Illinois state criminologist, called Nitti 'Professor' while Saul became his 'Student'. Alinsky came to believe his revered Communist Revolution had something to learn from organized crime. After all, the Mafia had historically targeted the 'rich' to rob, and they held tremendous power in the Chicago Political Machine, even in the 1930's. (5)

Alinsky, always obsessed with gaining power, and needing a rationale to justify and compensate for the Mob's evil ways, failed to consider the inherent stupidity of robbing the poor. Then, because he believed that society (especially Capitalist Society), *not* evil, was to blame for all criminal behavior, he was able to rationalize that robbing 'the rich' qualified the Mob as modern Marxist Robin Hood figures, i.e., 're-distributing wealth' from the hated 'Rich'. This, along with their power, obviously made them acceptable allies and role models for Alinsky's Socialist Revolutionaries. There's no denying you're in high class, deep-thinking company with the Alinsky Crowd! Not!

Alinsky, an educated, professional sociologist, fervently believed in Communism and considered Soviet Communists partners; however, he disagreed with the Soviet revolutionary tactics. Alinsky believed his own tactics to be smarter, and that his plan to overcome the United States with Communism was superior to theirs.

He also seriously believed that society; especially Capitalist society was to blame for all the evil that criminals performed, i.e. criminal behavior was generated only by the social environment, *not* by any evil intentions of the individual. Sounds like a great guy to have sitting on the parole board. If you're a vicious Felon!

Obama's 'Uncle' Frank Marshall Davis was a Stalinist Communist, as his (Second World) War-time record showed, first trying to keep the US out of the European War, then stridently working to get us involved after Hitler attacked Russia. After all, whatever was good for 'Uncle Joe' and bad for the USA was a worthy objective for Frank Marshall Davis' efforts. How can you wonder about his protégé?

There's a lot more about Alinsky you should know, but this simple book cannot include everything you never learned.

But, by Alinsky's "Rules", the Socialist's high-sounding goals were made to sound so principled and ever so important to the drowsing, unaware American public as to become, "Mom, Pop, and Apple Pie America". Yet virtually every one of these Socialist "Feel-Good Programs" are skins of good deeds, stuffed with lies, darkness, and potential slavery, for wage-earners, taxpayers, and welfare recipients alike. Remember, the issue is never the issue, the Revolution is The Issue! Alinsky's only goal was power for revolution!

As these Social(its) Programs continually skyrocketed out of control, both cost and management-wise, they added, to human degradation, vice, and corruption, yet these government programs lifespan are, as Ronald Reagan said, "the closest thing to eternal life we'll see here on this earth".

Look back over history. The high-sounding principles and the programs Socialist dreamers breed, once turned in to legislation and/or regulation, consistently erode the freedoms of any free or semi-free people, and eventually bankrupt their nations, both morally and economically. No exceptions, "Nothing New Under the Sun".

Consider this for instance, in the name of Health and Safety "Progressives" (Marxists hiding their identity) have turned our (at one time) 'best in the world' American Medical Care into a convoluted, corrupt, red-tape bound Bureaucracy, so expensive as to be priced out of *any* market.

In the name of Equal Treatment "Progressives" have regulated the housing and lending markets so deeply that banks were actually blackmailed by the Feds and Community Organized Groups, a la Alinsky and Obama, into making tens of thousands of loans for mortgages or business startups where both the bank and borrower knew the loan could only fail. This was the beginning of the collapse of the US Economy. Obama then, faithful to Alinsky, used and exacerbated this Progressive-manufactured "crisis" to rob, blackmail, and, nationalize huge portions of the US Financial Industry.

In the name of The Public Well-Being, Obama and his "Progressive" Congress have passed eighty one thousand pages of new Regulations on US business and industry last year. Currently, we have a "Regulation Czar", Cass Sunstien, in the Office of Information and Regulation, who once told a Chicago Class he was teaching, *"We don't need any more laws passed by congress, we can do everything we want to do with regulation"* (6). In other words, the United States now has a non-elected government of appointees and bureaucrats bypassing our elective government, regulating and controlling every facet of our lives. How different is that from a Fascist dictatorship? Very little, but give Obama another term as President and you will likely find out in detail!

In the name of Compassion, "Progressives" have created a 'generational welfare system' through which, like the wild animals in the parks, which you are told *not* to feed, some Americans have become so dependent on federal handouts, they can or will no longer fend for themselves. They receive federal checks to not work, to breed illegitimate children, to attend street demonstrations, or even to stay home stoned, and send someone to pick up their check.

These are part of a 'grand' Revolutionary strategy called "Overload the System" created by two 'Progressives' at Columbia University, who were so inspired by the riots, the destruction and the

'Progressive' successes following the Watts Riots they wanted to emulate it! Look it up! Google "Cloward-Pivin Strategy".

So, today, we have, "Government *of* the Ruling Class, *by* the Ruling Class, and *for* the Ruling Class!" No wonder US Business and Industry have degraded themselves into Crony-Capitalism with Obama. Look how well it rewarded General Electric, who landed tons of Federal work, yet *paid no corporate taxes in 2010*, because they did business the Obama Way. By kissing his imperial 'Ring'.

As discussed above, those who are working against, or even simply not supporting, these virtuous-sounding "Progressive" goals, like Health and Safety, Equal Treatment, Public Well-Being, or Compassion, will be immediately isolated, criticized, belittled, and generally made to look like a Troll in the public eye. That dirty little tactic gives a shining example of Lucifer's Kingdom from Alinsky's book, "Rules for Radicals" as follows:

> Rule Number 13. *"Pick the target, freeze it, personalize it, and polarize it. ... In conflict tactics there are certain rules that [should be regarded] as universalities. One is that the opposition must be singled out as the target and 'frozen.'... any target can always say, 'Why do you center on me when there are others to blame as well?' When you 'freeze the target,' you disregard these [rational but distracting] arguments.... Then, as you zero in and freeze your target and carry out your attack, all the 'others' come out of the woodwork very soon. They become visible by their support of the target..."*

That's just one of Alinsky's salute to Lucifer 'rules' Obama and the left are currently utilizing to pass their myriads of petty-fogging laws and regulations, get a favorite candidate elected, keep the USA dependant on foreign oil, or quash any opposition person or group. You only have to listen, it is rampant on today's Political Podiums and in the Government-Controlled (or Communist complicit) Lame-Stream-Media. You can hear these sound bites continually streaming from this smarmy President and his stable of Marxist Fascist revolutionary sycophants. Every bit of it straight from Saul

Alinsky's little book of filthy tricks designed to assist the cause of a Communist Revolution in the overthrow of the USA.

So, Alinsky's Revolutionary goal was to continually organize, inflame, and incite groups to clamor for more regulation, more taxation, more idiotic, Nazi environmentalism, more Marxism-based taxation and redistribution of wealth, nationalization of US Industry and Financial Institutions, and an enlarged role for bureaucratic (non-elected government again) intrusion into every facet of our lives. Thus they destroy freedom for every American individual and private business, while attain more latitude for our (yet) small-t tyrannical government.

As a tongue-in-cheek aside, it appears that Alinsky, in his 'Over the shoulder' acknowledgement of Lucifer in the forward of "Rules", was attempting to ingratiate for himself a little piece of Lucifer's Kingdom, which of course is *Hell!* As it turns out, Hell is a perfect definition of the kingdom that *Rules for Radicals* was written to attain. Unless, of course, you are its Dictator!

However, never, *never* forget, the ultimate goal of these people is *not, and never has been* benign. The goal forever in front of them, that which they seek, is nothing but the total slavery of all mankind.

Therefore, the underlying direction of Alinsky's "Rules" and its individual goals always nudge people, like a mass lemming migration, off the cliff, which is the statist's singular goal of totalitarian control of, and ultimate slavery for mankind. That thought is always uppermost in their minds as they work toward the final stage of communism, and its 'collective salvation' of mankind. Remember, *'the issue isn't the issue'*. The *Revolution* is the Issue! *Revolution* is the only issue!

No one who thinks atheistic Marxist Socialism is not a religion is thinking at all. Marxists worship their shrine cum vision of a world where all mankind works together in a "classless" society, always and only concerned with the common societal (or national) good, and without any feeling of individuality, or of personal wants or needs.

Such a "Utopian" society then, becomes the perfect mother, father, brother, sister, uncle and grandfather, and the *only* God to everyone. In addition, because no one has anything, no one *wants* for anything. Being Darwinian Socialists they actually believe that when they reach this point mankind will have *evolved to its highest state,* and to have achieved "Collective Salvation" and so can "live happily ever after".

To me that State is a permanent prison, slavery to mediocrity or worse, for every human being. What is *your* opinion of such a state? Would you want to live there? Could *you* survive there? Have you even thought about it? Well, when Obama's 'Fundamental Transformation' has completed, it will put you there, so you had better consider it!

It is critically important that anyone who doesn't want to live in that state of inhumanity must recognize that Socialism is *not* politics, it is a religion, whose adherents believe that they *must* gain those specific ends to achieve the salvation of all humankind. They also believe there are *no means*, which are not justified by the glorious end-state of their Communist, Utopian Hell.

Socialists believe the pain, the suffering, and the mass casualties of naysayers or opponents necessary to achieve the 'Utopian' Socialist State are merely 'collateral damage' and therefore a normal part of the evolutionary changes needed to bring it about. These are therefore totally justified, because this 'glorious end' justifies *'any'* means. Can you actually grasp a mentality that can believe this? Do you want to live in a world where that person rules? Well, you have been electing them to public office for almost a century. They are called "Progressives". The latest one promises "Hope and Change".

Do your own research. A simple Google search for the title 'Saul Alinsky, Rules for Radicals', gave me over three million hits. 'Saul Alinsky, Communist, Rules for Radicals' gave one million three hundred thousand hits. However, always remember that these are both pro and con responses. Today many Lefties out there love and revere Alinsky for becoming the "Lenin of the post-Communist Left" after the fall of the Soviet Union debilitated the Stalinists. In addition, there are certainly many Americans as well who don't despise Alinsky simply because they have never heard of him, and do not know anything about him.

But, after all, that's why God gave you a brain and power of reason. So you could make up your own mind. At least in today's USA.

~~~~~~~~~~~~

So, here we are. Barak Obama's Agenda of "Fundamental Transformation of America" was clear to those who could or would read his handwriting, his mentors, his family, his friends, and his history. Because he was elected along with a majority in both houses of congress, it indicated his radical agenda of "Fundamentally Transforming" America into a Marxist Socialist State could be realized.

To those who still believe in our Constitutional Republic, and the self-evident truths described in our Declaration of Independence, it came as a stern warning signal that our wall of protections had been breached and stood in severe jeopardy; that the very foundations of our nation were in danger of being broken, crumbled, and laid bare. That our freedom was in great peril.

Obama's election with a majority in congress was simultaneously a warning siren for us, and the trumpet sound to which our mortal enemy was advancing. For America, its meaning was not merely a fork in the road, but a potentially violent U-turn toward Marxist Tyranny and Slavery.

To the ultra-left, and all who hated America and worked tirelessly for the success of the Soviet Union and Communism as 'Uncle' Frank Marshall Davis had, and for the Alinskyites who believed they had a better set of tactics than the Stalinists, by using *Rules for Radicals* and *"Community Organizing"*, it was a clarion call to arms. It was a signal that the USA now had a sitting president *and* congress who were not interested in only ideological tweaking of Progressive or even viral Socialist reforms, but who were willing to completely destroy the gift of American freedoms through Fundamental Transformation.

It meant America now had a president and congress that were prepared to allow, or even create the untenable situations and atmosphere necessary to create and allow the revolution necessary to such fundamental restructuring of the United States of America. Moreover, that these people well understood such a fundamental restructuring meant replacing America's wealth, its world power, its capitalism, and its individual freedoms, with an ideology that has promised, but never furnished Utopia to billions, although it has certifiably delivered death to hundreds of millions.

It meant Obama, who clearly telegraphed his goals in his writings and by his words, was following his Stalinist father, who wrote,

> *"Theoretically, there is nothing that can stop the government from taxing 100 per cent of income so long as the people benefits from the government commensurate with their income which is taxed."*
>
> BHO Sr. East Africa Journal, 1965

This then answers the question of what Obama's "Fundamental Transformation" of America means. Neither of the two Obama's messages is vague if you understand Marx. It means the Government, not the individual, may take ownership of one hundred percent of the labors of each individual as long as *"the 'people' benefits from the government commensurate with their income which is taxed."*. The message is transparently spoken, it describes nothing but a descent into the Darkness of Marxist Statist Tyranny! However, just what does that mean? In the case of Stalinist Marxists, like Obama Senior and 'Uncle' Frank, the "People" is the Proletariat! Under National Socialism, the "People" is the Nation. It does not mean much when the Government comes with guns to take what you have and "Spread the wealth around" to those they think deserve part of what you made yourself. Remember Joe the Plumber?

True, neither Obama defined what *"...as long as the people benefits..."* actually meant, however both being Marxists, the above is exactly what they meant!

However, Stalinist Marxism had twice failed to co-opt the government of the People in the United States. In order to insure success, Obama pinned his hopes on Saul Alinsky's "Rules for Radicals". Alinsky did not write "Rules" to *supplant* Marx, but as a plan better adapted to winning the battle for Marxism in the United States, as shown in the following:

> *"A Marxist begins with his prime truth that all evils are caused by the exploitation of the proletariat by the capitalists. From this he logically proceeds to the revolution to end capitalism, then into the third stage of reorganization into a new social order of the dictatorship of the proletariat, and finally the last stage... the political paradise of communism."* ... *"The end is what you want, the means is how you get it."* ... *"The third rule of ethics of means and ends is that in war the end justifies almost any means"*... *"Change comes from power, and power comes from organization."* ... *"An organizer must stir up dissatisfaction and discontent..."* and,
>
> *"The first step in community organization is community disorganization. The disruption of the present organization is the first step toward community organization. Present arrangements must be disorganized if they are to be displaced by new patterns.... All change means disorganization of the old and organization of the new."*
>
> Selected excerpts from Alinsky's "Rules for Radicals"

So today, Barak Obama is using Alinsky's "Rules" to achieve his radical *"Dreams from My Father"* Fundamental Transformation, which becomes more clear when you understand that he spent a number of years in Chicago as an Alinsky organizer before being launched by the Chicago Political Machine into Politics. His goals are not so obvious to Americans, because those of us who studied communism years ago are mostly familiar with the Stalinist tactics espoused by Obama's 'Uncle' Frank.

However, the above shows without a doubt that Alinsky did not come to 'bury Marx, but to praise him'. Alinsky's rhetoric and actions are spoken in the American dialect, using familiar leftist and Progressive 'catch-phrases'. However, they are both fully Marxist, just not readily recognized *Stalinist* Marxist. This allowed Obama to speak directly to his sycophants in 'Alinsky-Speak', while his Marxism remained partially obscured to the average American. Handy for Obama, a tragedy for us and the US.

Today, Obama's 'Fundamental Transformation' of the United States from a free nation to a socialist dictatorship has progressed a long ways in three years. In his next step, he must incite and inflame his street-army of angry, hate-filled malcontents organized and educated by the Left, over the past generation into a "Democratic" Lynch Mob. These then, will go forth across the streets of America taking advantage of and exacerbating the public discontent and anger purposefully brought on by generations of "Progressive" Socialists and their class-warfare inciting legislation and regulation. Remember, *"All change means disorganization of the old and organization of the new."* Just watch the summer of 2012.

Following the Marx cum Alinsky roadmap, Obama's Fundamental Transformation can mean nothing less than purposefully undermining the laws and economy of the United States and collapsing the United States system of Constitutional Government, destroying its Capitalism, and following the roadmaps of Marx and Alinsky into the Slavery of Socialist Tyranny. These will include, but not be limited to:

- *Increased rhetoric for confiscatory taxation and redistribution of wealth from the American working class ("Do-ers" *) to the unemployed, unemployable, and generational welfare classes ("Gimme's" *) as wages for their populist support.*

    *Whereas Marx referred to the "Haves" and "Have-Nots" to commit his atrocities, I use the titles,"Do-ers" and "Gimme's", which are more realistic descriptions. - [rg]

- *Increased inflation, taxation, deficit spending and printing of "fiat" money to further erode the US Dollar and enrich the "Gimme's" at the expense of the "Do-ers".*

- *Continued Justice Department (sic) legal attacks and stonewalling of states, groups, and individuals, who try to force federal compliance with any pro-American agenda item, coupled with increased leniency and "Winking" at lawless and revolutionary riots, civil unrest, and other Marxist acts.*
- *Increased organization and subsidization of minorities, unemployed, generational welfare families, illegal aliens, and career troublemakers in return for their voice and their votes.*
- *Acceleration of Crony-Capitalism, Nationalization, and runaway Regulation of American Industry to bring "Social Justice".*
- *Continued abuse and prostitution of the American system of laws and freedoms.*
- *Tacit or outright support for Groups such as Occupy Wall Street (OWS), the New Black Panthers, corrupt unions, roving street gangs, and Marxist, or Alinskyite Revolutionaries.*
- *Continued funding and Oval Office tacit support for international terrorist and anti-American groups such as the Muslim Brotherhood, et.al, while verbally using them as a whipping boy to impress conservative Americans.*
- *Continued excoriation of Capitalism, calling it an 'Old, Outdated System and controlled by "Jew Bankers of Wall Street".*
- *Continued tacit or outright approval of increasing anti-Semitic rhetoric, both domestically, and worldwide, as well as US financial support of selected anti-Semitic Groups.*
- *Increasing legal and regulatory attacks on Christian, Jewish, and conservative religious groups in the USA, to break down the Judeo-Christian ethic upon which our national laws originated.*
- *Continued exacerbation and acceleration of racial, economic, and class hatred by well-chosen remarks at key moments.*
- *Support for groups fomenting violence in the streets, as they promote a Marxist Revolution in the streets to sweep the away American "Rule of Law" and replace it with Marxist "Social-Justice".*
- *Eventual replacement of the current US Constitution and Bill of Rights with one that more closely mirrors the Constitution of the Soviet Union (as demanded by the Marxist OWS Outlaws).*

These would have made no sense to Americans who had not read Alinsky's "Rules for Radicals", (originally titled, "Rules for Revolution"). Yet they are ongoing and increasing daily in the Obama Administration. Are you ready for the coming insurrection? Well, the alarm bells are ringing. It's time to wake up and look around.

Why do I believe this can happen? Look back at the definition of demagoguery! Barak Obama's election presented an engraved invitation to the numerous Communist factions in Labor Unions to create dissention, fear, and labor turmoil. It presented license to those purposefully disenchanted and disenfranchised over past decades to commence open rebellion. A clarion signal to those who teach, and to those who have been taught racial hatred and class warfare rhetoric over past decades, to come out of their Marxist 'mole-holes' and to begin rioting and radicalization in earnest (like the OWS movement and others).

It was a signal to international Communists and hate-America groups to organize and finance sister revolutions in their own or other nations, further destabilizing world peace and placing increasing pressure for a World Government, under which a new Marxist Socialist Oligarchy could rule the entire earth and its peoples.

It therefore came as a huge shock to these Leftists when the American People did not simply fall at their feet and worship them. However, the fact is that although Obama and his Democrat Congressional majority won the election handily, he did not have an ideological majority, merely a party majority of elected representatives, some of whom still wanted to remain re-electable. In addition, his electoral majority were simply Americans with different reasons and mixed loyalties who voted Democrat, or independents who simply wanted a change, and even some Progressive Republicans who always vote for the most socialist candidate.

But the American Democrat and Union loyalists were not all fools, the Independents wanted *some* change, not a train-wreck, and the

Republican Lefties were mostly Fabian, not Revolutionary Socialists. Even more disturbing, Conservative Americans actually organized for the first time in recent history, to regain some control in the congress, and even though the left had been organizing unions, street riots, sit-ins, and shout-downs for decades, there were enough gains made to frighten the Fabian Socialist Republican Hierarchy into defeating some conservative gains.

However, even though Obama won the election with a filibuster-proof majority in congress, some of those had to run for re-election, and the tone in the nation after the first year or so of Obama's Marxist Fascist arrogance was not happy.

Public response did not favor his Fascist nationalization of General Motors and Chrysler, by which he arrogantly backfilled the ludicrously out-of-control United Auto Workers Contract and Pension Plan, while giving Unions a likewise stolen portion of the ownership, all directly from taxpayer's pockets, all to re-pay the Union for supporting his election.

Additionally, the so-called Financial 'Bail-outs' were nothing but brazen taxpayer funded buy-outs, with more fascist nationalization of Obama's preferred Banks and Financial organizations. With these actions, Obama abrogated US Financial and Contract Law by Presidential Diktat so Obama could brazenly breach investor's financial contracts and steal their investment money, turning federal power into Federal (Fascist) tyranny.

At the same time, he was promising Unions he would pass the bill known as 'Card-Check', removing the secret ballot from unionization elections so his Union Goons could enforce "Chicago-Style" blackmail and coercion, creating a more union-friendly vote. If you think this kind of smells like Hitler's Brown Shirts at street meetings, or forcing all the Jews to wear the Yellow Star of David. What is the difference? These Obama actions were never legal, they simply occurred *because he utilized a manufactured crisis and the power of the federal government in a dictatorial operation, and the people did not revolt!* While that could never make it legal or proper, it is now an accomplished fact. Could this be what he and his father meant by,"*...so long as the people benefits...*" Maybe it depends on *which people* you are talking about?

Many Americans were also puzzled, if not outraged that on Obama's early Presidential trips, he acted as no leader of the free world had ever done, bowing and 'Kissing the Rings' of Muslim kings, holding deferential and chatty meeting with very questionable allies like Hugo Chavez, and endlessly apologizing for America. Yet all the while, he insulted traditional allies like England, by returning Churchill's Bust from the Oval Office, and giving the Queen of England an insulting childish trinket gift.

These could never be the actions of a benevolent Leader of the Free World, but of an arrogant, self-appointed "Leader of the ignorant masses", bent on damaging America. Welcome to the Fourth Reich!

Therefore, I find it to be a morbidly curious situation that most Americans have never read Marx or Alinsky, let alone both of them. Yet the importance of these two men's revolutionary manuals, both in the world history of the last hundred and fifty years, and for the coming century of human life, is staggering.

First because of Socialism's blood-soaked slaughter of some hundred fifty million people, and it's probable causality for the deaths by starvation of that many more, and its brutally enforced totalitarian slavery which today covers more than a billion human beings.

Secondly, because if Marx, Alinsky, and their current America-hating Socialist disciples continually succeed in their (now) openly flaunted Revolutionary tactics, of bringing the United States under Socialist Tyranny, there will remain no nation on earth with the strength and determination to offer a bastion of Freedom from the Tyranny we can already see enveloping the earth today. That Totalitarian Tyranny is today, just as it has historically been, the long-range plan of all self-appointed elites. Those who long to see the power and riches of all nations prostrated before themselves.

If Obama and his handlers are successful (no, I don't think he's acting alone, he came too far, too fast), Soviet-style Gulags and

Slave Labor Camps will eventually contain some twenty to thirty percent of the population of the earth. The rest will be only slightly better off, and in imminent danger of breaching some bureaucratic protocol, only to end up in the gulags or camps themselves. Life under Totalitarian Socialism has never been different. Read your history instead of your Union Pension Propaganda.

Can you now seriously ask me why this is important today? Think about that honestly for a few minutes. Remember the Kulaks and consider what happened to them as they entered the "Utopia" of Lenin's Marxist Socialism. Yet they are only one group out of multiple nations of people enslaved by the Soviet Union. Merely a *'Statistic'* as Stalin said. However, without a free people somewhere in free nations, such "statistics" as these, will never be recorded. Otherwise, they'll merely fertilize the ground with their blood.

While I would love to be proven wrong, I cannot deny what my lifelong study of history, politics and economics have taught me. Nor can I deny the number of historical events with predictable results, which are in the process of being repeated today.

CHAPTER THIRTEEN

Who blazed the trail we're following today?

I predict future happiness for Americans if they can prevent the government from wasting the labors of the people under the pretense of taking care of them.

Thomas Jefferson

"Society in every state is a blessing, but government, even in its best state, is but a necessary evil; in its worst state an intolerable one; for when we suffer or are exposed to the same miseries by a government which we might expect in a country without government, our calamity is heightened by reflecting that we furnish the means by which we suffer."

Thomas Paine

The most often told, the most often believed, and the most heinous lie of the Marxist Socialist crowd is that the "Filthy Rich" (who are likely dirty Jews as well) are to blame for all the plight of the poor! That all bankers and industrialists are an evil spawn of hell without humanity or compassion, and should be eradicated from the face of the earth by any means, the more horrendous the better. Historically this lie appears to be as old as western civilization, but it became a political ideology during the French Revolution and a political reality with the publication of the Communist Manifesto by Marx and Engels. (1)

It can be proven to have been both deadly and wrong in every nation in which it was instituted. However these lies are the bait charlatans use to net the greedy, the envious, and the foolish into a dictatorship from which millions will never survive.

Let us explain this simply, in the vernacular of plain-vanilla America. Marxist "Class Warfare" is based on the notion that there is a finite amount of wealth in the world, and teaches that wealth is not created, but simply stolen from or distributed between classes by the ruling authorities. Marxists state that monarchs and aristocracies had historically stolen it from Commoners, and that today Capitalists (Bourgeoisie) are still stealing it from the Working Class (Proletarians), by hoarding most of that "finite" wealth through the law and order rules of what most of us call Western Civilization.

Marxists historically use this concept to infect their revolutionary converts. It is then mixed with the poisons of greed, envy, class, racial, and economic hatred, and combined with a vision of gaining absolute power for revenge and retribution over theoretical enemies. This then is used to create a revolutionary army of "Useful Idiots" who will do the bidding of, and become the cannon fodder for the revolution in which the leader will ascend to power.

That this is a lie of universal proportions, is patently obvious to most rationally thinking people who have tasted some degree of freedom, and especially to Citizens of the United States, where we have historically enjoyed "Free-Enterprise" or Capitalism (The ability of anyone to create wealth by their labors), and seen it work.

Unfortunately, those who believe this lie can be manipulated by greed, envy, and hatred toward those who have more than they do, by those who simply lust for Power over other people. These scorn the idea of wealth creation, accepting the darkened vision and premise it involves. Also unfortunately, for them, like the millions of souls already slaughtered from Robespierre to Mao, the current superhero of many of Obama's appointees, and continuing through Castro, Pol-Pot, and Chavez, the victory dance for most of them will be a death-dance with Alinsky's hero, Lucifer.

That this Marxist thought process, a relic from the days of tyrant monarchies, has no meaning in even the poorest of free or partially free-enterprise economies, or even in a *democratic* socialist economy today. Yet it becomes impossible for these cannon-fodder draftees to understand because the dream of revenge and retribution clouds their minds and fills them with delusive visions of grandeur.

Obviously, if the United States economy were under the totalitarian control of a capitalist dictatorship, as the Marxists claim, there would never have been freedom for people born to less-than modest means to make wealth of any kind. This would have been the sole property of those in control, even as it is in the Statist Socialist's supposedly Utopian Dictatorship of the Proletariat.

Nevertheless, many millions of Americans of different races *have* come from poverty to attain middle-class status in their lives and many even to riches beyond anyone's dreams. Besides, capitalists did *not* slaughter a hundred and fifty million people while enslaving billions in the past century as Marxism has done.

From my own black and white point of view, it takes an idiot or a dictator 'wanna be' to believe in that kind of stupidity. Besides, what Marxist Dictator does not control all the wealth of the nation, and live like a Despotic Monarch? Who else has the power unless he gives it?

Therefore, a government under control by Marxists, like Lenin, Stalin, Hitler, Mao, Castro, Chavez, or any other person or group, is by definition a tyrannical regime, because Marxism and the human emotions of sympathy and compassion are proven incapable of co-existing in the minds of such people.

Still today the 'Big Lie' continues to be told by potential tyrants and thieves, and continues to be believed by the simpletons with whom they deceive it. It works because potential tyrants and thieves always know how to stroke the ego of the poor and unhappy with the envy of those who simply have more than they do.

However, when sufficient people are not poor and unhappy, Statist Socialists work to gain some degree of political power by whatever means, just as the "Progressive" Socialists did in America at the turn of the Twentieth Century. They can then manipulate legislation and regulation situations to create poverty, unhappiness, and disenfranchisement, just as the consolidated "Progressive," Socialist, Communist, Fascist Left in America has spent the past hundred years doing.

Today, with near transition of our Constitutional Republic into a fifty one percent lynch-mob 'Democracy', and the election of Barak Obama with his promised "Fundamental Transformation", they are very close to achieving the violence and civil war which may give them the ascension to power they lust for.

Today, by utilizing Marx and Alinsky's methods, in which Obama has majored, the power of class and racial tension, mixed with greed, anger, and hatred, can be abscessed into hatred and open rebellion leading to revolution. And today, Obama, has a coalition of corrupt elected officials, trade union leaders, Chicago Mafioso and criminal elements, power hungry Leftists, university students corrupted to Marxism by professors and leaders from the Sixties radicals, and carefully antagonized and angered ethnic minorities. These along with many youthful voyeurs from the streets, including communists, anarchists, druggies, and common criminals, create a Revolutionary Army with whose assistance he *can* Fundamentally Transform the United States from a Constitutional Republic into a Marxist Dictatorship, complete with the horrors, brutality, and deaths that have cursed every nation who entered that door.

~~~~~~~~~~~~~~~

So, let us choose, for example, a *special* item from the foundation of America to which Obama wishes to apply his "Fundamental" Transformations. What was its genesis, and how did it work out for those who previously tried it?

Universal Health Care (UHC) is Obama's "must-have, signature" legislation, the major one upon which he campaigned for election, so let us investigate that. There is likely a well-defined trail.

First, even though it was presidential candidate Obama's 'hard-sell' item, and he was elected with a veto-proof majority in Congress, in order to pass it he had to ram it forcibly through his own Congressional majority. He used backroom deals, multi-million dollar pay-offs, and even blackmail of members in his own party who felt the necessity to consider what results it might have on their re-election.

We have all heard about UHC for years, but most Americans have a healthy suspicion of it, because it just *might be "Socialism"*. Well, where, and by whom did it originate? Let us investigate who blazed the UHC trail that Obama, and by default, the United States and *You*, are currently travelling today.

The German Empire, the Weimar Republic, and Nazi Germany.
A powerful Chancellor of the German Empire or Realm (Deutsches Reich, 1871-1918), was Otto von Bismarck, a conservative Prussian/German who exerted much influence in Europe from the 1860's into the 1890's. Remember that the European definition of Conservative was one who wished to either remain under monarchy and aristocratic rule, or have the order and form of a military dictatorship, aka National Socialism or Fascism. Bismarck was not a Marxist Socialist, but believed by establishing a few 'agreeable' socialist programs; he could better defend against the less agreeable ones. (2)

Bismarck established one of Europe's first quasi-socialist welfare states, in which the German Social Insurance and Health Care System was likely the first large European national system. Key items of Bismarck's social legislation included the Health Insurance Bill of 1883, Accident Insurance Bill of 1884, and the Old Age and Disability Insurance Bill of 1889. (3)

In 1888, Kaiser Wilhelm I died, and his grandson Wilhelm II replaced him as Kaiser. Wilhelm II was a much more authoritarian ruler, and

Bismarck resigned as Chancellor in 1890. At a time in history when many monarchs and aristocrats were seeking to become constitutional figureheads, Wilhelm was re-asserting his ruling 'rights', including divinity. This attitude continued throughout his reign, until he had lost most of the German Empire's European allies, and even antagonized some of the territories or nation-states that made up the Empire, and eventually culminated in World War 1. It also gave weight to the Monarchist tyranny vs. Workers victimhood that had created Marxism in Europe to begin with. (4)

Wilhelm's autocratic and authoritarian monarch stance was fertile ground for Marxist agitators courting the German people, and while Socialism had not grown rapidly under Bismarck, by 1912 the Social Democrat Party won over 30% of the Reichstag, becoming the largest of the parties in Germany. As WWI commenced, Wilhelm increasingly relinquished command to Field Marshall von Hindenburg and General Ludendorff, until by 1916 Germany was essentially a Military Dictatorship, with Wilhelm the Kaiser in name only. This created even greater influence for Marxist agitators and the Social Democrats, as a military dictatorship was considered Right Wing", or Fascist in Europe. Ironically, after the German Empire was overthrown in 1918 by the Weimar Republic, von Hindenburg was elected president in 1925. There are excellent histories from this period on Wikipedia. I can't write the history of the whole world in this book, so look it up.

So, nationwide Universal Health Care, a 'social welfare' program, was likely instituted first in the German Empire under Bismarck in 1883 to 'forestall' institution of even greater problematic socialist programs.

> Welfare State: *a social system based on the assumption by a political state of primary responsibility for the individual and social welfare of its citizens*
>
> www.merriam-webster.com

Without going into detail, just like today, it quickly became apparent in Germany, that in both the short and long terms, UHC created budget crises during differing economic or political cycles.

In order to control costs, governments must necessarily control not only the actions, and even the very lifestyles of their citizen-patients (history repeats). (5)

In efforts to control duplication and waste, both in medical practice and in government bureaucracy, it became necessary to consolidate into a single agency for UHC cost-control. By the advent of the Weimar Republic in 1918, doctors had accepted bureaucratic cooperation, and being a partner of the Welfare State Apparatus.

This type of bureaucratization resulted in private practice becoming public health oriented, shifting the doctor's focus from *treating* diseases and ills to *public prevention*, including enforcement of ever-encroaching public laws to control people's lifestyles, behavior and habits. This shifted the role of physicians from being a healer to a functionary government partner, whose duty lay in protecting the government from suffering loss rather than the patient from suffering ill health, disease, or death. While this did improve some areas of public health, it slowed or halted treatment research and development of anything helpful to the patient that was not 'cost-effective' for the state. Therefore, the medical and bureaucratic cost of UHC was carried by the taxpaying public, however the price of that government "cost-effectiveness" was paid by the infirm, the weak, the diseased, the elderly, and the helpless, in pain, suffering and certain death. Bureaucracy and human compassion are an oxymoron, never belonging in either the same sentence or nation!

The worldwide Depression of 1929, created severe economic crisis in Germany, resulting in drastic reduction or dissolution of many formerly provided services, including Health Care. The only remaining residuals of "Health Care" were state mechanisms for regulation and inspection of doctors and their practices. Because of these bureaucratic mechanisms already in place, cost-effectiveness came to mean concentrating on the working strong, who were deemed to be "Worthy of support", and elimination of the weak or "unproductive".

Greatly simplified, as this was all happening, Darwin's 'survival of the fittest' theory gave rein to the political rationale that the protection of the strong, while 'allowing the weak to disappear', was simply part of the mankind's evolutionary refinement. The world scientific community, including many doctors, quickly embraced this new theory as technological advancements, and research began to be carried out to enlarge and further the idea, at the cost of replacing much or most medical research and development. (6)

Marxist Socialists, of course loved this theory, as it excused their mass-murders as simply being a part of the evolutionary progress of mankind, and so Social Darwinism was born to denigrate the capitalistic health and medical progress, and to increase the credibility of Marxist Theory into everyday dialogue.

Remember, it was Fabian Socialist, George Bernard Shaw, who said:

> *"You all must know a half dozen people, at least, who are no use in this world. Who are more trouble than they are worth. Just put them there and say, 'Sir, or Madam, now will you be just kind enough to justify your existence? If you can't justify your existence. If you're not pulling your weight in the social boat, if you're not producing as much as you consume, or perhaps a little bit more, then clearly we can't use the big organization of our society for keeping you alive, because your life doesn't benefit us, and it can't be of much use to yourself."* (7)

By the time the National Socialists came to power in 1933, the theory of protecting the strong and somehow 'getting-rid-of' the weak and infirm was firmly entrenched, and Hitler, already a Marxist as well as a hater of Jews and other "Lesser people" ('Unter-Mensch') became a strong proponent. (8)

Sterilization laws followed, then a plan of how to 'solve' the problem of those who managed to be born anyway, leading to the "Crown Jewel" of Universal Health Care, "Life unworthy of life" (Lebensunwertes Leben), which of course was the road which led to Hitler's "Final Solution". Is National Health Care not seeming such a great idea now, or do you really think it will be 'different this time'?

The Coming Fourth Reich

Remember, this statement also came from George Bernard Shaw, speaking of what Hitler called the 'Lesser People';

> *I appeal to the chemists to discover a humane gas that will kill instantly and painlessly. Deadly by all means, but humane, not cruel. (9)*
> British 'Humanist' George Bernard Shaw, 1934

In Nazi Germany, the term lebensuwertes leben (life unworthy of life) became an integral part of the Nazi "Public HealthCare" system. That term, used for those with problems that made their lives "unworthy" of life in the eyes of certain Nazi Bureau-Cretens, who were responsible to budget the funds for their healthcare. Therefore, when government-run health care began to break the budget, whether through treatment, certain types of behavior, illness, or even old age, a simple hypodermic needle with a few cc's of 'death' was a quick and cheap answer. Also, like used toilet paper, 'Lesser peoples' lives were considered necessarily disposable.

According to Wikipedia, lebensunwertes leben people included those who were mentally dead, human ballast and empty shells of human beings as follows:

> The brain damaged, mentally retarded, psychiatrically ill, Those considered 'racially impure,' 'inferior' according to Nazi thinking, "deviant" or a "source of social turmoil" including mentally ill, people with disabilities, political dissidents, homosexuals, interracial couples, and criminals. The "social turmoil" category included some clergy, Communists, Jews, Romani (Gypsy) people, Jehovah's Witnesses, "non-white" or non-Caucasian peoples, ethnic Poles and of course the hated Jews. (9)

Hitler and his minions 'erased' these "lebensunvertes leben" people to the extent of some 4% of the population, slaughtering some three hundred thousand who *were not* casualties of the War! I'll bet *that* helped Nazi health become more cost effective for the war-effort, as well as lowering prison costs! Notice that 'criminals' made the list last. You can bet that those who were healthy spent their last breath and efforts in concentration labor camps doing "their part" for the good of the "Father-Land" along with Jews, Gypsies, Poles, and other "Unworthy People". Good Socialists would never waste a resource like that!

By the way, four percent of the US population is more than twelve million people. Feeling lucky? Try Obama's HealthCare Lottery!

The only history of Socialism that was kept alive and well during the past seventy years is that of Fascist Nazi Germany. The Progressives have not airbrushed and whitewashed that history because Hitler scandalized the whole world, setting Marxists back in their own march to tyrannize the world. Therefore, Socialists merely claimed that National Socialism was not *really* Marxist Socialism. Did I mention, I have some swampland for sale cheap, and a couple of bridges too!

Therefore, Nazi history, in its nauseating completeness is available, although many Americans do not think it pertains to Socialism or Communism. However, if you study Socialism and Fascism, they are twins, one brown eyed, one blue eyed, but still twins nevertheless. So, research it and study it. It will tell you where you end up if you follow either. It is not a good place to be!

Now, concerning Marxist Communism and UHC in Soviet Russia:

> *"When Vladimir I. Lenin sought to remake Russian society into a "proletariats' paradise," he targeted three sectors for control: health care, banking and education. Sound familiar?"*   IBD Editorial (10)

Every Marxist Socialist dictatorship from Lenin to Castro has immediately 'gifted', their people with Universal Healthcare. In the case of Obama and the United States, it was jammed down our throats by an unresponsive and non-representative congress, which should rightly have been impeached to the last person!

However, after all, it is a "Fundamental" tenet of Marxism, and Marxist zealots like Harry Reid and Nancy Pelosi wanted their names in the Marxist Hall of Shame along with Obama's. Remember, we had to 'Pass it so we could find out what was in it'. Catchy phrase, huh? Yes, and deadly to your health and wellbeing, as well!

So what is so important about Universal HealthCare? Well, here is a definition from an expert in bringing Socialist "Utopia" to people:

> *"Socialized medicine is the keystone to the arch of the socialist state."*   Vladimir I. Lenin (12)

So then, State-run Healthcare is the Coup de Gras, so to speak, of Totalitarian Marxism, an absolute necessity to every Socialist Dictator and wanna-be, because it grants them absolute power and control over *every facet* of their subject's lives and deaths. Kind of like knocking out your gold teeth to sell to your enemy after they stabbed or shot you in the back. However, the 'Nation' must benefit, according to Marx! Fundamental Transformation in Spades!

To what end, you may ask. However, is it not simply a "whole-life" system of care, enacted by a benevolent and caring Leader? Well no, especially not if he's a Socialist "Leader", because Marxists must and will have total control over every facet of human life in order to create the true, brain-dead, automaton "Proletariat". Thus their Utopia of enforced mediocrity for all who have lost their individual wills. Actually, Frankenstein's Monster should be a symbol of the Proletariat, it fits! Parts of dead men sewn together, lacking a brain! Marxist Socialist Perfection!

Secondly, UHC creates personal dependency on the government from cradle to grave. Control over who is born, who lives, who dies, and even if and *when* that happens. And thirdly, because he who controls *your* life and death also controls *your* basic economy, *your* standard and style of living, *your* habits, how many children you may have (or whether), and *defines* your mental health. Sounds like true-life nurturing, does it not? Everyone should have an 'Uncle' Frank, or an 'Uncle' Joe (Stalin) to inflict this on them. Now you can understand why Obama was so willing to murder babies who survived abortions, it was just not cost-effective medical care!

So, just how did this "Key Arch-Stone" hype and change work out? Not for the murderers who installed it, but for the people whose lives it affected. Following is a short synopsis from the IBD Editorial quoted above: (13)

> (In 1918 Lenin) told the Russian people everybody would be able to afford going to the doctor, not just the "greedy rich." ... (that) centralized control of the medical industry would "reduce costs" and end the "waste" from "unnecessary duplication and parallelism" ... (in 1933 a report by American and British physician observers reported) ... "great shortage of physicians and hospitals", ... "Drugs are almost fabulously dear and scarce" ... "overworked Doctors" couldn't handle ... patients ... lack of hospital beds when needed ... not uncommon for patients to die while waiting in line to be admitted ... Rationing became necessary ... Elderly patients often turned away ... Death panels appointed by the health commissar decided their fate ... funds for this treatment (came) ... from general taxation."...(after 70 years) the USSR was infamous for ... the worst health-care system in the world.

If Lenin's sales pitch does not sound familiar, you need to think about Alzheimer's testing, but please, for your own good, please do not wait until after ObamaCare goes in effect in 2014! You might have just turned you into a "Lebensunwertes Leben" by then!

Obama laughed those exact points to scorn two years ago, as did almost everyone educated in our Marxist leaning Public School System. Who says teaching Marxism to the kiddies is a waste of time? Those who knew and understood their history were publically humiliated and destroyed by Obama's Marxist crowd, utilizing Alinsky's Rule Number 13, quoted earlier.

In fact concerning the infamous "Death Panels", the 'Obama Care' Law (which we "had to pass to find out what was in it) actually *did* set up such a Nazi, or Soviet -style panel, the Independent Payment Advisory Board (IPAB) (14), which is staffed by health *bureaucrats* appointed by our "Leader", Obama. How can you *really fake* surprise? Obama, Reid, Pelosi, et al, had to lie to get it passed! Now these panels are a done-deal, set up, staffed by Obama-Rat Appointees who are accountable only to his Arrogance, "Leader" Obama. They are unaccountable to Congress, therefore to the people. Therefore, you cannot 'reach-out-and touch' them unless you know someone to pay off, but you'd better have deep pockets! Still love ObamaScare? It's Obama's "Lottery" of your Life!

However, Obama's unelected Bureau-Cretens will make life or death decisions over lives of the weak, infirm, and elderly, such as whether to continue dialysis, chemotherapy, or even give treatment at all. *These recommendations go into effect in 2014!* They are, as presently established, binding and *CANNOT* be overruled. Now you know why Queen Nancy wanted to pass the thing, before you found out what was in it. Love ObamaDoesn'tCare yet? It's coming to a life near you soon!

In case you just can't believe that 'nice young man' could do anything so evil, check out the name and body of work of one Ezekiel Emanuel (brother of Rahm Emanuel), who was named top White House Health Advisor during the period Obama was 'Ramming it down our throats!'. This man wrote the *"Ezekiel Emanuel Complete Lives System"*. When I reviewed it a couple years ago, I immediately connected his work to another medical history I had studied, a Dr. Joseph Mengele, one of Hitler's chief MD's (Murdering Doctors).

Emanuel's system measures healthcare cost effectiveness like an Ebenezer Scrooge accountant. Each individual is considered only in the light of his or her value to the nation (see why I call it the "Fourth Reich"?). Sympathy, empathy, and humanity have no place in either Emanuel's or Mengele's twisted world of Bureaucratic Death-Panels, only cost effectiveness. If you are not 'worth' the cost of treatment, Mengele might just use the needle on you, or maybe do a few experiments, since you were 'going to die anyhow'. Emanuel didn't mention that part in his cold-blooded system, only the cost effective parts, but who knows where it'll end up when the government runs short of money for "R and D"? Remember,

Socialist nations *always* run short! Besides, there will be *so many* of them to 'put down', and it would not be 'fair' to waste them!

For more information, Google those names, but be aware that in Emanuel's case, I was reviewing and downloading articles about him during the healthcare debate. At that time they better defined his views than the whitewashed propaganda I can find today, so the Left has already been busily whitewashing, airbrushing, and hiding just what he really is, cause they don't want Americans to realize he would have fit into the Nazi hierarchy like a chain-mail glove or a Lugar pistol. Today the first five pages of links on his name are similarly written propaganda, defending him as a champion of people who pay too much for healthcare, and excoriating his opposition. Actually, if you re-read Lenin's promises on health care above, old Vlad himself might well have penned these defenses.

Additionally, most of the articles still available against to his Mengle stance are from radical-right websites like *larouchepac.com*, which is a strategy to tar any and all of his opponents with a bad smell.

By the way, did you know that too, is a Saul Alinsky tactic? The origins? On Alinsky's recommendation, some anti-Viet Nam Protesters, instead of shouting down George Bush Senior at a speech, came dressed up in KKK garb, carrying pro-Bush signs, and cheered when he made pro-war points. Thus, they were able to make Viet Nam War supporters look like some of the worst people America has ever suffered. This underhanded Alinsky tactic became a standard, but in what the Alinsky-trained Left considers a 'War', "The ends justify *any* means". So do not *ever* think you can negotiate or deal with people like this. Evil is as Evil does. We need to educate those who are ignorant of history to what they are assisting take place with their ignorance and silence or more deadly yet, support. That's why I wrote this book!

In Russia, Lenin had a position on health care as well. He said, *"Socialized medicine is the keystone to the arch of the socialist state."* Wow, do you suppose Obama learned that from his 'Uncle' Frank, or maybe from Saul Alinsky?

While it might appear Lenin and Stalin did not need Euthanasia during the first 20-30 years of 'their' Soviet Utopia, because they both slaughtered and starved people at a rate guaranteed to keep the population controlled and the hospitals empty of everyone but soldiers and police. However, because both were ruthless mass-murderers, they both also utilized executions, concentration camps, and gulags to destroy whole classes of people. It seems no method of meting out death was ever left wanting by any of the 'benign' Socialist Monsters.

Likely only Mao murdered more people than those two, but then he had a large quantity of souls to murder in order to match up the Communist Standard of 10-30 percent of the population

Here, because a number of Obama's Cabinet, Czars, and appointees appear to be ardent disciples of the late-great Mao Zedong, let us examine Mao's "Utopian" Socialist Health Care as well.

According to Wikipedia, Mao Zedong was a Chinese Communist revolutionary, guerrilla warfare strategist, Marxist political philosopher, leader of the Chinese Revolution, and was the architect and founding father of the People's Republic of China (PRC). (15)

According to an article from the British Broadcasting Company:

> "In China today, the old system providing near-universal access to basic healthcare has been dismantled, as the government tries to spread the cost of providing healthcare to more than one billion people."..."Our hospital's state funding isn't enough to even cover staff salaries for one month. Under the current system, hospitals have to chase profit to survive"..."A World Health Organization survey measuring the equality of medical treatment placed China 187th out of 191 countries"..."So they necessarily concentrate on those who have resources to spend. They provide excessive services to those who can pay, and limited services or no services at all to those who are unable to pay."..." But Dr Hu admitted hospitals have no choice but to

act the way they do"…"Our hospital's state funding isn't enough to even cover staff salaries for one month. Under the current system, hospitals have to chase profit to survive."…"The system has even been criticized by a government think tank, the State Council's Development Research Centre, which said healthcare reforms had basically failed"…"One World Bank study found 20% of China's poor blamed healthcare costs for their financial straits." (16)

As an "it would be funny if it weren't so deadly serious" aside, in China, Communist Revolutionaries like to brag that under "Mao-Care" China had a lower infant mortality rate than New York City by the Seventies. Even considering they are conscienceless Marxist liars, this is a Whopper! How can a nation that holds birth rates to one per family and forcibly aborts all other pregnancies, have any claim on infant mortality rates. Can you believe these butchers are claiming a compassionate success through infant mortality rates? In the whole annals of Marxist Demagoguery, this lie stands on its own! Besides, a Communist who believes the ends justifies the means would *never* lie about statistics would he.

> *The American youth have a term, "LOL", which means Laughing out Loud! This Chi-Com whopper may compete for* Lying out Loud, *but after all, it's just Classic Marxism.*   rg

Can you still claim to be a fan of Fundamental Transformation and 'Obama-Care'? Do you think it will be different this time for people outside of the 'Inner Circle'? Sure, so will the Bubonic Plague!

~~~~~~~~~~~~~~~~

Part Four:

So, Where are We Today?

CHAPTER FOURTEEN

The Map in the Mall says, *"You are Here"*.

"This year, Congress will spend $3.7 trillion dollars. ... $10 billion per day. Can we prey upon the rich to cough up the money? ... According to IRS statistics, ... 2 percent of U.S. Households have an income of $250,000 and above. ... (and) account for ... $1.97 trillion of the nearly $8 trillion of total household income. ... If Congress imposed a 100 percent tax, taking all earnings above $250,000 per year ... That would keep the government running for about 141 days ... problem ... there are 224 more days left in the year."
    "Eat the Rich" by Dr. Walter E. Williams, 4/13/2011

Politicians tax the middle class for the same reason robbers rob banks. 'Cause that's where the money is!
                    Attributed to Willy Sutton

The map in the mall, marked with an "X" in a circle can make finding a certain shop or your parked car simple. But, if you've been blindly following someone for a long time who was leading you into a swamp, there's nothing easy about waking up and recognizing you've been 'screwed' and may never find your way home again. That is just about where the American People are today, politically.

Where and for what reason did all these federal tax, spend, and give-away programs originate, and why are they so expensive? Who created them, who *actually* gains power or money from them, and how? *Most importantly,* how did they turn out where they were first tried? What tree did the rootstock come from? What kind of fruit did it bear; sweet, bitter, nutritious, or poisonous? Just how did the United States get from the richest nation on earth to "Broke" in a few decades?

These are all logical and proper question for any thinking person to ask, and questions to which we should be able to obtain an answer. The previous chapter showed you that the genesis of today's Universal Health Care was the Weimar Republic, Nazi Germany, and that butcher of the Kulaks and other Russian People, Vladimir Lenin.

However, the Federal Government, their Department of Education, and a majority of the US and world-wide Media Journalists have at best obscured, and at worst patently lied, in answering these questions. They have perverted both world history and the answers, hiding and obscuring from public view as best they could, the ugly truths of socialist tyranny and mass murder by such as Lenin, Stalin, Hitler, Mao, etc. Yet they are always on the attack against *any* alleged faults of America and its Capitalist System.

> *Note: The following are my own studied and deeply considered opinions, based on a lifetime of studying history and news. Believe them or laugh out loud. I don't care. I'd rather be wrong, so we could both stay free. However, if I'm right, maybe you should cared enough to study as well.* rg

Well, here is where I see the 'X' inside a circle on today's map.
Today, as I started this chapter, with the Dr. Williams quotation in front of me, President Obama appeared in a live News Conference to announce the one year 'repeal' of the "Bush" Tax Cuts on the filthy rich who make over two hundred fifty thousand dollars or more a year, because they're "not paying their fair share". I was thinking of looking for a stronger quote to use, but with that 'kiss' of Marxism from both Obama Senior and Junior, he convinced me to keep it. Imagine his hypocrisy in the presence of numerical

statistics. Of course, his sycophants in the audience were not seeing that. Unfortunately, neither were ninety-nine percent of the TV Audience. Americans have grown too familiar and comfortable with lying demagoguery from politicians, but they still reelect them. Why, because too many voters essentially get a paycheck for keeping such Cretins in power. Today Americans vote for the man who gives them the highest paycheck, and politicians like Obama pander to them and to those who join them. Mobocracy in action!

Obama said he did this to add jobs and defeat the Recession, but those listening knew it meant payday for them! Even though Socialist Political Hacks say it is not true a majority of people who make a quarter million dollars a year are the backbone of US Small Business. Nevertheless, I never got a job from a poor man! Increasing taxes while adding the ObamaDoesn'tCare burden to business costs will not create jobs. Quite the opposite in fact, but that's what Obama wants, a contracting and heavily taxed private sector side (the hated rich), while he borrows from China, electronically adds zeros to America's Treasury, and prints the difference. With this stolen money he buys more government sector workers, racing toward the fatal fifty-one percent "Tyranny of the Majority", to create his Mobocracy. If you want more of a thing, subsidize it, if you want less, tax and regulate it. Give 'paychecks' from the "Do-ers" tax-money to the "Takers" and they will vote for you every time!

Ultimately, of course, there's never enough money to pay the fifty-one percent with money stolen from the shrinking forty-nine. Marx or his Disciple then whine to their "Majority-Mob" that the "Rich aren't paying their fair share". Remember, it was Lenin who said, 'those who still had enough to eat were *Kulaks*, who deserved to be slaughtered! Today, Obama's target is those *'filthy'* rich who earn over two hundred fifty thousand dollars, but who knows when *you* as well might become a Kulak? Remember Marxists History!

"Nudging" each generation further into Marxism.
Toward totalitarian centralized government. Today we have a Department of Education, signed into law by Carter in 1979, which

ripped the control of local school districts from the hands of state and local control, and consolidated control federally. After all, what good is 'public education' if Progressives cannot spread their propaganda equally to all children across the nation. Besides, Lenin, Stalin, Mussolini, Hitler, Mao, and every Marxist Dictator since have controlled the education of 'his' children. Those results were discussed earlier. Catastrophic for the nation and their children, but a huge success for Tyrants of all stripes.

Today we have a US news media which ranges from the extreme left, those who 'feel a thrill, running up their leg' when Obama speaks, to the European-Social Democrat 'center-left' version, where talking heads, thoroughly trained in the Ivy Halls of Progressive 'dialectic', pontificate to the 'idiot masses' on America's faults, and "social justice" twenty four seven.

Then, of course, barely to the 'right' of these, we have "Balanced" news, meaning a stable of Marxist Progressives, spouting undiluted Marxism by interrupting and talking-over everyone else. 'Elites' talking down with sneering condescension to guests and the audience they obviously consider morons. A place where American Constitutionalism and Rule of Law, or Capitalism are continually excoriated as Neanderthal at best, and sublimely evil at worst, all the while, a "balancing" stable of Political Correctness neutered Republican Party hacks and Pseudo-Conservatives can't even defend the Founder's America because they're ineffectual at best and don't actually believe in it at worst. I am positively sick to death of Communism and Fascism being publicly lauded twenty-four seven, while Political Correctness threatens and blackmails even the most courageous souls. Blowback is necessary against Obama's open and arrogant Marxist rhetoric. Simple historical facts must report the amounts of innocent blood that flow and the depths of human degradation that *always* follow when such Marxists come to power.

Obama's Marxist Economics.
Today Obama has nationalized the Financial, Healthcare, and Auto Industries. He has used your tax-dollars to bail out and reimburse

his contributors and supporters like ACORN, UAW, etc. Obama has granted business success to his contributors and friends through Crony Capitalism, creating record length and depth unemployment through uncontrolled borrowing, printing, and spending, as he paid off and reimbursed his supporters to build a voting base for his reelection. That, coupled with industry-killing Regulatory Rules written by Obama's appointed bureaucrats, and selectively enforced by the President himself, has brazenly redistributed wealth from the despised "rich", into channels to assist his own reelection. But, *"The ends justify any means"* - Quote: Saul Alinsky.

Meanwhile, job-killing environmental regulations (remember who used environmentalism in the thirties, and why?) written by Obama's appointees, coupled with his out-of-control Union price, wage, and benefit packages continually price American Industrial jobs out of the world market, while Obama and his Leftists again blame the hated rich for "shipping jobs overseas to make more money". Why then are Obama's Mob Army the only profiteers?

Today, while Obama is pouring billions of your tax dollars into subsidization for the 'cutesy' sound-byte, "Alternative Energy", rewarding his sycophants and money bundlers with half billion dollar "Start-up, re-distribute this money, then Go-Bankrupt" 'deals. These "Alternative Rip-Off" businesses are set up to manufacture and distribute solar cells, wind turbines, and generators, etc. for our new, "Cheap Alternative Energy". The "funny little catch" is that all of these can more economically be manufactured overseas due to the aforementioned US and State Environmental Regulation, Union Shop wage and benefit packages, etc., all of which make them cost several times what China, for instance can manufacture them for. OOOOOPS! With Obama's business acumen, its obvious why he went to work for Tax Exempt Foundations and ACORN, etc, no one else could afford him. Neither can America, even if he were not a Marxist with a destructive agenda as well!

In addition, today the "Opposition" Republican Establishment, while politically whining about such hijinks, is too Socialist leaning and in addition, Political Correctness neutered to expose such a travesty to the American People as being blatant Marxism, because they have helped set this up for a century.

US Justice Department - Oxymoron?
Again, today we have an "Obama Justice Department", headed by the 'Congressionally Contemptible' Eric Holder, who never met an Anti-American person or group he wouldn't help, nor a 'cracker' he didn't think should be lynched. This situation makes the Term, "Obama Justice Department" a total Oxymoron! The term "Justice" could only belong in the same sentence with Holder's Department within the Lucifer-loving world of a Saul Alinsky or his disciples.

Some try to say that Holder ran the "Fast and Furious" Fraud, without Obama's knowledge. That makes no sense, Obama is a micro-manager and besides, he chooses his lieutenants carefully. If the US Justice Department was essentially "Running Guns" to the Mexican Drug Cartels trying to destroy the Second Amendment, Obama would be a fool *not* to know about that in case of 'blowback', and Obama is no fool! Again, when Holder brings suits against Arizona, to keep them from deterring illegal immigrants from flooding their state, or against Texas, and Florida to force them not to remove all Dead, Moved-away, Missing, Felons, and Illegal Alien voters *on* Registration Roles, Obama had to know, because of course, Obama needed and wanted those votes. But it was a different situation when uniformed, armed, and jack-booted Black Panthers threatened white voters outside a Polling Place. Holder would see black intimidation of whites to be 'Social Justice'.

Full disclosure. Yes, I do believe the man is totally driven by a blind hatred of whites! Liberals claim that cannot be Racist! Go figure!

Today, Holder's Justice Department is not merely an Oxymoron, it is a political reality and a warning of what happens when 'good-old' Democracy nearly reaches the fifty-one percent Mobocracy Level. A Charismatic Charlatan with a vision of buying votes from the fifty-one percent using the taxes of the other forty-nine percent can get elected, and remain elected, if allowed to control the people with Political Correctness, and an ever-growing majority of "Takers" who live off the "Do-ers". That is, of course, until after he has assumed power. Then devil take the hindermost! History shows that too.

Obama's Middle Eastern "Clean Hands" Final Solution.
Today, in the Middle East, which has been a hot spot for decades, a cataclysm is building steam to erupt into all-out war. This happened because of Presidential and US State Department tacit approval and assistance to the Muslim Brotherhood (MB), and eventually one-point-three billion dollars in foreign aid assistance. There was even unauthorized military help, for these Islamic Revolutionaries taking control of North African Nations, including Egypt, Tunisia, and Lybia. We covered some of the MB Rogues Gallery in Chapter Nine, and by now, you know they were historically a fountain of deadly Islamic violence, terrorism, and assassinations and in the Mid-East. They even assassinated Anwar Sadat in retaliation for his Treaty with Israel, after which the MB was outlawed to this day in Egypt.

MB was a strong ally of Adolph Hitler during WW II, and assisted Nazi War Criminals escape post-war Germany to hiding places around the world. Today, as the MB is afloat with America's tax dollars, courtesy of the Obama State Department, and controls over seventy percent of the Egyptian government, terrorist attacks and rockets are again 'incoming' into Israel. Meanwhile, Kamal al-Halbawi (first Egyptian Muslim Brotherhood leader to visit Tehran) announced his wishes for "Egypt (are) what Iran has today: "a true Islamic state."

> "Egypt and the world of Islam as a whole need leaders like ... Ahmadinejad ... Egypt should join 'a new world order with Iran and Venezuela plus Hezbollah and Hamas to chase away the Americans.' ... Every night when I go to bed, I pray to wake up the next day to see Israel is wiped off the map."   (1)

This was a great strategic move by Obama, at least great for the MB! While Israel is considered a *'Satan'* by the MB and other Mid-East Terrorist groups, the US is considered the *"Great Satan"*. Yet Obama's 'Propaganda Minister', James Clapper described them as a *"largely secular"* organization to mislead the American People while our State Department assisted them in taking control. A lie so patent that recently Five Egyptian Secular Parties condemned US support for the MB. (2)

Also recently, Muhammad Badi, whom some have portrayed as the true power behind Egypt's presidency, with Morsi acting as his puppet, called on all Muslims to wage jihad with their money and their selves to free al-Quds" (Jerusalem) - the same exact language one finds in al-Qaeda's tracts. (3)

So, today's Obama-assisted Regime Change in the Mid-East over the past year has hugely shifted the balance of power from Muslim Rulers and 'Dictators' who had grown used to dealing with the United States (for a price), while continuing a formal 'Peace Treaty' with Israel. Now it appears the MB may also either topple or absorb the Kingdoms of Jordan and Saudi Arabia. (4)&(5) So, if the Muslim Brotherhood continues receiving money, assistance, and international approval from President Obama, as it did last spring, and the Kingdoms of Saudi Arabia and Jordan fall into the MB Terrorist Regime, Obama will be a step ahead of Adolph Hitler in the "Final Solution to the Jewish Problem". With continued aid and comfort to the MB as they increasingly gain control of the nations surrounding Israel, Obama can simply sit back and watch while the MB, with or without Iran "Wipe Israel off the Map". That way, he can see Israel gone and quit "putting up" with Netanyahu without getting the 'Stink of Hitler's Ovens' on his hands. A very evil and smooth tactic worthy of Adolph Hitler! However, remember, after 9/11 Obama said in his book, *'Audacity of Hope'*, "I will stand with them (Muslims) should the political winds shift in an ugly direction."

Do not get me wrong, I do not believe Obama is a Muslim any more than I believe he is a Christian. I do not personally believe Obama bows at any alter than the one dedicated to Barak Obama. Besides, if he believes in anything at all, he is a believer in Liberation Theology. Marxists believe the final stage of Marxism will result in the "Collective Salvation" of all mankind. You know, that Marxist 'Thousand Year Utopian Reich' where "Your eyes will be opened, and you will become as gods" (6). Who had that idea earlier?

The Dangers of "Party Politics and Politicians"

Today, even though the Founders warned strictly of its dangers, "Party Politics" has taken the place of "American Politics". People now end up voting for the "Lesser of two evils" in one Party or the other, instead of voting for whoever is best for America. Note that the lesser of two evils is still evil, just less so. That reminds me of the Marxist Agenda, "two steps forward and one step back". That is why even though it took a century to get here; today we have a virtual Democracy, just one-quarter step from Mobocracy and another quarter step to Revolution and Tyranny. Today we have a two Party System, which is essentially the right and the left wing of the Democratic Socialist Party of America. That is, Revolutionary Socialists vs. Fabian Socialists, brothers who agree on the ends, but not the means to achieve it. These both work against the American Public, who if they have somehow escape the Marxist brainwashing of Federal Education and actually *understand* the difference between both Parties and true American Principles, still has no voice, and no choice, being given none. In Nineteen Sixty Four, we called this situation, "Pete, 'n Re-Pete". Today, is there another choice? No, but as we said, history repeats!

The 2010 Election showed that the Republican Party no longer is a champion of the American Republic, even though some Republican Elected Officials, just as some Democrats, still are. However, the Republican Establishment was willing to lose seats to Democrats (Fellow Socialists) rather than allow those seats to go to the Tea Party, who represented a large grass-roots portion of Conservative, Freedom-loving Americans. The Republican Establishment used their power to betray that constituency for their own gain.

Today, the Tea Party still exists, but it is older and wiser. Parts were co-opted by the Republican Establishment, some decided to 'moderate' their views, and surrender, meaning they were never seriously willing to fight for Freedom, just 'Good-time Charley's'.

Some, like me, lost faith in both American Political Parties as being more interested in grasping and retaining their power base than protecting Freedom for all Americans. They (we?) mostly dropped out of all Party memberships, including donating. To what or whom would we donate? That means the Republican Establishment, as brother Socialists to the Democrat Establishment, are now still in the American Political Arena, but have cut Constitutional Americans adrift in order to save their own positions in the power structure, just as they did in 2010. Their major Role, even if they win against Obama, can only be as the continued major 'Whipping-Boy" for Socialists who now rule both Parties. With the loss of Constitution-believing Americans, who feel seriously betrayed, the Republican Party will likely never again be anything but a "stop-gap" vote, because that's about all they can be counted on for. Terribly sad, however unfortunately true.

The Proof of this is that we have a "Socialist-Lite" running for President on the Republican Ticket against a Marxist Socialist, because the Republican Party pulled every possible legal and dirty trick to disenfranchise Americans who wanted to discontinue sliding from Democracy into Mobocracy, and the Republican Establishment wanted their piece of the 'Dark Kingdom' along with Democrats.

So where are we Today?
Well, Romney at least, does believe in a 'Socialist Lite' Version of Capitalist America, so he is a choice, but certainly not a first choice to those of us who weep to see where America is going under Obama's Marxist Regime. First, Obama has already shot Romney in the 'foot' over 'Romney-Care', which was bound to happen. Second, Romney's Fabian Socialist leanings keep him from fighting back with anything but the usual Politically Correct Party-Line Rhetoric, placing him at a great disadvantage because he totally lacks Obama's Populist and Demagogic talents. So, it is going to be a long, 'windy' campaign season, with an Alinsky-trained 'Street Agitator using street-proven Marxist talking points, and "end justifies any means" lies and half-truths, battling the 'usual' weak-kneed, Politically Correct Republican Rhetoric. Where can those who truly love and care about America and Freedom turn today?

Also, today some people do not want to get too involved because they believe it is a moral battle and do not want to get involved with 'religion'. Well, news flash, religion designates morality, but morality is not necessarily religion. There is right, and there is wrong, and most people know the difference, whether Christian, Buddhist, or Agnostic, or nothing.

Besides, it is *already* a religious battle, because both Fascism and Communism, being Marxism *are* a religion. Some believe Marxism, because it is Atheistic, is not therefore religious. The awkward truth is that Atheism *is* definitely a religion, merely one without a god. Marxism as a religion is much more personally controlling than Christianity, which is based on personal choice. To achieve Collective Salvation for their Nation or World, Marxists not only limits personal choice, it is a heresy punishable by death, just as is any other type of individuality! Welcome to *their* world!

Additionally, Obama declared open war on one of American's "Self-Evident" Constitutional Rights, Freedom of Religion and Worship by cutting the amount of donations that can be written off taxes, then with his signature legislation, ObamaDoesn'tCare, forcing Catholics, among others to obey *his* laws rather than personal religious convictions. Hitler would have been proud. I had a college professor from Germany who had spent time in prison under Hitler because he was a Methodist Pastor. History repeats, and repeats, etc.

Even so, the battle is critical for both camps. The Republican Establishment and Romney are battling for permission to continue America's long, slow slide into Democratic Socialism. Obama and his Left-Wing sycophants are battling for a license to complete his 'Fundamental Transformation' of America, and bring about the Revolution, which will Socialize us so he becomes *"The Leader"* to achieve the 'Collective Salvation' of America, and maybe the whole World! A new Fourth Reich, a new Kingdom of Marxist Fascism!

Additionally, there is another serious danger possible for America. Because Obama is so close to his goal, he and his handlers may do something desperate, which has never happened in America. Many will smirk or laugh at the idea, but if things become ugly, and it looks as if Obama might lose the election, I firmly believe he may simply cancel it. By that, I mean, in that position, Obama might declare or even create an emergency, impose Martial Law, and cancel the election "Until the Crisis is over". This happened in Germany, during six weeks in 1933, when Adolph Hitler, upon winning some forty four percent of the vote, created a coalition giving him the majority, then with the 'assistance' of several crises, suspect, but never proven to be manufactured, Hitler passed 'emergency' legislation he had pre-written, making him the acting 'Dictator' of Germany. This is a role he only gave up when he 'ate his gun' in the bunker in 1945. During the intervening years, much horrible world history was acted out and written, as was a large portion of the total evil recorded in human history.

Does Obama have the stomach to murder millions of people? Do not forget, his premier act as an Illinois Legislator was to make certain he locked in the votes of the Democrat Party and NOW by fighting for legislation making certain, not just the guaranteed freedom to kill a fetus (baby), but that no child should survive. That is to say, he specifically worked for legislation that any 'fetus' which survived an abortion was thrown in the trash to expire there. No sympathy, no help, just Obama's Law of Death. Also, Obama has stepped comfortably into the role of 'Executioner in Chief' with his 'Committee of Death', glorying and enjoying 'Air-Time' in the death of Bin Laden and Al Awlaki and family. Think he does not have what it takes to wipe out you or your family? I won't be betting with you.

Throughout this book, I have explained to the best of my ability exactly how we got here, based on my study of history and current events. Many do not want to hear that, many do not want to believe it, and many will do neither. That is human nature.

But the stakes are high. Not only for your freedom, but your life, and as well that of your children's. Study carefully, think clearly and carefully, and then vote wisely. While I really want neither of the above options, there is a universe of difference in the two.

But even if Obama loses, America must not merely stop, we must seriously reverse our slide into Socialist Mobocracy or the results will only be delayed, not halted! Tyranny will eventually come under the Fabian Socialists as well. Socialism brings only Tyranny!

Research and Reference Notes

I have endeavored to perform the majority of my research for this book from simply "Google Searching" terms on the Internet. This was purposefully done for several reasons. First and foremost, so you can look up your own sources and do your own research. Don't simply repeat mine. Second, to show there is a lot of information easily researched, at least for now. There is a 'ton' of information out there on the internet, which spans the spectrum from wild-eyed anarchists, neo-Nazis, Maoists, Stalinist and Trotskyite Communists to the disgustingly lukewarm and ineffectual moderates, all the way to constitutionalists and libertarians so radical they're nearly anarchists.

We all must thread our way through these diverse groups, however, having studied history, I almost instantly recognize political slant. If you have not kept abreast of things, your task will be more difficult. *However, you must find your own way.* I have neither reason nor intent to brainwash you to my opinion, merely to point out the road we are travelling and place some warning signs where you can see them. Like highway driving, the rest is up to you.

Finally, I need to show you my opinions exist somewhere besides in the dark corners of my mind or imagination. But unlike a Progressive or Socialist, to me the ends could *never* justify shady or even questionable means. So I not only have no reason to lie to you, I *specifically do not want to* lead you astray, even accidently.

My wish is merely to lead you to where you can weigh my view against your own research, and then come to your own conclusion. On the other hand, you will never be anything but a bottle-fed baby until you use your own time and talent to research, and formulate your own point of view. If it differs from mine, so be it. A long time tongue-in-cheek comment of mine is that God made us all individuals so He would not get bored with us. If you do not agree after doing your own research, more power to you, just do not remain (propaganda) bottle-fed.

Seriously, we all come from different, genetics, environments, and experiences. The only "Equality" humans can ever have comes from the rights "endowed upon us" by our Creator. To my knowledge, the first and only historical government to enumerate those rights, then write legislation to institute them with a rule of Law, not of Men, came into being at the founding of United States of America.

Unfortunately, I believe we now have leaders who are purposefully deceiving and misleadingly us into trading our Creator Endowed Constitutional Freedoms and Rule of Law for a false sense of financial and personal security. False, because the crisis situations seen as a danger were created by the very people now offering to 'fix the problem'. If you understand this, you must also realize they created these crises for the disingenuous purpose of "fixing them". Such people will likely never "waste a good crisis", but will fix it to suit their own ends. Historically, those ends are Tyranny.

Who blazed that trail before them? How did that turn out? Do *you* want the same outcome? Good luck in your research. I hope you find who blazed the trail, and find where you are, so you can decide which way you want to go while such a decision is still free to make. Good luck and Good Hunting!

The Coming Fourth Reich

Chapter 1: Why Call it the Fourth Reich?
(1)(http://en.wikipedia.org/wiki/Karl_Marx)
(2) http://necrometrics.com/20c5m.htm.

Chapter 2: Right vs. Left. What is Right and What is Left?
(1)http://en.wikipedia.org/wiki/Left-right_politics
(2)http://en.wikipedia.org/wiki/John_Reed_(journalist)

Chapter 3: America: Constitutional Republic, or Democracy?
(1) http://www.stopthenorthamericanunion.com/NotDemocracy.html
(2) http://en.wikipedia.org/wiki/Constitutional_republic
(3) http://www.lexrex.com/enlightened/AmericanIdeal/aspects/demrep.html

Chapter 4: Americans, What do we believe now?
(1)http://www.huffingtonpost.com/2011/12/29/young-people-socialism_n_1175218.html
(2) http://pjmedia.com/zombie/2011/10/31/the-99-official-list-of-ows/?print=1)
(3) http://www.libertyzone.com/Communist-Manifesto-Planks.html

Chapter 5: Just what is Fascism?
(1) https://www2.bc.edu/~weiler/fascism.htm

Chapter 6: Revolution? It couldn't happen here could it?
(1)http://www.huffingtonpost.com/2011/12/29/young-people-socialism_n_1175218.html
(2)http://nation.foxnews.com/president-obama/2012/01/10/obama-usa-not-nation-founded-principle-survival-fittest
(3) http://www.foxnews.com/story/0,2933,580414,00.html

Chapter 7: How did the Seeds of Marxism come to the USA?

Chapter 8: How do you start a Socialist Revolution? Part One
(1)http://www.huffingtonpost.com/2011/12/29/young-people-socialism_n_1175218.html
(2)http://www.thefreemanonline.org/columns/education-in-colonial-america/print/
(3)http://www.usatoday.com/news/education/2009-01-08-adult-literacy_N.htm
(4)http://www.reuters.com/article/2009/03/02/us-usa-prisons-idUSTRE5215TW20090302
(5)http://wiki.answers.com/Q/National_average_cost_per_student_in_public_school
(6) www.wcwonline.org/pdf/ekates/ATISummary9.11.pdf
http://en.wikipedia.org/wiki/Woodrow_Wilson
(8) http://www.tldm.org/news7/CommunismInAmerica.htm
(9) http://bitchesinblue.blogspot.com/2009/06/1968-convention-truth.html
http://www.archive.org/stream/subversiveinvolv01unit/subversiveinvolv01unit_djvu.txt

(10) http://en.wikipedia.org/wiki/History_of_the_hippie_movement

Chapter 9 Footnotes: How do you start a Socialist Revolution? Part Two

(1) http://en.wikipedia.org/wiki/First_they_came

(2) http://www.spartacus.schoolnet.co.uk/GERsa.htm
http://en.wikipedia.org/wiki/Sturmabteilung

(3) http://www.youtube.com/watch?v=mVh75ylAUXY&feature=player_embedded

(4) http://www.americanthinker.com/2011/04/the_green_nazis.html

(5) Book: How Green Were the Nazis?: Nature, Environment, and Nation in the Third Reich (Ecology & History) Franz-Josef Bruggemeier.
http://www.amazon.com/How-Green-Were-Nazis-Environment/dp/0821416464

(6) http://www.americanthinker.com/printpage/?url=http://www.americanthinker.com/2011/01/why_we_should_fear_the_moslem.html
http://www.jewishvirtuallibrary.org/jsource/Terrorism/muslimbrotherhood.html

(7) http://en.wikipedia.org/wiki/Federal_Farm_Loan_Act

(8) http://en.wikipedia.org/wiki/Agricultural_Adjustment_Act

(9) http://www.oyez.org/cases/1940-1949/1942/1942_59
http://en.wikipedia.org/wiki/Wickard_v._Filburn

(10) http://farm.ewg.org/progdetail.php?fips=00000&progcode=corn
http://grist.org/article/2010-03-25-corn-ethanol-meat-hfcs/

Chapter 10 Footnotes

(1) www.sparknotes.com/history/european/frenchrev/summary.html
http://en.wikipedia.org/wiki/French_Revolution

(2) http://en.wikipedia.org/wiki/Revolutions_of_1848

(3) http://en.wikipedia.org/wiki/The_Black_Book_of_Communism#Comparison_of_Communism_and_Nazism
http://en.wikipedia.org/wiki/Mass_killings_under_Communist_regimes

(4) http://www.spartacus.schoolnet.co.uk/RUSlenin.htm
http://en.wikipedia.org/wiki/Vladimir_Lenin

(5) http://en.wikipedia.org/wiki/Congressional_Progressive_Caucus
http://cpc.grijalva.house.gov/

(6) http://en.wikipedia.org/wiki/Kulak
http://freemencapitalist.com/communist-countries/kulaks/
http://en.wikipedia.org/wiki/Lenin's_Hangihg_Order

(7) http://en.wikipedia.org/wiki/The_Black_Book_of_Communism#Comparison_of_Communism_and_Nazism

(8) http://en.wikipedia.org/wiki/The_Black_Book_of_Communism#Comparison_of_Communism_and_Nazism

(9) http://www.eisenhowermemorial.org/stories/death-camps.htm

(10) http://www.eisenhowermemorial.org/stories/death-camps.htm

(11) http://ironicsurrealism.com/2010/06/10/video-undercover-fbi-agent-infiltrated-and-exposes-bill-ayers-weather-underground-genocidal-plan/

(12) http://www.discoverthenetworks.org/individualprofile.asp?indid=2169
http://en.wikipedia.org/wiki/Bill_Ayers

(13) http://www.digitaljournal.com/article/261511
http://voices.yahoo.com/prairie-fire-william-ayers-revolutionary-manifesto-2136210.html
(14) http://www.youtube.com/watch?v=hQvsf2MUKRQ
http://www.youtube.com/watch?v=4R7jL0_JANY&feature=related
http://www.youtube.com/watch?feature=endscreen&NR=1&v=mW-iy-9m9SU

Chapter -11- Footnotes
(1) http://www.youtube.com/watch?v=1G1hPq1ARc4
(2) http://nlpc.org/stories/2009/11/18/seiu-president-andrew-stern-frequent-white-house-visitor-may-have-violated-lobbyi
http://www.realclearpolitics.com/articles/2009/05/13/big_labors_investment_in_obama_pays_off_96469.html
(3) http://www.tedmontgomery.com/remarks/08.1-12/ObamaClinton/Barack'smother/index.html
http://rottie-refugees.com/2011/11/02/the-little-red-schoolhouse/
(4) http://rottie-refugees.com/2011/11/02/the-little-red-schoolhouse/
http://www.americanthinker.com/2008/12/obama_from_unitarian_to_libera_1.html
(5) http://en.wikipedia.org/wiki/Ann_Dunham
http://www.youtube.com/watch?v=hhhOMSV3xUQ
(6) http://www.usasurvival.org/docs/hawaii-obama.pdf
http://www.hawaiifreepress.com/main/ArticlesMain/tabid/56/articleType/ArticleView/articleId/500/July-7-1935-Moscow-orders-first-Communists-to-Hawaii.aspx
(7) http://www.usasurvival.org/docs/hawaii-obama.pdf
http://en.wikipedia.org/wiki/Harry_Bridges
http://www.scribd.com/doc/71024656/Obama-and-Communism-in-Hawaii
(8) http://keywiki.org/index.php/Gus_Hall
http://www.aim.org/aim-column/soviets-funded-black-freedom-journal/
(9) http://www.discoverthenetworks.org/individualProfile.asp?indid=2323
http://freedompub.org/profiles/blogs/black-america-s-gains-and-losses
(10) http://www.powells.com/biblio?isbn=9780821415979
(11) http://tinyurl.com/4rdgv5
http://www.vdare.com/posts/barack-obama-srs-mugabeist-plan-for-kenya

Chapter -12- Footnotes
(1) http://www.youtube.com/watch?v=KrefKCaV8m4
(2) http://www.crossroad.to/Quotes/communism/alinsky.htm
(3) http://en.wikipedia.org/wiki/Saul_Alinsky
http://www.crossroad.to/Quotes/communism/alinsky.htm
(4) http://en.wikipedia.org/wiki/Saul_Alinsky
http://www.discoverthenetworks.org/Articles/Rules%20for%20Revolution%20(2).pdf
http://www.crossroad.to/Quotes/communism/alinsky.htm

(5) http://www.americanthinker.com/2008/09/barack_obama_and_alinskys_rule.html
(6) http://www.discoverthenetworks.org/individualProfile.asp?indid=2422

Chapter -13- Footnotes
(1) http://www.gutenberg.org/ebooks/61
(2) http://en.wikipedia.org/wiki/German_Empire
(3) http://en.wikipedia.org/wiki/Otto_von_Bismarck#Health_Insurance_Bill_of_1883
(4) http://en.wikipedia.org/wiki/German_Empire#Wilhelmine_era
(5) http://en.wikipedia.org/wiki/Weimar_Republic
(6) http://www.thefreemanonline.org/columns/national-health-care-medicine-in-germany-1918-1945/
(7) http://www.youtube.com/watch?feature=endscreen&NR=1&v=OBZsTf6oLfY
http://www.youtube.com/watch?v=4R7jL0_JANY&feature=related
http://www.youtube.com/watch?v=mW-iy-9m9SU&feature=related
http://www.youtube.com/watch?v=7WBRjU9P5eo
(8) http://en.wikipedia.org/wiki/Life_unworthy_of_life
(9) http://www.youtube.com/watch?feature=endscreen&NR=1&v=OBZsTf6oLfY
(10) http://en.wikipedia.org/wiki/Life_unworthy_of_life#Nazi_categorization
http://www.youtube.com/watch?v=1G1hPq1ARc4
(11) http://news.investors.com/article/607800/201204131846/obamacare-ominously-similar-to-soviet-socialized-medicine.htm
(12) IBID
(13) IBID
http://conservativebase.com/716761/obamacare-vs-lenincare-u-s-copies-soviets-by-anna-ebeling/
(14) http://spectator.org/archives/2011/04/22/ipab-is-an-acronym-for-death-p/print
(15) http://en.wikipedia.org/wiki/Mao_Zedong
(16) http://news.bbc.co.uk/2/hi/asia-pacific/4763312.stm

Chapter -14- Footnotes
(1) http://ivarfjeld.wordpress.com/2012/02/20/muslim-brothers-lets-wipe-israel-off-the-map/
(2) http://english.ahram.org.eg/NewsContentPrint/1/0/45933/Egypt/0/Egypts-secular-forces-condemn-US-support-for-Musli.aspx
(3)) http://amoraloutrage.wordpress.com/2012/07/09/muslim-brotherhoods-supreme-leader-calls-for-jihad-on-israel/
(4) http://www.americanthinker.com/2012/01/jordans_king_and_the_muslim_brotherhood_an_unholy_marriage_1.html
(5)) http://arabsaga.blogspot.fr/2012/07/morsy-in-saudi-arabia-brothers-in-islam.html?m=1
(6) Genesis 3:5

ACKNOWLEDGEMENTS

I would like to acknowledge several key sources from which I have historically searched for information.

The Heritage Foundation (http://www.heritage.org), of which I'm a member, is a rock-solid organization, tirelessly serving Conservative policy research and analysis needs.

Discover the Networks (http://www.discoverthenetworks.org/groupProfile.asp?grpid=7030) is dedicated to describing the networks and agendas of the political Left. It's Founder, David Horowitz, is soundly despised by the Left, having been raised as a Communist, but who saw through their nefarious agenda and has dedicated his life to exposing it.

Investor's Business Daily (IDB), (http://www.investors.com/default.htm Probably one of the best, pro-American newspapers in the nation. Their series, Perspectives of a Russian Immigrant (http://www.investors.com/search/searchresults.aspx?Ntt=reminiscences+of+a+russian+immigrant) is many issues long at this point. The author, **Svetlana Kunin** lived in the Soviet Union until 1980, working as a civil engineer. She is now a retired software developer living in Connecticut. While you'll have to subscribe (on the net) to download the whole thing, it's a real eye-opener to those who think Obama is just a 'Lefty, and not a Marxist Ideologue.

Another immigrant, **Kitty Werthmann** is in her 80's, she was 12 when Hitler 'annexed' Austria. She has directly compared Hitler to Obama. The Left has gone looney throwing their paper-bags full of feces at her, but I was studying what happened in Germany while these Lefty's were still soiling their own 'didies', and she tells it just like history did before the Marxists began airbrushing it. Google her name, you'll find a lot of paper bags full, but if you're not afraid to listen to her, I for one am certain she's telling the complete truth. Like me, she has nothing to gain by lying.

Just to get a taste of what we're paying Marxist University Professors to do, Google "Cloward Piven Strategy" and prepare to be sickened. These Marxists were so impressed by the human misery and destruction caused by Watts Riots that they developed a strategy to use them as a Template for Marxist Revolution in America.

ABOUT THE AUTHOR

Ray Grace is a retired Professional Engineer and Construction Manager who worked on projects in the United States, the Middle East, South America, and the Pacific Rim. In 1995, he retired to Eastern Oregon, where he worked locally as Resident Engineer on small and medium Infrastructure projects. During his world travels, he worked, communicated, and interacted with numerous races and cultures. He is conversant or familiar in several languages, including Spanish, German, Arabic, and Russian. Elected County Commissioner in 2002, he served one term during the startup and operational phase of incineration for the nerve gas and blister-agent containing chemical weapons stockpile stored at the Umatilla Chemical Depot. He then received a Governor's appointment to the Citizen's Advisory Commission, continuing to monitor the public safety aspect of incineration until its recent completion. He and his wife of thirty-seven years want to protect and pass on the same Inalienable Rights and Freedoms all American's have through the U.S. Bill of Rights and Constitution to their children, grandchildren, and great-grandchildren.

The Coming Fourth Reich

Made in the USA
San Bernardino, CA
19 February 2013